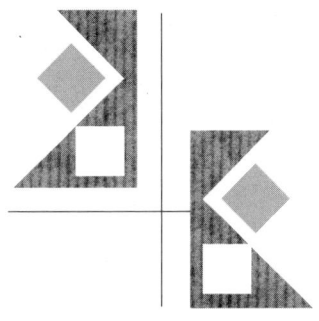

INFLUENCING CHANGE

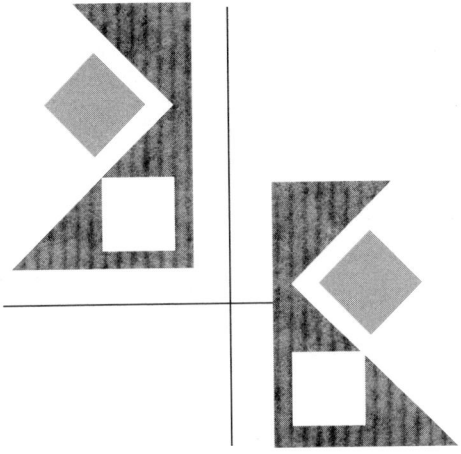

INFLUENCING CHANGE

Building Evaluation Capacity to Strengthen Governance

Ray C. Rist
Marie-Helene Boily
Frederic Martin

THE WORLD BANK
Washington, D.C.

© 2011 The International Bank for Reconstruction and Development / The World Bank
1818 H Street NW
Washington DC 20433
Telephone: 202-473-1000
Internet: www.worldbank.org

All rights reserved

1 2 3 4 14 13 12 11

This volume is a product of the staff of the International Bank for Reconstruction and Development/The World Bank. The findings, interpretations, and conclusions expressed in this volume do not necessarily reflect the views of the Executive Directors of The World Bank or the governments they represent.

The World Bank does not guarantee the accuracy of the data included in this work. The boundaries, colors, denominations, and other information shown on any map in this work do not imply any judgement on the part of The World Bank concerning the legal status of any territory or the endorsement or acceptance of such boundaries.

Rights and Permissions

The material in this publication is copyrighted. Copying and/or transmitting portions or all of this work without permission may be a violation of applicable law. The International Bank for Reconstruction and Development/The World Bank encourages dissemination of its work and will normally grant permission to reproduce portions of the work promptly.

For permission to photocopy or reprint any part of this work, please send a request with complete information to the Copyright Clearance Center Inc., 222 Rosewood Drive, Danvers, MA 01923, USA; telephone: 978-750-8400; fax: 978-750-4470; Internet: www.copyright.com.

All other queries on rights and licenses, including subsidiary rights, should be addressed to the Office of the Publisher, The World Bank, 1818 H Street NW, Washington, DC 20433, USA; fax: 202-522-2422; e-mail: pubrights@worldbank.org.

ISBN: 978-0-8213-8403-9
eISBN: 978-0-8213-8497-8
DOI: 10.1596/978-0-8403-9

Cover design: Naylor Design, Inc.

Library of Congress Cataloging-in-Publication Data
Influencing change : building evaluation capacity to strengthen governance / Ray C. Rist, Marie-Helene Boily, Frederic Martin, editors.
 p. cm.
 ISBN 978-0-8213-8403-9 — ISBN 978-0-8213-8497-8 (electronic)
1. Organizational change. 2. Administrative agencies—Evaluation. 3. Executive departments—Evaluation. 4. Bureaucracy—Evaluation. I. Rist, Ray C. II. Boily, Marie-Helene. III. Martin, Frédéric.
 HD58.8.I5378 2011
 658.4'06—dc22
                                                                    2010037927

CONTENTS

Preface	xiii
About the Contributors	xv
Abbreviations	xix

Introduction. Evaluation Capacity Building: A Conceptual Framework — **1**
Ray C. Rist, Marie-Helene Boily, and Frederic Martin

Results-Based Management	2
Structure of This Book	9
Notes	10
Bibliography	11

Chapter 1. Working toward Development Results: The Case of Sri Lanka — **13**
Dhara Wijayatilake

Monitoring and Evaluation as of 2006	14
The Policy Framework as of 2006	15
Institutionalizing MfDR in the Whole of Government	15
Lessons Learned after Three Years	19
Accomplishments as of the End of 2009	21
Future Plans	21
Conclusion	22
Notes	22

Chapter 2. The Evaluation of Macroeconomic Institutional Arrangements in Latin America   23
Eduardo Wiesner

The Evaluation of Institutions and the Evolving Frontiers of Evaluation Priorities	24
The Evaluation of Macroeconomic Institutions and Arrangements	26
Linking Performance with Nominal Institutional Characteristics	28
Demand-Driven Evaluation and the Role of Incentives	29
Accountability with Respect to Learning and the Role of Incentives	30
The Demand-Driven Requirements of Capacity Building	30
Evaluative Implications of the 2008–09 World Crisis	32
Conclusion	34
Notes	34
Bibliography	37

Chapter 3. From Evaluating Projects toward Assessing Institutional Performance   41
Todor Dimitrov

Broadening the Scope of Evaluations	42
Closing the Gap between Reality and Intentions	42
Ensuring an Environment that Facilitates Systemic Institutional Performance Evaluations	43
Seven Steps for Preparing a Systemic IPE	45
Conclusion	54
Notes	55
Bibliography	55

Chapter 4. Evaluation Systems as Strategy Management Tools: Building Dubai's Institutional Learning Capacity   59
Mohammad A. Jaljouli

Strategy Management Concept and Processes	60
Evaluation versus Strategy Management	64
How Can Strategy Management and Evaluation Processes Be Integrated?	71
Building Dubai's Institutional Learning Capacity	73
Notes	83
Bibliography	83

Chapter 5. A Conceptual Framework for Developing Evaluation Capacities: Building on Good Practice   85
Caroline Heider

Evaluation Principles	86
Developing Capacity at Three Levels	88
The Importance of the Process of Capacity Development	96
Where to Start?	98
Conclusion	104
Notes	106
Bibliography	107

Chapter 6. Supporting Evaluation Capacity on Environment and Development   111
Rob D. van den Berg

Upgrading Evaluation of Sustainable Development: How to Identify Best International Practices	111
Partnering and Preparatory Work for the International Conference	113
Building Up an Inventory of Evaluations	115
The International Conference on Evaluating Climate Change and Development	116
Publication of Conference Papers and Further Studies Envisaged	117
A Virtual Community of Practice	119
Collaboration with IDEAS and Other Evaluation Associations	120
Note	121
Reference	121

Chapter 7. Capacity Building: The Indian Experience   123
Rashmi Agrawal and Banda V L N Rao

Utilization of Evaluations: Various Viewpoints	124
Institutional Mechanism for Development Evaluation in India	126
Factors Influencing Utilization of Evaluation Results: The Indian Experience	128
On-the-Job Capacity Building: A Case Study	134
Conclusions	136
Note	137
Bibliography	138

Chapter 8. The Environmental/Rural Development and Food Security Program in Madagascar   141
Balsama Andriantseheno

The Stocktaking Exercise	143
Roles and Responsibilities	144
Issues Raised	145
Lessons Learned	146
Recommendations	147
Conclusions	149
Bibliography	149

Chapter 9. Recognizing "Helping" as an Evaluation Capacity Development Strategy   151
Stephen Porter

Definitions	153
The Components of Helping	154
Applying Helping to Understand an Evaluation of the Bana Barona/Abantwana Bethu Project	158
Conclusion	168
Notes	168
Bibliography	169

Chapter 10. Building Capacities for Results-Based National M&E Systems   171
Gilles Clotteau, Marie-Helene Boily, Sana Darboe, and Frederic Martin

Challenges in ECB	173
Lessons Learned and Best Practices	176
Improving M&E Information Systems and Knowledge Management	187
Conclusion	193
Notes	193
Bibliography	194

Chapter 11. Where Is Development Evaluation Going?   195
Robert Picciotto

The Origins of IDEAS	196
What Is IDEAS About?	196
A New Context for Evaluation	198
A New Spirit among Evaluators	200

Conclusion	205
Bibliography	205

Chapter 12. Old Challenges and New Frontiers 207
Elizabeth J. McAllister

Defing ECB	208
New Areas for Exploration	209
Conclusion: Confronting a Political and Leadership Vacuum	222
Notes	222
Bibliography	223

Chapter 13. Perspectives on Evaluation Capacity Building 225
Steffen Bohni Nielsen and Karin Attström

The Literature on Evaluation Capacity Building	226
ECB Perspectives Offered by the Contributors	228
Key Findings in a Common ECB Framework	234
Conclusion	239
Notes	240
Bibliography	240

Chapter 14. Lessons Learned in Capacity Building: Where Do We Go from Here? 243
Stefan Dahlgren

Working toward Development Results: The Case of Sri Lanka	245
The Evaluation of Macroeconomic Institutional Arrangements in Latin America	246
From Evaluating Projects toward Assessing Institutional Performance	247
Evaluation Systems as Strategy Management Tools: Building Dubai's Institutional Learning Capacity	249
A Conceptual Framework for Developing Evaluation Capacities: Building on Good Practice	250
Capacity Building: The Indian Experience	252
The Environmental/Rural Development and Food Security Program in Madagascar	255
Recognizing "Helping" as an Evaluation Capacity Development Strategy	256
Building Capacities for Results-Based National M&E Systems	256

Where Is Development Evaluation Going?		258
Discussion		258
Note		260
Bibliography		260

Index   **263**

Boxes

3.1	The First IPE of the Black Sea Trade and Development Bank	53
4.1	Where Does the Strategy Management Concept Apply?	64
4.2	How Is Public Value Created and Measured in This Model?	79
5.1	Ensuring Evaluators' Structural Independence	90
5.2	Selecting the Head of Evaluation	102
9.1	The OECD Definition of Evaluation	153
9.2	The Core Principles of Helping	154
12.1	New Zealand Road Authority	221

Figures

1	Components of Results-Based Management	3
2	Demand and Supply Framework for Evaluation Capacity Building	5
3	Framework for Assessing Evaluation Capacity	6
2.1	Per Capita Income Relative to the OECD, 1870–2000	26
2.2	Volatility of Real GDP Growth, 1960s–90s	27
2.3	Annual Percentage Changes in World GDP, 2005–09	32
3.1	Framework for Institutional Performance Evaluations	44
3.2	Activities to Be Performed to Plan IPE	47
4.1	Generic Strategy Map Structure for a Public Organization	61
4.2	Process Custodianship and Governance in Different Contexts	69
4.3	High-Level Integrated Strategy Management and Evaluation Process	73
4.4	Architecture of Dubai's Strategy Management Framework	75
4.5	Dubai's Strategy Map	77
4.6	Strategy Execution Support Team	81
4.7	Dubai's Strategy Execution Measurement Challenge	82
5.1	Evaluation Principles	87
5.2	The Three Levels of Capacity	89
7.1	Institutional System for Evaluation in India	127
8.1	Relationship between Nature, Health, Wealth, and Power	142
9.1	Project Data Flow for AMREF Project	161

9.2	The Barefoot Collective's Phases of Organizational Development	162
10.1	Areas of Monitoring and Evaluation and Their Relationship with the Public Value Chain	172
10.2	Ten Steps to Designing, Building, and Sustaining a Results-Based M&E System	177
10.3	ECB Public Value Chain	181
10.4	A Structured Approach to Assessing Training Needs	183
10.5	Nine Steps to the Implementation of a Results-Based M&E Information System	188
10.6	Baldrige Criteria for Performance Excellence Framework	191
10.7	Key Components of the Balanced Scorecard Approach	192
13.1	Evaluation Capacity Building Issues Covered by the Authors	235

Tables

2.1	Growth of per Capita GDP in Latin America and Selected Comparators, 1960–2000	26
2.2	Actual and Projected Output in Selected Areas	33
4.1	Evaluation, Strategy Management, and Potential Areas of Integration	72
5.1	Evaluation Principles and the Three Levels of Capacity	93
5.2	Evaluation Capabilities at the Three Levels of Capacity	95
5.3	Tips for Reinforcing an Enabling Environment for Evaluation	100
5.4	Tips for Developing an Institutional Framework for Evaluation	101
5.5	Tips for Developing Evaluators' Skills and Knowledge	104
9.1	Schein's Four Forms of Inquiry	157
9.2	Examples of On-Site Support Linked to Helping Roles and Inquiry	164
10.1	Checklist of Questions to Consider in Designing and Implementing a Results-Based M&E System	180
10.2	Levels of Training Evaluation	182
10.3	Checklist of Criteria for Effective Training	187
13.1	Main Features of Each Chapter	229
13.2	Methods for Evaluation Capacity Building Prescribed or Applied by the Authors	237

PREFACE

This book takes on an elusive yet frequently mentioned concept in development evaluation: *evaluation capacity building* (ECB). The term is knocked about and used as if its meaning were recognized by all. The reality is quite different. Differences and divergences were apparent in the spring of 2009, when the International Development Evaluation Association (IDEAS) held its biannual global assembly in Johannesburg, South Africa, around the theme of "Getting to Results: Evaluation Capacity Building and Development." What became apparent was that a number of challenges had already been identified, but that trying to capture lessons learned on effective strategies was difficult, because of the failure to agree upon a unique and coherent definition of ECB, its various objectives and wide scope, and the diversity of institutional contexts in which it takes place.

This book brings together the key papers from that global assembly, as well as new papers that reflect on what was learned and shared at the conference. We hope that readers will appreciate the intellectual contributions and thorough discussions made since the groundbreaking volume by Boyle and Lemaire (1999, Transaction Publishers), *Building Effective Evaluation Capacity: Lessons from Practice*. A decade of unpacking the concept, looking for concrete strategies of application, and learning from experience took place between the publication of that volume and the global assembly in 2009. We trust that readers will benefit from our returning to this concept, updating the conceptual understandings and frameworks, and bringing to the fore the most recent and insightful intellectual reflections in this area.

This book was published with the support of five donors, each of which was a key sponsor of the 2009 global assembly. We wish to thank the Swedish International Cooperation Agency Development (Sida), the Department for International Development (DfID) of the United Kingdom, the Belgium Development Cooperation, the Ministry of Foreign Affairs of

Denmark, and the African Development Bank. We are also grateful to the Canadian International Development Agency (CIDA), which funded an expert conference in the fall of 2009 in Quebec City to improve selected papers. Without the support of these donors, this book would not have become a reality. Finally, we would like to acknowledge the support and encouragement we gained from working with all of the contributors, who come from a wide range of countries. Although bringing this book to fruition was not easy, it was worthwhile, not the least for the pleasure of having gotten to know one another and to learn to work together.

Ray C. Rist
Washington, DC

Marie-Helene Boily and Frederic P. Martin
Quebec City

ABOUT THE CONTRIBUTORS

Rashmi AGRAWAL is the chief and head of research at the Institute of Applied Manpower Research in Planning Commission, in New Delhi. She has many years' experience in project management, evaluations, and capacity building. She holds a Ph.D. in psychology.

Balsama ANDRIANTSEHENO became interested in monitoring and evaluation in 1995, while involved in an environmental impact assessment training program. He has served as national coordinator of a governance program for the government of Madagascar.

Karin ATTSTRÖM is a manager and evaluation specialist at Ramboll Management Consulting, in Copenhagen, where she focuses on development of evaluation capacities and evaluation systems for clients such as the European Commission and international donors. She has worked extensively in both developed and developing countries, promoting the use of evaluative knowledge in policy development and decision making. She serves on the board of directors of the European Evaluation Society.

Steffen BOHNI NIELSEN is director of evaluative knowledge at Ramboll Management Consulting, in Copenhagen, where he is responsible for the knowledge and quality management of evaluation services. He has worked extensively with evaluation capacity building and results-based management, managed numerous evaluation studies, and published extensively on these topics. He is a former board member of the Danish Evaluation Society.

Marie-Helene BOILY is senior economist and training program coordinator at the IDEA International Institute, in Quebec. She has more than a decade of experience supporting the implementation of monitoring and evaluation systems in public policies, programs, projects, and training in Africa, Latin America, and Asia. She holds a master's degree in rural economics from University Laval, Quebec City.

Gilles CLOTTEAU is vice-president of the IDEA International Institute and the head of its Nairobi Regional Office. A certified project management professional, he has supported national teams in implementing results-based management approaches and tools, including monitoring and evaluation systems, in Africa, Asia, Europe, and Latin America and the Caribbean for more than 15 years. He holds a master's degree in science from the University of Quebec in Rimouski, Canada, and a master's degree in project management from the University of Quebec in Montreal.

Stefan DAHLGREN is the head of evaluation at Swedish Sida. He has significant field experience in Afghanistan, Pakistan, Sudan, Tanzania, Vietnam, and other countries. His has conducted evaluations of infrastructure, health, and natural disasters interventions; country policies and programs; and modes and methods of development cooperation.

Sana DARBOE is the director of the Dakar Regional Office of the IDEA International Institute. He has 17 years of experience in the public sector of The Gambia. Since 2007, he has supported capacity building in results-based management of country teams in Western, East, and Southern Africa. He holds an MBA from the University of Durham Business School, in the United Kingdom.

Todor DIMITROV is head of the Evaluation Office of the Black Sea Trade and Development Bank. He has 20 years of experience in international development evaluation. He worked in development evaluation in more than 30 countries, focusing on projects funded by multilateral and bilateral institutions, including the World Bank and the European Commission. He was as a board member of the International Development Evaluation Association.

Caroline HEIDER is the director of the Office of Evaluation at the World Food Programme. She has more than 20 years of international experience in the development and humanitarian field, having held a variety of posts, including deputy director of the Office of Evaluation at the International Fund for Agriculture Development. She plays an active role in international evaluation networks, such as the United Nations Evaluation Group, of which she is the vice-chair.

Mohammad JALJOULI is a strategy management adviser to the government of Dubai. He led the design and development of Dubai's Strategy Execution System and Guidebook and served as a senior public sector consultant to the World Bank in the West Bank and Gaza, Yemen, and Jordan. As the head of Jordan's Public Sector Reform Program, he pioneered the deployment of monitoring and evaluation concepts and practices within the government of Jordan.

Frederic P. MARTIN is a co-founder and co-president of IDEA International Institute, in Quebec. He holds a Ph.D. in agricultural economics from Michigan State University.

Elizabeth McALLISTER has served in leadership positions in the international development community for more than 25 years. At the World Bank, she served as director of the Operations Evaluation Department, director of the External Affairs Department, and United Nations Relations and Special Adviser to the Vice Presidency for East Asia and Pacific. At the Canadian International Development Agency (CIDA), she served as director general of performance review, director general for Latin America and the Caribbean Region, director of the China country program, and director of women in development. She holds a master's degree in public administration from the Kennedy School of Government at Harvard University.

Robert PICCIOTTO is a visiting professor at Kings College, London. He has held many senior management positions at the World Bank Group, including vice-president of corporate planning and budgeting and director-general of evaluation. He is a member of the International Advisory Committee on Development Impact of the United Kingdom, a council member of the United Kingdom Evaluation Society, and a board member of the European Evaluation Society.

Stephen PORTER is a lecturer at the School of Public and Development Management at the University of the Witwatersrand in South Africa. He holds a master's degree in public policy from the University of Cape Town.

Banda V L N RAO is a consultant to national and international organizations in project evaluation activities. He served in the Ministry of Labour and Planning Commission of the government of India in various positions involving project appraisal, management, and evaluation. He also worked for the Indian Statistical Service. He holds a master's degree in mathematics from the Indian Statistical Institute, Kolkata.

Ray C. RIST is an adviser to the Independent Evaluation Group of the World Bank. His career includes 15 years in the U.S. government, with appointments in both the executive and the legislative branches. Dr. Rist has held academic appointments at Cornell University, Johns Hopkins

University, and George Washington University. He has written, edited, or co-edited 25 books and 135 articles and lectured in more than 75 countries.

Rob D. VAN DEN BERG is director of the Evaluation Office of the Global Environment Facility in Washington, DC. Over the past 30 years he worked in various positions in Dutch development cooperation and as an advisor to the European Commission in Brussels, most recently as director of evaluation of the Dutch Ministry of Foreign Affairs. He was chairman of the OECD/DAC Network on Development Evaluation and involved in various joint international evaluations. He has co-edited several books and published articles on various aspects of policy formulation, research, evaluation, history, and development cooperation. He holds an master's degree in contemporary history from the University of Groningen in the Netherlands.

Eduardo WIESNER is a consultant to the World Bank, the United Nations, and the Inter-American Development Bank. He served as minister of finance of Colombia, director of the National Planning Department, dean of the School of Economics of the Universidad de los Andes in Bogotá, director of the Western Hemisphere Department of the International Monetary Fund, and member of the Executive Board of the World Bank.

Dhara WIJAYATILAKE is a member of the Law Commission of Sri Lanka. A lawyer by profession, she served as secretary to the Ministry of Justice and secretary of the Ministry of Plan Implementation. She has been a key actor in institutionalizing managing for development results in the Sri Lankan government.

ABBREVIATIONS

AEA	American Evaluation Association
AFD	Agence Française de Développement
Afrea	African Evaluation Association
AMREF	African and Medical Research Foundation
ARF	Agency Results Framework
ASK	Association for Stimulating Know-How
CGIAR	Consultative Group on International Agricultural Research
CIDA	Canadian International Development Agency
COMPAS	Common Performance Assessment System
CONEVAL	National Council for the Evaluation of Social Development Policy
CREAM	clear, relevant, economic, adequate, monitorable
DAC	Development Assistance Committee
DANIDA	Danish International Development Agency
DEAC	Development Evaluation Advisory Committee
DFID	Department for International Development
DSP	Dubai Strategic Plan
DWACRA	Development of Women and Children in Rural Areas
ECB	evaluation capacity building
EDMS	Electronic Documentation Management Systems
EIS	Evaluation Information System
ENAREF	Ecole Nationale des Régies Financières
e-PMS	electronic project monitoring system
FAO	Food and Agriculture Organization
FFEM	Fonds Français pour l'Environnement Mondial
GDP	gross domestic product
GEF	Global Environment Facility

GNI	gross national income
IAMR	Institute of Applied Manpower Research
IDB	Inter-American Development Bank
IDEAS	International Development Evaluation Association
IDRC	International Development Research Centre
IFAD	International Fund for Agricultural Development
IPDET	International Program for Development Evaluation Training
IPE	institutional performance evaluation
IPEN	International Program Evaluation Network
IT	information technology
IUCN	World Conservation Union
LAC	Latin America and the Caribbean
M&E	monitoring and evaluation
MDG	Millennium Development Goal
MfDR	managing for development results
MPI	Ministry of Plan Implementation (Sri Lanka)
MTEF	Medium-Term Expenditure Framework
NGO	nongovernmental organization
OECD	Organisation for Economic Co-operation and Development
OVE	Office of Evaluation and Oversight
PEO	Program Evaluation Organisation
PIU	project implementation unit
PMRY	Prime Minister Rojgar Yojana
POP	Persistent Organic Pollutant
RBM	results-based management
SEDESOL	Ministry of Social Affairs (Mexico)
SFP	Ministry of Public Service (Mexico)
SGSY	Sampoorna Grameen Swarozgar Yojana
SHCP	Ministry of Finance (Mexico)
Sida	Swedish International Development Cooperation Agency
SMART	specific, measurable, achievable, relevant, timebound
ToR	Terms of Reference
TRYSEM	Training of Rural Youth for Self-Employment
TYDF	Ten-Year Development Framework
UEMOA	Union Economique et Monétaire Ouest Africain
UN	United Nations
UNDP	United Nations Development Programme

UNEP	United Nations Environmental Programme
UNICEF	United Nations Children's Fund
USAID/PEPFAR	U.S. Agency for International Development/U.S. President's Emergency Plan for AIDS Relief
WBI	World Bank Institute

INTRODUCTION

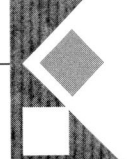

Evaluation Capacity Building: A Conceptual Framework

Ray C. Rist, Marie-Helene Boily, and Frederic Martin

Evaluation capacity building (ECB) is an often-discussed topic in developing countries and their partner international institutions. However, a quick review of the ECB literature will quickly convince readers that there is no unique way of defining and approaching ECB and its related concepts. If readers deepen their review of the ECB literature since the major publication by Boyle and Lemaire in 1999, they will note the close correlation between the evolving debate about the role of evaluation as a scientific and professional endeavor and its contribution to the development process. This correlation was clearly visible in the debates during the International Development Evaluation Association (IDEAS) Global Assembly held in Johannesburg in March 2009.

Chapters 1 through 10 of this book present selected contributions made during the 2009 IDEAS Assembly. Chapters 11 through 14 includes a set of discussions and reflections by senior development evaluation specialists. The book reviews how evaluation can lead the change process in policy and institutional development, presents a variety of good practices and lessons learned in building up evaluation capacities, and introduces new perspectives on ECB.

Results-Based Management

Monitoring and evaluation (M&E) are essential components of results-based management (RBM). It is therefore important to begin with a quick review of key concepts related to RBM.

RBM of public programs is a management approach oriented toward

- achieving development targets
- clarifying the roles and responsibilities of public servants
- increasing transparency and accountability in public affairs and budgets
- using good-quality data to improve decision making.

Although there are some variations in the main components of RBM in the public sector, there is consensus (and evident overlap) on the major pillars of RBM, as exemplified by two commonly used definitions. The Organisation for Economic Co-operation and Development (OECD) Development Assistance Committee (DAC) distinguishes the following five pillars: leadership, accountability and partnerships, monitoring and evaluation, planning and budgeting, and statistical capacity. The Inter-American Development Bank (IDB)/PRODEV identifies the following five pillars: strategic planning, budgeting for results, financial management (including auditing and procurement), program and project management, and monitoring and evaluation. Figure 1 outlines the components and relationships from the vantage point of the IDB.

Two important concepts at the heart of RBM are those of performance and accountability. *Performance* means actual achievements measured against defined goals, standards, and criteria. Performance measurement is the ongoing M&E of the results of a program, policy, or initiative, in particular, progress toward preestablished goals. Performance of a policy, program, or project can be measured in terms of its relevance, effectiveness, efficiency, sustainability, and impact (expected and unexpected). *Accountability* can be defined as a relationship based on the obligation to demonstrate and take responsibility for performance in light of agreed-upon expectations (Office of the Auditor General of Canada 2002). Performance can be measured only through a good M&E system. Therefore, M&E is at the heart of RBM.

Definitions of Monitoring and Evaluation

This book presents contributions by authors from four continents. As one might expect, it includes different approaches and understandings of ECB.

Figure 1 Components of Results-Based Management

Source: Garcia Lopez and others 2007.

One area of discussion is whether ECB should encompass the monitoring function. Monitoring and evaluation are two interrelated concepts that are important to define and distinguish.

Monitoring can be defined as a "continuing function that uses systematic collection of data on specified indicators to provide management and the main stakeholders of an ongoing development intervention with evidence of the extent of progress and achievement of objectives and progress in the use of allocated funds" (OECD 2002, 27–28). *Evaluation* refers to the "process of determining the worth or significance of an activity, policy, or program, as systematic and objective as possible, of a planned, on-going, or completed intervention" (OECD 2002, 21).

As an ongoing internal function, monitoring is used to collect information on a program's activities, outputs, and outcomes to track performance. As a periodic and largely external function, evaluation addresses key issues of relevance, targeting efficiency, effectiveness, beneficiary assessment, national ownership, sustainability, and so forth. Evaluations try to answer the "why" question behind the "what" question at the heart of monitoring (Morra Imas and Rist 2009). However, aggregated monitoring data feed into evaluation, and the two overlap to some extent in yearly performance reports—what is sometimes called the review function—hence, the suggestion to include monitoring in the concept of ECB.

Building Evaluation Capacity

A literature review by Nielsen and Lemire (n.d., 3) reveals the following trends when referring to ECB: "widespread conceptual pluralism, differing opinions regarding the purpose of ECB, the lack of a comprehensive empirical base for the various models, and a significant focus on approaches and methods for tackling capacity building, with less attention being paid to the nature of ECB."

Boyle and Lemaire (1999, 5) define evaluation capacity as the "human capital (skills, knowledge, experience, and so forth) and financial/material resources" needed to undertake an evaluation. ECB refers to "activities and initiatives taken to implement an evaluation regime" (Boyle and Lemaire 1999, 6). Stokdill, Baizerman, and Compton (2002, 8) define ECB as "a context-dependent, intentional action system of guided processes and practices for bringing about and sustaining a state of affairs in which high-quality program evaluation and its appropriate uses are ordinary and ongoing practices within and/or between one or more organizations/programs/sites."

A broader definition by Mackay (2002, 83) suggests that ECB should ensure that knowledge from M&E is applied as part of sound public governance and that it should encompass "a broad range of evaluative tools and approaches that include but go beyond program evaluation," capacity building being one step along a "results chain." He suggests a more complete definition of evaluation capacity as "an organization's ability to bring about, align, and sustain its objectives, structure, processes, culture, human capital and technology to produce evaluative knowledge that informs ongoing practices and decision-making in order to improve organizational effectiveness" (p. 14).

Conceptual underpinnings and field experience show that demand for evaluation and supply of evaluation products are equally important to ensure that good-quality evaluations are produced and used in the decision-making process. ECB should not only emphasize building capacities of suppliers of evaluation products, but also aim at improving capacities on the demand side (Picciotto 1995; Boyle and Lemaire 1999). Figure 2 suggests four possible scenarios.

Developing an Evaluation Capacity Assessment Framework

A good assessment of existing evaluation capacity is the starting point to the elaboration of a good ECB plan (figure 3). The move toward RBM in the public sector in developing countries comes from a growing social demand for government to demonstrate results as well as from demand by donors

Figure 2 Demand and Supply Framework for Evaluation Capacity Building

		Evaluation demand	
		Strong	Weak
Evaluation supply	Strong	High evaluation capacity, high utilization	High evaluation capacity, limited utilization
	Weak	Limited evaluation capacity, high utilization of studies produced	Little evaluation capacity, little utilization of evaluation studies

Source: Boyle and Lemaire 1999.

for greater accountability.[1] This change in the public management culture requires reforms to revise the legal framework for greater governance, such as an accountability law, a financial responsibility law, or both. The governance framework must be conducive to the implementation of a results culture in the whole of government (Grob 2010). The governance framework affects both the demand for and the supply of M&E results. It must ensure that preconditions exist to guarantee the production of good M&E results and the use of these results in decision making.

A functioning and performing M&E system requires that the supply of M&E information respond to demand from decision makers and other stakeholders, that the information be communicated on time and in an adequate format, and that a minimum capacity exists to analyze and process this information for decision making at the level of both suppliers and users of M&E information. Consequently, the components of the evaluation capacity assessment framework should take into account the demand side and the supply side, with the objective of producing results of the M&E system that will feed back into the change management process through better planning, policy making, and program budgeting.

Evaluation capacity can be assessed in terms of four dimensions: institutional capital, human capital, technical capital, and financial capital. Each is described below.

Institutional capital

On the demand side, institutional capital includes objectives of decision makers and accountability requirements, as expressed by the M&E legal framework and the M&E policy if it exists. The objectives of decision makers should be divided into various information needs at the strategic level

Figure 3 Framework for Assessing Evaluation Capacity

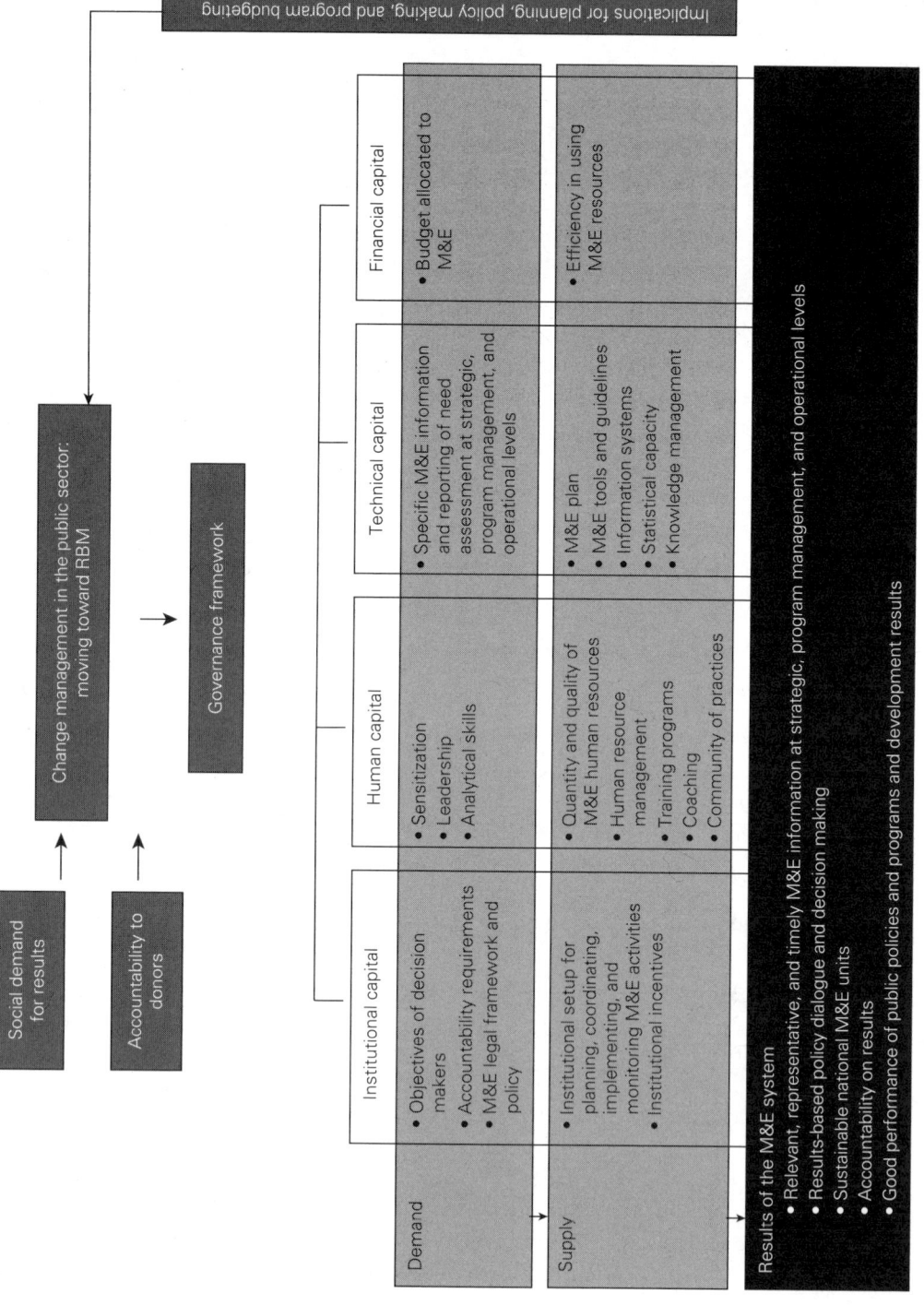

Influencing Change: Building Evaluation Capacity to Strengthen Governance (the cabinet, the national development planning commission, line ministry planning and M&E units, and so forth); the program management level (technical department in line ministries); and the operational level (line ministry institutional activities and investment projects). A good understanding of the information needs of decision makers will ensure that the supply of information meets the demand for results-based information and promotes greater use of M&E results in decision making. Accountability to parliament, civil society, citizens, and donors will also stimulate the demand for results-based information. The existence of an M&E legal framework or policy will institutionalize and reinforce the importance of using M&E results in decision making (see Kusek and Rist 2004).

On the supply side, institutional capital includes the institutional setup as well as institutional incentives implemented to ensure the adequate production of M&E information. The institutional setup includes the mechanisms implemented for planning, coordinating, implementing, and monitoring M&E activities. It deals with the definition of the M&E function and the position of this function at different levels (from the president or prime minister's office down to the project level) (Leeuw 2006). Institutional incentives for good performance—and, when necessary, sanctions for bad performance—also need to be put in place. Incentives can be established by linking future budgetary allocations to performance, for instance. Mechanisms also need to be implemented to ensure proper follow-up to evaluations (that is, monitoring the implementation of proposed corrective measures).

Human capital

There needs to be adequate human resources on the demand side, including decision makers, civil society, and citizens, all of whom need to be sensitized to the importance of performance measurement through M&E. For decision makers, leadership must be ensured to support M&E. For instance, if a minister does not believe in the importance of measuring results, there is a high probability that little importance will be given to M&E activities within the ministry and that the minister's decisions will not be based on results. Decision makers must have at least minimal analytical skills to be able to interpret results-based information and make decisions based on that information.

Human capital is of primary importance for the production of M&E results. There needs to be good capacity in terms of the quantity and quality of M&E human resources, both within the organization (M&E staff) and outside the organization (external evaluators). Proper training and experience as well as the establishment of a multidisciplinary team is needed to ensure good M&E. Human resource management is also important to ensure the stability of M&E staff through greater retention, including the implementation of measures such as tailor-made career paths, individual incentives, and performance contracts.[2] Finally, access to existing training programs, coaching activities, and communities of practice within the public sector, the country, the region, or even at the international level needs to be assessed (see the discussion of the readiness assessment diagnostic in Kusek and Rist 2004).

Technical capital

Global information needs for decision-making and accountability purposes should lead to more-specific assessments of needs in terms of indicators, the degree of precision, the disaggregation level, frequency, and information flows and data bases at the three key levels (strategic, program management, and operations). Existing technical capital and gaps with respect to the needs identified above have to be assessed, including the existence of an M&E plan; M&E tools and guidelines; information systems and statistical capacity to ensure data quality; data collection process; survey systems; and data processing, validation, storage, analysis, and dissemination. Technical capacity also encompasses knowledge management, which includes mechanisms that ensure the sharing, storage, and dissemination of M&E results. The incorporation of knowledge management is increasingly being understood as critical to good M&E practice.[3]

Financial capital

The availability of adequate financial resources should reflect actual demand for M&E results, just as with other management systems in the public sector, be they budget systems, audit systems, human resource systems, or information technology systems. Resources should enable public sector organizations to properly implement mechanisms and activities to ensure the production of good-quality M&E information and develop M&E capacity in a reasonably remunerative and sustainable way. Undersourcing efforts leads to staff mobility and loss of quality, with negative consequences for decision making and development results. At the same time, M&E staff and external evaluators should be able to demonstrate the efficient use of M&E financial resources, with consideration for the relevance and timeliness of results versus the cost of various methodologies and the desired degree of statistical precision and disaggregation levels.

This evaluation capacity assessment framework should be interpreted in a systemic and dynamic way, in which the concepts presented in different boxes in figure 3 are interrelated. Every country and institution is a specific case study for which different issues are relevant and significant. However, some issues tend to be more important than others, as exemplified by a recent ranking conducted during a 2010 International Program for Development Evaluation Training (IPDET) workshop that identified the following priority issues, in order of decreasing importance:

1. lack of or inadequate M&E policy framework, legislation, and procedures; insufficient coordination among donors to support national M&E systems
2. insufficient skills within M&E units, compounded by staff mobility and the lack of local training institutes in M&E
3. limited demand for evaluation and lack of interest from politicians
4. limited financial resources allocated to M&E
5. inadequate follow-up on evaluation reports
6. positioning of M&E units within a ministry organization with limited power; lack of recognition of M&E as a professional career within the public administration
7. lack of systematic baselines; excess or inadequate numbers of indicators, limited and low-quality information systems
8. resistance to change within the bureaucracy to results-based M&E.

Structure of This Book

The first four chapters explore how evaluation can influence and interact with the change process in policy and institutional development. In chapter 1, Dhara Wijayatilake recounts a riveting story about how evaluation was introduced in Sri Lanka and the striking results that were achieved in a few years through a progressive and pragmatic approach coupled with strong leadership. In chapter 2, Eduardo Wiesner reviews the role of evaluation in the formation of macroeconomic policy in Latin America, outlining the role of demand for improved results and performance and of accountability from politicians, the private sector, civil society, and, in the end, the population. In chapter 3, Todor Dimitrov proposes a seven-step approach for tackling institutional performance evaluation and applies it to the case of the Black Sea Trade and Development Bank. In chapter 4, Mohammad Jaljouli addresses the challenge of integrating development strategy and the evaluation process, using Dubai as a case study.

Chapters 5 through 10 present a variety of lessons learned and good practices in ECB. In chapter 5, Caroline Heider presents a structured approach to capacity development at three levels (individual training, institutional development, and creation of an enabling environment) and suggests moving from capacities to capabilities. In chapter 6, Rob van den Berg illustrates how evaluation capacity has been developed and could be further developed in a critical area for the future in environment and development. In chapter 7, Rashmi Agrawal and Banda VLN Rao identify various factions influencing the use of evaluation results and show how capacity building was used in India to increase this use. In chapter 8, Balsama Andriantseheno examines how an M&E system for a major development program can be set up as part of a programmatic approach using the case study of the Environment/Rural Development and Food Security program in Madagascar. In chapter 9, Stephen Porter outlines the potential of the "helping" approaches in evaluation capacity development strategy, using the Bana Barona/Abantwanu Bethu project in South Africa to prove his point. In chapter 10, Gilles Clotteau, Marie-Helene Boily, Sana Darboe, and Frederic Martin review major challenges in ECB and present a variety of ECB strategies for designing and implementing national results-based M&E systems, building on experiences in Africa, Asia, and Latin America.

Chapters 11 through 14 offer a stimulating comparative analysis of the chapters 1 through 10. In chapter 11, Robert Picciotto outlines a path for the future of development evaluation on the basis of a review of emerging endogenous and exogenous trends. In chapter 12, Elizabeth McAllister explores the interface between the evaluation function and organizational leadership in setting results strategy and the limitation of results approaches as implemented by the international development community. In chapter 13, Steffen Bohni Nielsen and Karin Attström map the perspectives offered by the contributors in terms of scope, purpose, definitions, and methods and relate key findings and recommendations to the ECB framework offered by Heider in chapter 5. In chapter 14, Stefan Dahlgren underlines that building evaluation capacity requires not only competence and quality but also taking into account the political and institutional context, costs, relative importance of learning and accountability, and differences and similarities between monitoring and evaluation.

Notes

1. For an excellent discussion of how this demand is growing and evolving in South Asia, see Carden (2010) and Hay (2010).
2. Bangladesh, for example, has more than a 30 percent vacancy rate for M&E officers in its national M&E bureau (ADB 2010).

3. For two informative discussions on this topic, see Perrin (2006) and Spinatsch (2006).

Bibliography

Asia-Pacific Community of Practice on Managing for Development Results. 2010. "Workshop on Monitoring and Evaluation Framework for Public Sector Development Projects." Dhaka, Bangladesh, May 2–3.

Boyle, R., and D. Lemaire 1999. *Building Effective Evaluation Capacity: Lessons from Practice*. Piscataway, NJ: Transaction Publishers.

Carden, F. 2010. "Introduction to the Forum on Evaluation Field Building in South Asia." *American Journal of Evaluation* 31 (2): 219–21.

Garcia Lopez R., R. Garcia Moreno, J. Kaufman, and S. Rodriguez. 2007. "Managing for Development Results in the Public Sector: An Analytical Tool, PRODEV Evaluation System," PRODEV, Inter-Amercian Development Bank.

Grob, G. F. 2010. "Evaluation Field Building in South Asia: Insights from the Rear View Mirror." *American Journal of Evaluation* 31 (2): 241–45.

Hay, K. 2010. "Evaluation Field Building in South Asia: Reflections, Anecdotes, and Questions." *American Journal of Evaluation* 31 (2): 222–31.

Kusek, J. Z., and R. C. Rist. 2004. *Ten Steps to a Results-Based Monitoring and Evaluation System: A Handbook for Development Practitioners*. Washington, DC: World Bank.

Leeuw, F. L. 2006. "Managing Evaluations in the Netherlands and Types of Knowledge." In *From Studies to Streams: Managing Evaluative Systems,* ed. R. C. Rist and N. Stame, 81–97. Piscataway, NJ: Transaction Publishers.

Mackay, K. 2002. "The World Bank's ECB Experience." *New Directions for Evaluation* 93 (Spring): 88–99.

Morra Imas, L. G., and R. C. Rist. 2009. *The Road to Results: Designing and Conducting Effective Development Evaluations*. Washington, DC: World Bank.

Nielsen, S. B., and S. Lemire. n.d. "Measuring Evaluation Capacity: Results and Implications of a Danish Study." Copenhagen.

OECD (Organisation for Economic Co-operation and Development). 2002. *OECD Glossary of Key Terms in Evaluation and Results-Based Management*. Development Assistance Committee, Paris.

Office of the Auditor General of Canada. 2002. *Report of the Auditor General to the House of Commons. Chapter 9. Modernizing Accountability in the Public Sector*. Ottawa.

Perrin, B. 2006. "How Evaluation Can Help Make Knowledge Management Real." In *From Studies to Streams: Managing Evaluative Systems,* ed. R. C. Rist and N. Stame, 23–45. Piscataway, NJ: Transaction Publishers.

Picciotto, R. 1995. "Introduction: Evaluation and Development." *New Directions for Evaluation* 67 (Fall): 13–23.

Spinatsch, M. 2006. "Management of Evaluative Knowledge in National Health: Some Comparative Observations." In *From Studies to Streams: Managing Evaluative Systems*, ed. R. C. Rist and N. Stame, 49–64. Piscataway, NJ: Transaction Publishers.

Stockdill, S. H., M. Baizerman, and D. W. Compton. 2002. "Toward a Definition of the ECB Process: A Conversation with the ECB Literature." *New Directions for Evaluation* 93 (Spring): 7–26.

CHAPTER 1

Working toward Development Results: The Case of Sri Lanka

Dhara Wijayatilake

This chapter describes Sri Lanka's experiences in institutionalizing managing for development results (MfDR) using a "whole of government" approach. It highlights the strategy adopted, the challenges faced, and the lessons learned in the three years since the initiative was launched in 2007. It also describes plans for the future.

Sri Lanka is blessed with an abundance of human and natural resources. Translating these resources into tangible benefits for the people is a challenge that many administrations have taken on.

In recent years, a highly literate constituency was becoming increasingly eager to see a government that works. It was looking for meaningful progress by the country as a whole and for value additions that would improve the quality of their own lives. The government was keen to deliver. It is in this context that a focus was placed on the need for a better management strategy to enhance the efficacy of government and to allow it to respond more meaningfully to the aspirations of the people.

Sri Lanka is a lower-middle-income country with social indicators that are among the best in the region. Much progress had been made in literacy (91 percent), girls' education, and maternal and infant mortality. At the national level, the education and health sectors have shown commendable achievements, supported by strong institutional frameworks.

Reducing poverty and bridging regional disparities were identified as urgent national priorities. The development of infrastructure outside the Western Province was viewed as a necessary response to achieve a regionally balanced economy.[1] Hence, significant investment was made to improve roads, increase the power supply, provide access to clean water, and enhance education. Because many development projects were implemented with donor funding, there was a clear need to ensure aid effectiveness.

If sustainable development was to be achieved, implementation of these projects had to be effective and efficient, and it had to produce meaningful results. A system based on the use of information and evaluation findings to make better decisions and improve policies and performance was seen as a means of improving government performance. The approach was to introduce a management system that focused on results at all levels of the development cycle: planning, implementation, and evaluation.

Monitoring and Evaluation as of 2006

The Ministry of Plan Implementation (MPI) was mandated with, among other functions, monitoring and reviewing the progress of all plans, programs, and projects of the government as well as public sector investment programs. As of 2007, MPI was reporting quarterly progress to the cabinet of ministers with an analysis of the expenditure progress of ministries as well as the physical progress of development projects. This reporting merely monitored expenditure and reported on physical progress as reported by the implementing agency. The role of monitoring focused on outputs; there was no integrated system with a focus on results.

MPI also had an electronic project monitoring system (e-PMS), which was capturing project progress data online. Although the system had all the features necessary for project monitoring, it faced two significant challenges. First, although monthly updating was mandatory, project management staff were not always entering data periodically and without delay, undermining the quality of the information available in the system. Second, the information entered in the system was not being read with a view to extracting information that would lead to appropriate and timely interventions to improve performance. Instead, e-PMS was perceived largely as a tool of MPI and was not being accessed by others. An excellent system was in place, but stakeholders had yet to appreciate its potential.

There was also inadequate appreciation of the value of evaluations. There was no accepted evaluation policy and no focus on impact evaluations. Almost all project evaluations were conducted at the insistence of donors. Although evidence-based decision making was evident in all other spheres, there was a lack of sensitivity to the need for evidence to make decisions within the development regime. The need to highlight the value of evaluations and to motivate the use of evaluation findings as evidence to improve government programs was urgent.

The Policy Framework as of 2006

As of 2006, Sri Lanka had an ambitious national development program, the Ten-Year Development Framework (TYDF), known as the Mahinda Chintana, which set out the development agenda for 2006–16 and a serious commitment to realize that agenda. A three-year Medium-Term Expenditure Framework (MTEF) was based on the TYDF. As a policy, resource allocation to line ministries was determined in terms of the TYDF, and all projects financed with foreign funds had to be in compliance with this strategy. Expected outcomes and key performance indicators were set out for important sectors.

Institutionalizing MfDR in the Whole of Government

Sri Lanka signed the Paris Declaration on Aid Effectiveness in 2005, thereby committing to introduce MfDR to achieve foreign aid effectiveness. MPI saw MfDR as a valuable strategy that could be adopted not only to enhance foreign aid effectiveness but also to improve the way the government does business. The ministry had to match the ambition with which the development program had been embarked upon with effectiveness and ensure that all investments yielded results that could be sustained. The focus on outputs alone had to change. MfDR was introduced in the whole of government, with a strong results-based monitoring and evaluation (M&E) component. The initiative commenced in early 2007.

Assumptions and Strategy

MPI based its plan on the following assumptions:

- *Required infrastructure.* To build a workable system, it was accepted that each agency should have a multiyear strategic plan, a sound data collection system, and an annual activity plan. Performance evaluation and a reporting framework to measure performance were of the essence.
- *Political support.* MPI was conscious that support from the highest level of political leadership would be vital.
- *Capacity.* The public service had the capacity to engage in a change process. Hence, it would be possible to build capacity while implementing MfDR.
- *Difficulty of task.* The proposed effort was ambitious. MPI recognized that it would face many obstacles and make many mistakes. It proceeded on the assumption that there was adequate commitment within MPI to initiate and sustain the task as well as the wisdom and willingness to admit mistakes and take remedial action.

The strategy had to be formulated with sensitivity to the ethos of the public service, the aspirations of the political leadership, and the existing capacity of those who would function as change agents. Toward that end, the following decisions were made regarding management of the process:

- For assurance that stakeholders assumed ownership for the strategy, a core group of stakeholders was appointed.[2] This "think tank" group was tasked with steering the process of institutionalizing MfDR throughout the government. As the secretary of MPI, I chaired the group and developed a plan of action to institutionalize MfDR based on the key strategies proposed—namely, that the initiative would be introduced through a phased-out program; that it should adopt a whole-of-government approach; and that in the final stage, the budget should be linked to results and the audit should focus on a performance (value for money) audit rather than a mere regulatory compliance audit.
- All things considered, it was decided that it would be advantageous to introduce the strategy at the level of line ministries. Doing so would require engaging with key officers who would be initiated into the program at the earliest stage, leaving room for their own development and enhancement of their capacity over time.
- Vertical and horizontal alignments and cascading below the level of the line ministry would be done subsequently.
- Given MPI's own capacity as well as the need to use the introduction phase as a learning exercise, it was decided to introduce the strategy to

ministries in stages. Four key ministries (education, health, agriculture, and highways) were selected for the pilot phase. The selection was based on several factors. All of the selected ministries had mandates that had a direct impact on the lives of the people, they had to show results, and they had committed leadership. It was necessary to work with believers, and the senior staffs of these ministries were believers.

- The program was introduced in steps. First, the mandate to redefine, if necessary, the vision and mission of the ministry was reexamined. Second, each ministry developed its own Agency Results Framework (ARF), which set out the thrust areas and goals and targets for a medium term of five years as well as key performance indicators with which to measure progress. The thrust areas and goals were required to be identified with reference to the mandate of each ministry; the TYDF; and where relevant, the Millennium Development Goals (MDGs). All activities of the ministry were henceforth to be based on the ARF, and resources were to be sought to achieve the identified targets. A scorecard based on the achievement of the targets identified in the ARF was compiled for each ministry. Each ministry then had a monitorable results framework.
- The approach in formulating the ARF was a process rather than a product approach. The process approach required the active involvement of the staff of each ministry in formulating the ARF. The framework was to be developed and owned by each ministry and periodically revised to improve its content. It was important that each ministry assume ownership for its ARF. Had the product approach been used, each ministry would have been handed an ARF developed by an external source, which ministry officers may have rejected.
- Recognition and acceptance at the highest level of political leadership were obtained through a note from MPI to the cabinet of ministers outlining the initiative, with the assurance that its objective was to make government more efficient and to yield results that would improve the quality of life of the Sri Lankan people. As a follow-up, the cabinet was advised of the proposal to introduce performance agreements with key officials.
- The next stage of the initiative was to secure vertical alignment of outcomes with sector-level outcomes.
- Linking resource allocation to results would be ensured after all ministries had been introduced to the MfDR strategy and developed their ARFs. The Ministry of Finance and Planning would have the ARF and the key performance indicators to assist in resource allocation.
- A performance-based audit rather than a mere regulatory audit would be conducted.

Supportive Measures

MPI took the following steps in support of the initiative:

- A database, the Evaluation Information System (EIS), was launched. Because a results-based M&E system relies heavily on learning from evaluation findings, it was considered necessary to enhance a belief in evaluations and to provide an accessible database containing evaluation findings. A synthesis of evaluation reports is collated in the EIS with features that provide easy access to specific areas through an effective search engine.
- As a means of keeping the newly established community of stakeholders (officers in the ministries) well informed of MfDR–related news (happenings within the country, global events, and so forth), MPI created a quarterly newsletter, *Results Focus*, to share news and views. The newsletter is posted on the ministry Web site and forwarded to all ministries and other stakeholders. We hope that, through this effort, it will be possible to engage with the community, which will sustain an interest in this initiative not only as a mere function undertaken by the ministry but as an inspiring exercise that will contribute to more effective development.
- The process of working with other ministries was continued. As of the end of 2008, 35 ministries, including MPI, had been introduced to MfDR in two more phases. When the ARF of a ministry was finalized, it was posted on the Web site of that ministry as well as on the MPI Web site. Not all ministries have been able to finalize their ARFs. Some have struggled because of the lack of baseline data. We are patient with these ministries and continue to work with them.

Results-Based Budgeting

The 2010 budget call issued by the Ministry of Finance and Planning in July 2009 included a requirement that all ministries submit a results framework with identified key performance indicators with their budget estimates. At this stage, MPI worked with ministries to help them refine or formulate their ARFs. The MfDR initiative of MPI thus received recognition, with the Ministry of Finance and Planning confirming that the first steps had been taken toward results-based budgeting.

Incentives

A performance appraisal system is in place for public officers. Even with the new management strategy, these officers will be engaged in the same volume of work and will be appraised accordingly.

The scorecard system will identify ministries that have worked well. These ministries' efforts will be recognized. Apart from that, no additional incentives are considered necessary. I do not believe that we need to reward public officers to perform at their optimum levels and make their own contribution to the country's development with anything other than the promise of recognition for good work done. I hope I am proved correct.

Lessons Learned after Three Years

As expected, the challenges have been many. The most important challenge is to remember that even this initiative should be results based. There is a tendency at times to follow "best practices" and lose sight of the importance of ascertaining whether the adoption of such practices has actually yielded the desired results.

Ensuring the Quality of the ARFs

Ministries do not always formulate good ARFs. It is necessary to improve quality as a continuing exercise. We cannot rest on our laurels and merely count the number of ministries that have finalized their ARFs without assessing their quality. An ARF has to be treated as a flexible document that can be improved.

Gathering Data

The Department of Census and Statistics conducts periodic surveys and has a rich collection of data. However, the MfDR initiative requires data that are specific to the targets identified in ministries' ARFs. Many ministries had no baseline data and had difficulty identifying measurable indicators because of the absence of systematic data collection in relation to targets. The fact that data should be accurate and authentic must be constantly emphasized.

Reporting

All ministries continued to treat progress reporting as an irritant. Although MPI assumed this role with more diligence than ever, with new software systems to facilitate data collection, inspiring ministries to pay attention to the accuracy of the information provided proved to be a challenge. More serious was the concern that data were being collected only for the purpose of submission to MPI rather than for internal use in monitoring performance. On a positive note, MPI was able to improve project data submission on e-PMS.

Securing Buy-In from the People's Representatives

To elected representatives of the people, a focus on a system that measures real results may not be an exciting proposition. How can they be inspired to believe in a performance measuring system? It is a challenge to explain that an M&E system will offer proof of development that can, in turn, be used to convince voters of the effectiveness of their representatives.

Political support from the highest level is always an asset. We had that support, which was enhanced by recognition of the effort at meetings of ministry secretaries. We were conscious that it was necessary to keep ministers engaged in a meaningful way by constantly highlighting the advantages of the systems being introduced. The initiative cannot be sustained without their support.

Acknowledging that Change Takes Time

The statement that we had put in place a results-based management system with an M&E system in 35 ministries needed to have some meaning. We needed to take stock of what we had actually succeeded in doing. Had we succeeded in implementing the theory of change? The stocktaking made us realize that although MfDR had become a buzzword within the ministries we had worked with, it was necessary to improve the quality of the work done before proceeding further. We had engaged with the ministries that were assigned responsibilities with respect to the most important functions. We therefore decided to develop sector outcomes and address the issue of alignment in important sectors such as agriculture, education, and health before proceeding to work with the other ministries. Doing so became our new focus by the end of 2009. We checked our impatience and decided that it would be good to take some time lest the initiative end up as an output with no outcome.

Fostering Leadership

We realized the importance of the lead ministry being taken seriously. Unless it is perceived as a force to be reckoned with, other ministries will not respond with any degree of seriousness. The role of MPI as an oversight ministry, rather than a line ministry, proved to be an appropriate institutional arrangement to take this change management initiative forward.

We also realized that leadership at all levels is vital to secure success in an initiative such as this. To date, the ministries that have responded well to this initiative are those that have sound leadership.

Accomplishments as of the End of 2009

MfDR with a strong focus on M&E has now been introduced in 35 ministries, 28 of which have completed ARFs, which are posted on the Web site of MPI.[3] In the wake of the 2010 budget call, all ministries have now had some introduction to MfDR. Results frameworks are being formulated with respect to certain high-value development projects, and an instruction manual for the training of trainers has been prepared. The M&E function has been enhanced through capacity building of officers in MPI and other ministries. An EIS has been launched to collate evaluation findings, and the evaluation capacity of public officers is being strengthened.[4] *Results Focus*, our newsletter, continues to be released quarterly. Through its many activities, MPI has been able to secure recognition for MfDR and, among public officers, to inspire a belief in its value. Academic courses that teach MfDR have been introduced at the postgraduate level.

Our initiative has attracted international interest. As a result, we have had many visitors—from Afghanistan, Bangladesh, Yemen, IPDET, and the Asia-Pacific Community of Practice on Managing for Development Results—all of whom have spent time at MPI looking at what we have done. We at MPI are inspired and encouraged by this interest, although at this stage, our initiative needs to be valued more for its vision and ambition than for its actual achievements.

Future Plans

MPI has identified the value of an integrated system. Gaps will be identified and addressed to ensure an integrated system that will recognize a results focus throughout the development cycle, commencing from the planning stage through budgeting, implementation, and auditing.

Alignment of ministry outcomes and indicators with sector outcomes and indicators is under way. Total vertical alignment will be achieved. MfDR will also be introduced at the subnational level, through the provincial councils.

Conclusion

The kings who ruled our country centuries ago engaged in development that was truly amazing. They were responsible for constructions that today are regarded as engineering marvels.

Some may argue that there was no dependence then on any of the systems now viewed as necessary. To them, my response is this: achievements of the past were based on good judgment, common sense, gut feeling, and wisdom, all of which remain relevant today. What is offered as sophisticated systems in impressive packages is, in a sense, old wine in new bottles. Those who were successful in the past made decisions that proved to be the right ones. There are instances when wrong decisions were taken and success did not follow: wells were dug in the wrong locations; schools were constructed that had no staff to teach in them; marketplaces were constructed that were too small to be of value. The strategy proposed here is, in essence, a sophisticated presentation of the collective wisdom that was used to be successful, a collection of good sense with minimum risks. This disciplined process ensures decision making based on real evidence.

We continue to be inspired by the splendid response we have received from the ministries with which we have worked. The excitement we have been able to generate is real. We have every reason to be hopeful that we will succeed.

Every country needs to identify the strategy that works best for it. I never believed we had the ideal setting to embark upon this initiative. Although our initiative amounts to administrative reform, we embarked upon it without using that label. All we had was a dream and a homegrown strategy. We have made a start and are committed to make a success of what we have started.

Notes

1. The Western Province is home to the administrative and commercial capitals of Sri Lanka.
2. The group consisted of the secretaries to the five pilot-phase institutions (the Ministry of Finance and Planning, the Department of Census and Statistics, the Office of the President, the Office of the Prime Minister, and the Information and Communication Technology Agency) as well as representatives of stakeholder institutions (the central bank and the auditor general). Ministry secretaries are officers who function at the highest level of the administration and are the chief executive officers in ministries.
3. See http://www.mpi.gov.lk.
4. See http://www.mpi.gov.lk.

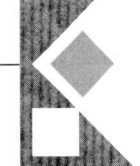

CHAPTER 2

The Evaluation of Macroeconomic Institutional Arrangements in Latin America

Eduardo Wiesner

The central idea of this chapter is to suggest a common analytical evaluative framework that may be useful in addressing specific evaluation issues across varied evaluation settings. The chapter offers the view that there is a modicum "universal" core of analytical concepts and templates with, prima facie, useful general applicability for addressing different evaluation challenges. This core framework evolves from plausible causality and endogenous relationships between rules, incentives, information, and accountabilities. The discussion is based largely on the results of an empirical evaluation conducted in 2007–08 of macroeconomic performance in several Latin American countries (Weiner 2008).[1]

The chapter offers two main messages. The first is that the effectiveness of evaluation in enhancing results and policies is largely a function of the degree to which it is driven by the demand for improved results and performance. From this perspective, demand-driven evaluation acts as an incentive to encourage the search for new information and evaluability rules to improve accountability and learning.[2] Furthermore, demand-driven evaluation is a highly effective way to configure the "right" evaluation capacity development from the supply side of the institutional arrangement. As Boyle, Lemaire, and Rist (1999, 12) note, "Achieving a suitable balance between the demand for and the supply of evaluation becomes a key issue in evaluation institutionalization."

The second main message is that accountability in the private, public, and even political markets is ultimately the key incentive driving the quality of evaluations and the effectiveness of capacity building.[3] Capacity building thus requires—and results from—the generation and use of information on the specifics of the "transaction costs"[4] of alternative institutional arrangements.[5] Within this context, evaluation capacity building is also largely a function of the demand for—and use of—the most relevant information on the determinants of what is being evaluated.

These are not new discoveries, but their importance is such that they deserve to be reiterated and their policy implications underscored. After all, without the private or political demand for a given result and the attendant incentives to reward the provision of what is being demanded, it is very difficult for evaluation to be effective and to contribute to the achievement of the desired results. Given the important evaluative implications of the current world financial crisis, the chapter ends with a brief discussion on how this core analytical evaluative framework can enhance the effectiveness of development evaluation in general and contribute to a better understanding of the causes of crises.

The Evaluation of Institutions and the Evolving Frontiers of Evaluation Priorities

Evaluation priorities are evolving from individual projects to programs, sectors, policies, countries, and institutions in general. Within this process, country program evaluations are becoming the unit of analysis, as country developmental effectiveness is the ultimate goal of both bilateral and multilateral institutions and countries themselves.[6] The emerging paradigm in social and economic development is that institutions—and the incentives they contain—are the main determinants of long-term country prosperity. If institutions are what matters most, assessing institutional developmental performance becomes a distinct evaluation priority.[7] According to Ostrom,

Schroeder, and Wynne (1993, 112), what matters is the sustainability of institutional arrangements.

Notwithstanding the empirical problems related to measuring the links between the "right" and the "wrong" institutions on the one hand and development on the other, the "institutional hypothesis" has come to be regarded as the key explanatory variable for overall long-term economic, social, and political results across developed and developing countries. The notion that institutions are the crux of development has led to—and resulted from—an analytical framework called "new institutional economics," the central concepts of which are that incentives, history, politics, and beliefs play a major role in determining which institutions end up prevailing in a given society at a given moment in time (Williamson 2000). Within this context, the research agenda of development and of evaluation for development is not so much to further the notion that institutions matter or that they influence—and result from—policies but to "unbundle" this finding into its causal effects and the identification of which institutions matter most and why (Acemoglu 2005).

Within institutions as a whole, the macroeconomic institutional arrangements regulating the interaction between central banks, ministries of finance, and financial sector supervision seem to be the most critical, because they determine macroeconomic volatility, affect private and public revenues and expenditures, and, hence, provide the overall incentive environment. More important, they determine macroeconomic performance and growth and, hence, employment and poverty levels as well as poverty and distributive justice in general.

On both growth and equity, the record for Latin America is a dismal one. Some rapid growth periods notwithstanding, Latin America's growth record has been slow and volatile. From 1960 to 2000, the average annual real per capita rate of growth was 1.3 percent. Over the same period, Asia's annual per capita gross domestic product (GDP) grew 4.6 percent (table 2.1).

Figure 2.1 shows that Latin America's relatively slow rates of economic growth go back as far as 1870 and decline sharply after 1980. Why this is so is a subject of debate, particularly concerning the role of institutions.[8]

Figure 2.2 shows that Latin America has also recorded higher GDP volatility than most regions since the 1960s.

In brief, although some institutional arrangements, such as those regulating the interface between education and health or between infrastructure and environmental protection, are important, the arrangements determining the rates of economic growth, macroeconomic volatility, and the redistributive effectiveness of social expenditures appear to be the most critical ones. They deserve special evaluation priority.

Table 2.1 Growth of per Capita GDP in Latin America and Selected Comparators, 1960–2000
(percent)

Country or region	1960s	1970s	1980s	1990s	1960–2000
Argentina	2.3	1.4	−3.9	4.2	1.0
Chile	2.2	1.2	1.3	4.8	2.4
Japan	9.3	3.1	3.5	1.1	4.2
United States	2.9	2.7	2.2	2.3	2.5
Latin America[a]	2.3	2.1	−1.8	1.6	1.3
East Asia[b]	4.7	5.4	4.5	4.0	4.6

Source: De Gregorio and Lee 2003.

a. Includes 15 countries with largest GDP (Argentina, Bolivia, Brazil, Chile, Colombia, Costa Rica, the Dominican Republic, Ecuador, El Salvador, Guatemala, Mexico, Paraguay, Peru, Uruguay, and República Bolivariana de Venezuela.

b. Includes China; Hong Kong SAR, China; Indonesia; the Republic of Korea; Malaysia; the Philippines; Taiwan SAR, China; and Thailand.

Figure 2.1 Per Capita Income Relative to the OECD, 1870–2000

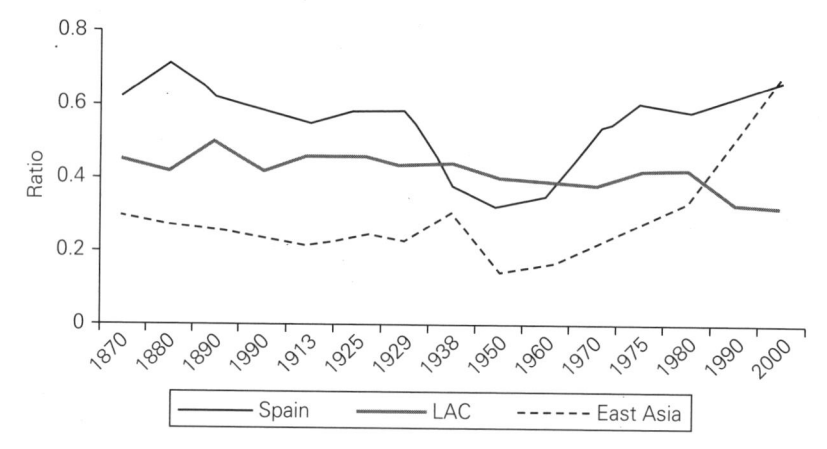

Source: Perry and others 2006.

Note: Latin America and the Caribbean includes Argentina, Mexico, Uruguay, and República Bolivariana de Venezuela. East Asia includes Hong Kong SAR, China; Korea; Singapore, and Taiwan SAR, China. LAC = Latin America and the Caribbean.

The Evaluation of Macroeconomic Institutions and Arrangements

The literature on the evaluation of institutional performance is vast and varied. This is understandable given the complexity of the issues

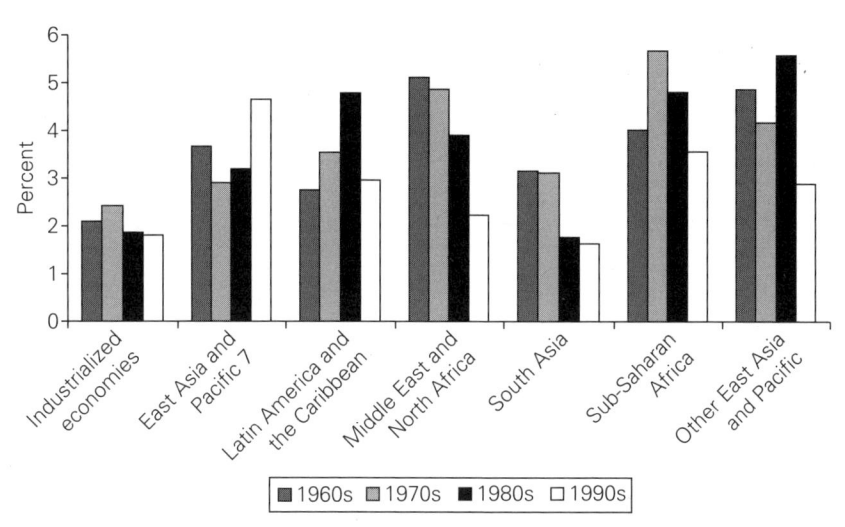

Figure 2.2 Volatility of Real GDP Growth, 1960s–90s

[Bar chart showing percent volatility of real GDP growth by region across decades (1960s, 1970s, 1980s, 1990s) for: Industrialized economies, East Asia and Pacific 7, Latin America and the Caribbean, Middle East and North Africa, South Asia, Sub-Saharan Africa, Other East Asia and Pacific.]

Source: De Ferranti and others 2000.

involved and the endogenous nature of the exercise. After all, as Stiglitz (1998, 287) has pointed out, "Evaluation itself is an institution . . . and an incentive." Evaluation performance criteria (for example, efficiency, equity, accountability, adaptability, and sustainability); the broad contextual settings (public, private, regulated markets); and the purposes for the evaluation can all differ, as in the cases of comparative institutional analysis, new comparative economics, and official development aid (see the Paris Declaration and the Accra Declaration).[9] Last but not least, it should be remembered that evaluation is seldom if ever conducted in an environment free of political economy restrictions or political interests.[10] This is particularly true in the case of evaluating particular institutional configurations.[11]

Notwithstanding these limitations, the evaluation of institutions in general is an exercise that includes the examination of the relationship between actual results or outcomes on the one hand and the specific designed[12] "performance characteristics" that were (theoretically) supposed to deliver a given product on the other.[13] This first phase of the exercise involves establishing the nominal "first-order" baseline scenario—that is, linking results with institutional characteristics and coming to a preliminary conclusion on the initial fit between intended and actual results.[14]

A second and related phase involves deepening the analysis to try to establish attribution and direction of possible causalities between expected performance characteristics and what actual performance information seems to reveal. If there are different results from the same characteristics, what can explain those differences? This understanding or learning phase is the most difficult one, as it is fraught with enormous informational and methodological challenges. And yet it is here that priority should be placed, as it is in the link between evaluation and research that most of the information required for capacity development will come (Picciotto and Rist 1995).

Linking Performance with Nominal Institutional Characteristics

For the six Latin American countries studied, the evaluation criteria were to assess macroeconomic performance in terms of the capacity of the institutional framework to deliver, with low transactions costs, the following interdependent results: price stability and sustainable growth, gains in equity and employment, exchange rate stability and low long-term rates of interest, the application of monetary and fiscal countercyclical policies, and financial sector depth.

In general, different macroeconomic results can be explained by different institutional characteristics, such as the degree of central bank credibility and independence, the existence of effective fiscal rules, the information agents have, and the strength of the regulatory body and policy credibility in general. Other institutional characteristics include policies with regard to disclosure of information, rules governing the decision-making processes, the use of independent evaluations, and the evaluable history and verifiability of states of nature.[15]

One of the most important findings of the evaluation was that when the specific country differences in macroeconomic performance were linked to the corresponding institutional characteristics, it was not possible to discern sufficient differences in attribution or correspondence between the two. In other words, two countries could have similar macroeconomic arrangements with hardly different institutional characteristics but different macroeconomic results. This finding led to the notion of "nominal" characteristics, such as central bank independence with respect to "real" characteristics on central bank independence. The subsequent evaluation question was "what could explain the differences between nominal and real institutional characteristics?"

The answer was related to the different degrees of political demand for macroeconomic stability. Political demand appeared to be the main and ultimate independent explanatory variable and the key source of the effectiveness of the "real" institutional characteristics. Any country can nominally, for instance, adopt inflation targeting. The real test is to have enough fear of inflation to provide political support for the "right" interest rate, fiscal, and exchange rate policies. The policy implication is that to enhance macroeconomic performance, the strategy should be to focus more on the underlying determinants of the political demand for macroeconomic stability than on nominal compliance with "stylized" institutional characteristics.

The conclusion was that information and a well-informed society are the critical underlying determinants of the demand for macroeconomic stability and performance. Information becomes the critical algorithm that links the demand for macroeconomic stability, macroeconomic performance, and, ultimately, distributive justice.

Demand-Driven Evaluation and the Role of Incentives

The conceptual and analytical core of most evaluation exercises can be structured around the relationships between rules, incentives, and accountability.[16] Rules are incentives; they matter because they frame the process through which accountability and the relevant information can be established. Formal (and real) rules configure the real incentives that reward or sanction individual or collective behavior.[17]

Accountability requires rules to govern the processes through which attribution, causality, or possible association can be established. Just as there are rules governing the separation of powers in constitutional frameworks (which assumes a modality of hierarchical political governance structure and an incentive compatibility framework), there is a need for rules to link ex post results with the ex ante decisions that led to those results.[18] At this point, the questions that arise are "What were the process and the underlying real incentive structure that led to the existing rules? How can new rules be established?"

These are not easy questions to answer. One way to create new and more efficiency-enhancing rules is to establish rules, such as evaluable history and paper trails as sources of accountability, behind the veil of ignorance.[19] Evaluators can do so through verifiable baselines and observed end results. But rules are needed to reduce random or deliberate ambiguity between the intervening factors and actors. In this interaction, accountability and rules spawn the institutional and political incentive structures determining decision-making behavior. The incentive structure is the main determinant of effectiveness in most organizational constructs. Accountability, rules, and incentives need to be understood not as three separate concepts or factors but comprehensively in their mutual interactions and effects (Wiesner 2008).

Accountability with Respect to Learning and the Role of Incentives

What about the elusive balance (or trade-off) between learning and accountability? To what extent can the search for accountability adversely affect the need to learn? These are difficult questions to answer. Both involve the role of incentives. One way out is to focus on the learning that will induce the most relevant policy changes. A focus on accountability seems to provide the most critical learning. From this perspective, Picciotto's insight (2005, 348) seems valid: "If evaluation is only about learning, it does not make authority responsible. If it must churn out lessons to justify itself, it will generate an oversupply of simplistic and pious exhortations and platitudes. Worse: evaluators that do not encourage accountability for results fail to provide incentives for learning."

The Demand-Driven Requirements of Capacity Building

Most of the literature on the definition of evaluation capacity building agrees that it is a context-driven process involving a number of dimensions that include the use of evaluation results to inform decision making and policy formulation for learning and accountability purposes.[20] This process-intensive definition says little about where and why the process arises or begins. It is not clear what it says about the quality of the emerging evaluation capacity. In brief, the question is "What are the sources of that process?" A related question is "What are the requirements for that evaluation capacity to be relevant and effective?"

Two main interdependent factors determine the sources of this process—namely, the existence of demand for lower transactions costs in the delivery of the good, service, or intended result and a rules-based framework to ensure the "right" incentives, evaluable history, and accountability. But if the demand for evaluations is the main explanation for the quality of evaluations and of capacity building, how can such demand be developed?

To strengthen demand, the following requirements need to be met:

- Information on possible lower transactions costs of the intended result needs to be provided.
- A close link must be established between research and evaluation to provide independent empirical diagnostics on the most binding restrictions.[21]
- Technical knowledge of the particular context must be mastered.

The demand-induced approach to institutional change comes from the recognition that existing arrangements leave margin for potential gains (Feeny 1993), that transactions costs may be too high, and that a Coasian solution may be worked out by the actors to lower transactions costs.[22] Analogous to the theory of the demand for technological change (Hicks 1963), the demand-induced theory of institutional change is based on the search for lower transactions costs (Coase 1960). This search, in principle, will induce successive autonomous new institutional arrangements on the supply and demand side of the process.

Within the scope of an evaluation of the effectiveness of macroeconomic frameworks, the application of the demand-induced approach for the "right" institutional arrangement would require recognizing that transactions costs are too high and that an alternative modality of institutional arrangement is possible. More specifically, it would mean that under the existing institutional arrangement, for example, inflation, unemployment, or long-term real interest rates are too high. If these are the conditions generally prevailing, it is likely that there may be political demand, for example, for a more independent central bank or for fiscal correction under a special modality of institutional arrangement. That demand would shape the capacity supply response to the demand for institutional change and potentially lower transactions costs. In principle, a tentative theorem linking the political demand origin of institutions with the transactions costs of the extant institutional arrangement could be framed as follows: "The lower (higher) the real political demand for macroeconomic stability the higher (lower) will be the transaction costs of coordination between fiscal and monetary policy and the less (more) macroeconomic stability will result" (Wiesner 2008, 27).

Although the key requirement for reform and economic transformation is the emergence of the political demand for change, the development on the supply side in terms of the "right" capacity response is not automatically ensured. For any given institutional change proposal, the potential losers may not engage in a successful cooperative collective action. On the contrary, if they end up being politically or economically stronger, institutional change will not occur and a country may find itself with the "wrong" institutions and without an effective political demand for evaluation to drive policy reform. To a large extent, this is what has happened in several Latin American countries. This is also what can happen in many organizations (private, public, multilateral, and bilateral) when evaluations are conducted in the hope that their results will inform and drive reforms.

Evaluative Implications of the 2008–09 World Crisis

Figure 2.3 illustrates the steepness of the reduction of world output in 2008–09. The world crisis—marked by a drop in the growth of world output from 5.2 percent in 2007 to –1.1 percent in 2009 (table 2.2)—has already caused a major evaluation-accountability-learning exercise to determine its causes, implications, and policy changes.

In Latin America, the world crisis appears to have led to an even more severe drop in output, from a 5.7 percent rate of growth in 2007 to –2.5 percent in 2009. Mexico's GDP may have fallen from 3.3 percent to –7.3 percent over the same period.

The evolving world macroeconomic crisis and its impending deleterious impact in Latin American countries have important evaluative

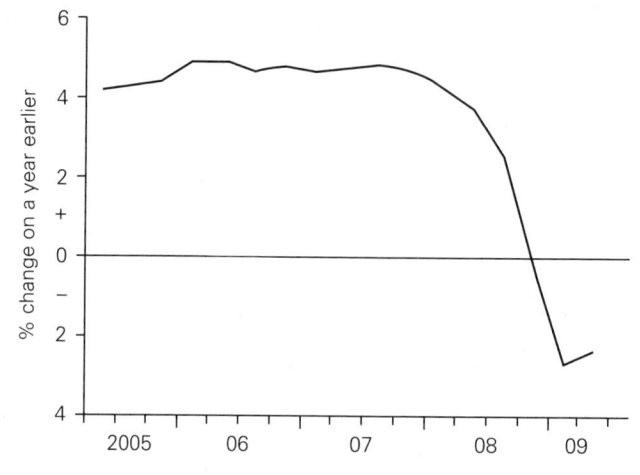

Figure 2.3 Annual Percentage Changes in World GDP, 2005–09

Source: Economist 2009.

Table 2.2 Actual and Projected Output in Selected Areas

	Actual		Projected	
Output	2007	2008	2009	2010
World	5.2	3.0	−1.1	3.1
Advanced economies	2.7	0.6	−3.4	1.3
China	13.0	9.0	8.5	9.0
Western Hemisphere	5.7	4.2	−2.5	2.9
Brazil	5.7	5.1	−0.7	3.5
Mexico	3.3	1.3	−7.3	3.3

Source: IMF 2009.

implications. First, an original flaw that may have gone undetected in the foundational governance framework may explain current crisis developments. Second, and perhaps more important, the current crisis can yield lessons on strengthening future evaluation capacity development of the macroinstitutional domestic and systemic arrangements. To a large extent, the relative vulnerability of Latin American countries to global growth and to capital market volatility reflects an "evaluation failure," in the sense that countries have not been able to adopt timely reforms to build institutional resiliency against, for instance, sudden stops or to implement effective countercyclical fiscal and monetary policies. The question that now emerges is whether there will be sufficient political accountability for the impending welfare loss and sufficient political demand to support better evaluations of macroeconomic institutions and performance.

There are three interdependent implications for evaluation capacity development. First, insufficient political demand for macroeconomic stability may have been a large part of the explanation for preexisting evaluation flaws in the assessment of macroeconomic institutional arrangements. Second, if the political demand for macroeconomic reforms is a function of the demand for and supply of information, then targeted and strategic evaluations may play a major role in identifying possible responses to macroeconomic volatility. Third, from a political economy perspective, vulnerability to external shocks, which prima facie is considered a function of exposure and risk taking, becomes a function of political accountability. It becomes a function of who can be politically blamed for unpreparedness or for the consequences of the shocks. In this case, new information derived from independent evaluations is an effective way to unmask the lack of political accountability and lead to policy reform.

Conclusion

Four main conclusions emerge from this chapter. First, there is a core evaluative analytical framework that has general theoretical validity as well as practical application across varied environments. This framework evolves from plausible causality and endogenous relationships between rules, incentives, information, and accountabilities. Although this core is far from ideal, it seems much less imperfect than relevant alternatives.

Second, the effectiveness of evaluation in enhancing results is a function of the degree to which it is driven more by the demand for improved results than by supply-side considerations and origins. Demand-driven evaluations are more effective than supply-driven ones, because they contain incentives that encourage and reward the search for new information.[23] Accountability is the ultimate incentive driving the quality of evaluations and attendant learning.

Third, evaluation capacity building is a process that requires—and results from—the demand for improved results. Such demand is driven by information on the specifics of transactions costs of alternative institutional arrangements.

Fourth, the macroeconomic and distributive implications of the world crisis on Latin America will depend largely on the quality of previous evaluations of the performance of macroeconomic institutions. The evaluative implications of the current world crisis will depend largely on the political accountability that can be extracted from the ongoing evaluation of the causes of the crisis.

It is striking to observe that what have long been recognized as the key analytical precepts to guide evaluation exercises at the level of projects, programs, sectors, and even countries—that is, that they be driven more by demand than supply incentives—are the same ones that frame the evaluation of macroeconomic institutions at the highest level of policy making. Both endeavors respond to higher-order principles of incentive and information theory and to recent research findings in the political economy.

Notes

1. The evaluation was conducted for the Office of Evaluation and Oversight (OVE) of the Inter-American Development Bank in 2007–08. It covered the macroeconomic arrangements of Argentina, Brazil, Chile, Colombia, Costa Rica, and Peru.
2. Wiesner (2008, 45) posits that "information is the critical algorithm that links together the demand for macroeconomic stability, macroeconomic performance and, ultimately, distributive justice."

3. On the importance of political accountability, see Chelimsky (2008). According to Kusek and Rist (2004), incentives can be political, institutional, or personal. They raise different questions, such as what political entity is driving the need for an evaluation system, who will benefit from the system, and who will not.
4. According to Williamson (1985), the level of transactions costs determines the modality of the institutional arrangements.
5. On the overall criteria for evaluating institutional performance, see Ostrom, Schroeder, and Wynne (1993).
6. For a useful analytical distinction between country performance, multilateral institutional performance, and country outcomes, see Lele (2005).
7. On the challenges of using evaluation to assess developmental effectiveness, see Gariba (2005).
8. Prados de la Escosura (2007, 44) offers the following view of the causes of Latin America's long-term economic and social development. "The empirical findings presented here seriously challenge conventional assessments that locate Latin America economic retardation in the early nineteenth century and link it to geography, initial inequality of the wealth and power, colonial heritage, and post-independence political instability and turmoil. They all certainly hindered long-run growth and a counterfactual scenario with law and order, lower inequality, and British-like institutions would have cast a higher growth rate in Latin America. However, blaming Latin America's long-term backwardness on the post-colonial epoch seems farfetched. Contrary to a widely held view, Latin America's retardation appears to be a late-twentieth century phenomenon that should be explored if we want to understand why Latin America remains a backward region in a global world."
9. On the evaluation of alternative institutional arrangements, see Ostrom and others (2002). On issues related to the evaluation of public policies, see Scriven (2001). On aid effectiveness, see Easterly and Pfutze (2008).
10. Wiesner (2005, 352) posits that "we should evaluate both the economic system and the political system."
11. Referring to the building of an evaluation and monitoring system, Kusek and Rist (2004, 40) posit that it "is first and foremost a political activity with technical dimensions rather than vice versa."
12. Leonid Hurwicz was the pioneer scholar who, since 1960, advanced the concepts of "design mechanisms" for institutional configuration when markets would not, on their own, engender an efficient framework. In 2007, he received the Nobel Prize for his work in this area. See Maskin (2008), another Nobel laureate, on the conditions for appropriate institutional design to achieve desirable outcomes.
13. According to Weiss (2000, 103), "Theory-based evaluation is a mode of evaluation that brings to the surface the underlying assumptions about why a program will work."
14. According to Wiesner (1998, xiv), the "effectiveness of evaluation is determined largely by how quickly and accurately it can link policy, project, and program outcomes to specific public sector characteristics. In fact, evaluation effectiveness can be judged in terms of its efficiency in identifying public sector

institutional obstacles and in contributing to the productive meditation between the demand for and supply of the 'right' institutional arrangements."

15. See Ostrom (2000) on the role of externally enforced rules to induce particular results.

16. According to Arrow (quoted in Laffont and Martimort 2002, 264), "The most important development in economics in the last forty years has been the study of incentives to achieve potential mutual gains when the parties have different degrees of knowledge."

17. Scholars (Buchanan 1991; Acemoglu and Robinson 2000; Rodrik 2003; Persson and Tabellini 2004) use the concept of rules as well as that of institutions as restrictions that can have a formal expression in constitutions and laws as well as in informally accepted norms regulating societal organizations and exchanges. Another line of research relates rules to cooperative and uncooperative games. This approach has spawned the field of game theory and of economic development as a learning cooperative game in which some societies prosper by designing the "right" rules (North 1990; Weingast 1995; Bardhan 2001) and restrictions.

18. An incentive compatibility framework is one designed to reconcile and balance different interests and information asymmetries within a structured rules-based game to be played and replayed in which the collective gain is increased without any detriment to others. Such a framework disincentivizes shirking and other collective action problems. The necessary information must be gathered to design mechanisms that are incentive compatible. On the theory of mechanism design, see Maskin (2008) and Myerson (2008).

19. In *A Theory of Justice*, John Rawls (1971) develops the concept of the veil of ignorance behind which welfare-enhancing results are the more likely policy outcome.

20. To Picciotto (1998, 39), evaluation capacity development "is the ability of institutions to manage information, assess program performance, and respond flexibly to new demands."

21. To Scriven and Coryn (2008), the link between evaluation and research is more to establish the performance of the evaluation framework than to explain how or why it works or fails to work. In the case of building capacity for evaluating macroeconomic institutional arrangements, the Scriven and Coryn position is the appropriate one. In this particular case, research would have to pursue the understanding of why one arrangement worked or not.

22. Coase's economic theorem holds that "efficiency" will be achieved as long as property rights are fully allocated and completely free trade of all property is possible. The importance of the theorem is in demonstrating that it does not matter who owns what initially but only that all property be owned by someone (Coase 1937, cited in Williamson and Winter 1991).

23. Hoff and Stiglitz (2001, 397) warn that "although the institutions that arise in response to incomplete markets and contracts may have as their intention an improvement in economic outcomes, there is no assurance that improvement will actually result. Institutions may be part of an equilibrium and yet be dysfunctional."

Bibliography

Acemoglu, D. 2005. "Constitutions, Politics, and Economics: A Review Essay on Persson and Tabellini's 'The Economic Effects of Constitutions.'" *Journal of Economic Literature* 43 (4): 1025–48.

Acemoglu, D., and J. A. Robinson. 2000. "Political Economy, Governance, and Development: Political Losers as a Barrier to Economic Development." *American Economic Review* 90 (2): 126–30.

Alesina, A. 2007. "Political Economy." *NBER Reporter* 3, National Bureau of Economic Research, Cambridge, MA.

Bardhan, P. 2001. "Distributive Conflicts, Collective Action, and Institutional Economics." In *Frontiers of Development Economics: The Future in Perspective*, ed. G. M. Meier and J. E. Stiglitz, 269–90. Washington, DC: World Bank.

Boyle, R., D. Lemaire, and R. C. Rist. 1999. "Introduction: Building Evaluation Capacity." In *Building Effective Evaluation Capacity: Lessons from Practice*, ed. R. Boyle and D. Lemaire, 1–19. Piscataway, NJ: Transaction Publishers.

Buchanan, J. 1991. "The Domain of Constitutional Political Economy." In *The Economics and the Ethics of Constitutional Order*, 3–18. Ann Arbor: University of Michigan Press.

Chelimsky, E. 2008. "A Clash of Cultures: Improving the 'Fit' between Evaluative Independence and the Political Requirements of a Democratic Society." *American Journal of Evaluation* 29 (4): 400–15.

Coase, R. 1937. "The Nature of the Firm." *Economica* 4: 386–405.

———. 1960. "The Problem of Social Cost." *Journal of Law and Economics* 3 (1): 1–44.

De Ferranti, D., G. E. Perry, S. G. Indermit, and L. Servén, with F. H. G. Ferreira, N. Ilahi, W. F. Maloney, and M. Rama. 2000. *Securing Our Future in a Global Economy*. Washington, DC: World Bank.

De Gregorio, J., and J.-W. Lee. 2003. "Growth and Adjustment in East Asia and Latin America." Working Paper 245, Central Bank of Chile, Santiago. http://ideas.repec.org/p/chb/bcchwp/245.html.

Easterly, W., and T. Pfutze. 2008. "Where Does the Money Go? Best and Worst Practices in Foreign Aid." *Journal of Economic Perspectives* 22 (2): 29–52.

Economist. 2009. "Economic and Financial Indicators." October 3, 121.

Feeny, D. 1993. "The Demand for and Supply of Institutional Arrangements." In *Rethinking Institutional Analysis and Development*, ed. V. Ostrom, D. Feeny, and H. Picht, 159–209. San Francisco: Institute for Contemporary Studies.

Gariba, S. 2005. "Trends in the Evaluation of Efforts to Reduce Poverty." In *Evaluating Development Effectiveness*, ed. G. K. Pitman, O. N. Feinstein, and G. K. Ingram, 331–36. World Bank Series on Evaluation and Development, vol. 7. Piscataway, NJ: Transaction Publishers.

Hausmann, R., and M. Gavin. 1996. "Securing Stability and Growth in a Shock-Prone Region: The Policy Challenge for Latin America." Working Paper 315, Inter-American Development Bank, Washington, DC.

Hicks, J. 1963. *The Theory of Wages.* London: St. Martin's Press.

Hoff, K., and J. E. Stiglitz. 2001. "Modern Economic Theory and Development." In *Frontiers of Development Economics: The Future in Perspective,* ed. G. M. Meier and J. E. Stiglitz, 389–459. New York: Oxford University Press.

IMF (International Monetary Fund). 2009. *World Economic Outlook: Sustaining the Recovery.* Washington, DC: IMF.

Kusek, J. Z., and R. C. Rist. 2004. "Conducting a Readiness Assessment." In *Ten Steps to a Results-Based Monitoring and Evaluation System: A Handbook for Development Practitioners,* 39–55. Washington, DC: World Bank.

Laffont, J–J., and D. Martimort. 2002. *The Theory of Incentives: The Principal-Agent Model.* Princeton, NJ: Princeton University Press.

Lele, U. 2005. "Comments on the Papers by Lindahl-Catterson and Johnson-Lamdany." In *Evaluating Development Effectiveness,* ed. G. K. Pitman, O. N. Feinstein, and G. K. Ingram, 174–76. World Bank Series on Evaluation and Development, vol. 7. Piscataway, NJ: Transaction Publishers.

Lucas, R. 2009. "Economics Focus: In Defence of the Dismal Science." *Economist,* August 8, 67.

Mackay, K. 2002. "The World Bank's ECB Experience." *New Directions for Evaluation* 93 (Spring): 88–99.

Maskin, E. S. 2008. "Mechanism Design: How to Implement Social Goals." *American Economic Review* 98 (3): 567–76.

Myerson, R. 2008. "Perspectives on Mechanism Design in Economic Theory." *American Economic Review* 98 (3): 586–603.

North, D. C. 1990. *Institutions, Institutional Change and Economic Performance.* New York: Cambridge University Press.

Ostrom, E. 2000. "Collective Action and the Evolution of Social Norms." *Journal of Economic Perspectives* 14 (3): 137–58.

Ostrom, E., C. Gibson, S. Shivakumar, and K. Andersson. 2002. "Appendix A: The Institutional Analysis and Development Framework." In *Aid, Incentives, and Sustainability: An Institutional Analysis of Development Cooperation,* ed. E. Ostrom, C. Gibson, S. Shivakumar, and K. Andersson, 273–300. SIDA Studies in Evaluation 02/01. Gothenburg, Sweden: Elanders Novum.

Ostrom, E., L. Schroeder, and S. Wynne. 1993. "Evaluating Institutional Performance." In *Institutional Incentives and Sustainable Development: Infrastructure Policies in Perspective,* 111–26. Boulder, CO: Westview Press.

Perry, G., O. S. Arias, J. H. López, W. F. Maloney, and L. Servén. 2006. *Poverty Reduction and Growth: Virtuous and Vicious Circles.* Washington, DC: World Bank.

Persson, T., and G. Tabellini. 2004. "Constitution and Economic Policy." *Journal of Economic Perspectives* 18 (1): 75–98.

Picciotto, R. 1998. "Evaluation Capacity Development: Issues and Challenges." In African Development Bank and World Bank Operations and Evaluation Departments, *Evaluation Capacity Development in Africa: Selected Proceedings from a Seminar in Abidjan,* 39–46. Washington, DC: World Bank.

———. 2000. "Concluding Remarks." In *Evaluation and Poverty Reduction: Proceedings from a World Bank Conference,* ed. O. Feinstein and R. Picciotto, 355–61. Washington, DC: World Bank.

———. 2005. "Use of Evaluation Findings to Improve Development Effectiveness: Panel Discussion." In *Evaluating Development Effectiveness,* ed. G. K. Pitman, O. N. Feinstein, and G. K. Ingram, 347–54. World Bank Series on Evaluation and Development, vol. 7. Piscataway, NJ: Transaction Publishers.

Picciotto, R., and R. C. Rist. 1995. *Evaluation and Development: Proceedings of the 1994 World Bank Conference.* Washington, DC: World Bank.

Prados de la Escosura, L. 2007. "When Did Latin America Fall Behind?" In *The Decline of Latin American Economies: Growth Institutions, and Crises,* ed. S. Edwards, G. Esquivel, and G. Márquez, 15–58. National Bureau of Economic Research Conference Report. Chicago: University of Chicago Press.

Rawls, J. 1971. *A Theory of Justice.* Cambridge, MA: Harvard University Press.

Reinhart, C. M., and K. S. Rogoff. 2009. *This Time is Different: Eight Centuries of Financial Folly.* Princeton, NJ: Princeton University Press.

Rist, R. C. 1999. "Linking Evaluation Utilization and Governance: Fundamental Challenges for Countries Building Evaluation Capacity." In *Building Effective Evaluation Capacity: Lessons from Practice,* ed. R. Boyle and D. Lemaire, 111–32. Piscataway, NJ: Transaction Publishers.

Rodrik, D. 2003. *Search of Prosperity Analytic Narratives on Economic Growth.* Princeton, NJ: Princeton University Press.

Scriven, M. 2001. "Evaluating Global Public Policies and Programs." In *Global Public Policies and Programs: Implications for Financing and Evaluation: Proceedings from a World Bank Workshop,* ed. C. D. Gerrard, M. Ferroni, and A. Mody, 219–22. Washington, DC: World Bank.

Scriven, M., and C. L.S. Coryn. 2008. "The Logic of Research Evaluation." In *Reforming the Evaluation of Research,* ed. C. L. S. Coryn and M. Scriver, 89–105. *New Directions for Evaluation* 118 (Summer).

Stewart, F. 2005. "Evaluating Evaluation in a World of Multiple Goals, Interests, and Models." In *Evaluating Development Effectiveness,* ed. G. K. Pitman, O. N. Feinstein, and G. K. Ingram, 3–28. World Bank Series on Evaluation and Development, vol. 7. Piscataway, NJ: Transaction Publishers.

Stiglitz, J. 1998. "Evaluation as an Incentive Investment." In *Evaluation and Development: The Institutional Dimension,* ed. R. Picciotto and E. Wiesner, 287–90. Washington, DC: World Bank.

Weingast, B. R. 1995. "The Economic Role of Political Institutions: Market-Preserving Federalism and Economic Development." *Journal of Law, Economics and Organization* 11 (1): 1–31.

Weiss, C. H. 2000. "Theory-Based Evaluation: Theories of Change for Poverty Reduction Programs." In *Evaluation and Poverty Reduction: Proceedings from a World Bank Conference,* ed. O. Feinstein and R. Picciotto, 103–11. Washington, DC: World Bank.

Wiesner, E. 1998. "Introduction." In *Evaluation and Development: The Institutional Dimension,* ed. R. Picciotto and E. Wiesner, xi–xiv. Washington, DC: World Bank.

———. 2005. "The 'Resource Restriction Condition' for Evaluation Effectiveness." In *Evaluating Development Effectiveness*, ed. G. K. Pitman, O. N. Feinstein, and G. K. Ingram, 337–46. World Bank Series on Evaluation and Development, vol. 7. Piscataway, NJ: Transaction Publishers.

———. 2008. *The Political Economy of Macroeconomic Policy Reform in Latin America: The Distributive and Institutional Context*. Northampton, MA: Edward Elgar.

Williamson, O. E. 1985. *The Economic Institutions of Capitalism: Firms, Markets, Relational Contracting*. New York: Free Press.

———. 2000. "The New Institutional Economics: Taking Stock, Looking Ahead." *Journal of Economic Literature* 38 (3): 595–613.

Williamson, O. E., and S. Winter, eds. 1991. *The Nature of the Firm: Origins, Evolution, Development*. New York: Oxford University Press.

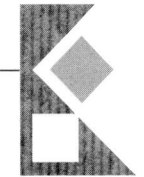

CHAPTER 3

From Evaluating Projects toward Assessing Institutional Performance

Todor Dimitrov

Although the importance of evaluations above the project level is widely recognized, such assessments rarely reach the overall institutional level of development organizations. In contrast to evaluations of nongovernmental organizations (NGOs), usually demanded by their donors, there are very few systematic full-fledged evaluations of development organizations. Only a small number of the dozen multilateral development banks have ever performed such evaluations; where such evaluations were conducted, they were rarely done repeatedly as a matter of policy.

There is consensus that higher-level evaluations are instrumental if development evaluation is to have broad impact. It is therefore beneficial to review the causes for the modest success in this area and to propose some mitigation of the most common barriers, based on a recent hands-on experience.

This chapter highlights the key factors that make a high-level institutional review impossible, difficult, or unused and unrepeatable. Various lessons learned are presented from the perspective of an independent internal evaluation unit operating under typical resource and regulatory constraints.

Broadening the Scope of Evaluations

During the past few years, interest in and demand for information about the performance of international development institutions has increased substantially. The focus of this interest is the search for evidence of *development effectiveness and results on the ground,* as per the implicit orientation of the Millennium Development Goals, adopted by 189 countries in 2000, and the 2005 Paris Declaration on Aid Effectiveness.

After 2005, most development banks adopted a new term, *managing for development results* (MfDR), which constitutes an adaptation of the terms *performance management, results-based management,* and *managing for outcomes* with an emphasis on contributions rather than attributions to outcomes. The new term implies a results focus in all aspects of management and includes accountability and lessons learned.

A growing number of recent publications and initiatives aim in this direction. For example, the Multilateral Development Banks' Working Group on Managing for Development Results, set up in 2003 to exchange experiences, produced a series of reports on the Common Performance Assessment System (COMPAS) of seven institutions, listing a system of indicators on development effectiveness performance.[1]

Closing the Gap between Reality and Intentions

Despite the paradigm shift toward coordinated reporting on institutional performance—embraced by many multilateral development banks as a management approach and a set of tools for strategic planning, monitoring, and evaluation—the actual use of systemic in-depth institutional evaluations is still modest and far from institutionalized. Although many recent evaluations have focused on management for results in general and deal with the higher levels of programs, countries, and sectors, very few comprehensive evaluations look beyond these levels to address and reshape overall organizational performance.[2] This is unfortunate, because without systemic, if not harmonized, institutional performance evaluations and a commitment to their rigor, impartiality, and follow-up at the highest levels, the use of the evaluation work will remain fragmented and underutilized.

There is consensus about the benefits and importance of conducting and using development evaluations at the institutional level (Lusthaus, Anderson, and Murphy 1995; Patton 2008). But doing so is easier said than done. Theories, methodologies, and training courses on the subject, some of which are listed in the bibliography, are a necessary but not sufficient condition for conducting institutional-level evaluations on a periodic basis. In addition to such resources and experiences, it is essential to bring the issue of systematic institutional performance to the core of results-based evaluation discussions, with the ultimate goal of highlighting and mitigating the hidden obstacles to a wider and better use of institutional assessments.

A first step in closing the gap between intentions and reality would be to reveal some of the key planning and implementation challenges that a potentially useful institutional evaluation faces from the perspective of an internal independent evaluation unit (the same step can be applied to organizations without such a unit). A next step would be to overview ideas on how to mitigate such challenges, based on specific practical experience. These two steps are outlined later to initiate a constructive discussion and exchange of experiences on the subject rather than propose a silver-bullet prescription.

The theme of institutional performance evaluations (IPEs) is reviewed in the context of a framework provided and used by the International Development Research Centre (IDRC) and the Universalia Management Group (Universalia 1985). This chapter and the proposed practice-based approach center on how to prepare the institutional ground and the regulatory framework for a sound, replicable IPE. The chapter does not deal with the specific methodological aspects and techniques of organizational performance measurement. The main effort is devoted to sharing some experience in preparing, launching, and using a successful pioneering IPE, which should become a precursor for more systemic evaluations at the corporate level.

Ensuring an Environment that Facilitates Systemic Institutional Performance Evaluations

The relatively poor record in conducting and using IPEs in international development as a matter of policy indicates major deficiencies in the area that are not mitigated by theory and practice in organizational assessment in general (Universalia 1985). Although some organizations made a substantial contribution in the area of organizational assessment and related research and training, the use of such resources remains limited mostly to NGOs and a few pioneering development institutions.³ IPEs are far from being institutionalized, much less harmonized.

The IDRC and Universalia Management have developed, used, and disseminated a framework for organizational self-assessment, thus mitigating the lack of theory and shared practice in this field as far as international development evaluation is concerned (Lusthaus, Anderson, and Murphy 1995; Universalia 1995). This framework, along with other recent concepts of dealing with organizational analysis (Patton 2008), allows for an effective IPE that covers multiple aspects of institutional performance. Although the actual use of the framework should be adapted to the particular structure, mandate, and issues of the organization, it is important to ensure that the multiple layers of the analysis are integrated to provide a good overall picture of performance. This is achieved by analyzing three key aspects of the organization (motivation, operating environment, and capacity) to derive the four aspects of institutional performance (effectiveness, efficiency, relevance, and financial viability) (figure 3.1).

It is also essential to adopt a comprehensive IPE approach and conduct comprehensive planning that reflect the actual institutional context while maintaining relatively transparent and multidimensional methodology and evaluation rigor. Thus, the IPE will be tailored to the specifics of the institution but will also serve for interinstitutional comparisons and eventual

Figure 3.1 Framework for Institutional Performance Evaluations

Motivation
History
Mission   Culture
Incentives   Rewards

Performance
Effectiveness
Efficiency
Relevance
Financial viability

Environment
Political
Economic
Technological
Administrative
Social / cultural
Stakeholder

Capacity
Structure
Leadership
Financial
Technology
Infrastructure
Human resources
Program / services
Linkages

Source: Universalia 1985; IDRC 1991.

replications, with the ultimate goal of achieving a common ground for shared good practice standards and international harmonization.[4]

The main obstacle to the effective use of IPEs is that although most development institutions seek and use peer comparisons and feedback on their performance and structure in several ways, they seldom use systemic overall organizational reviews to do so. A key reason why is that such reviews, if performed, are rarely institutionalized or required by policies and procedures; if done at all, they are typically undertaken on an ad hoc basis. Hence, in addition to understanding how to conduct an IPE, it is critical to ensure a critical mass of prerequisites for such evaluation to be feasible, replicable, and utilized. These prerequisites, constituting the gap from a practical perspective, are addressed in this chapter through a seven-step approach.

The choice of an IPE methodology and the approach used depend on each situation. Therefore, the attention is on creating and sustaining an IPE–conducive environment. Naturally, most if not all IPEs face numerous resource and cultural challenges. Thus, a one-size-fits-all methodological framework is considered unrealistic and therefore not discussed. That said, it is necessary to aim for a commonly agreed upon terminology and validity of results, if not a set of minimum standards, and broader harmonization within the international development evaluation context and the current effort to set some professional benchmarks. The ongoing debate about what constitutes methodological soundness in more trivial evaluations only illustrates that there may be a long way to go before consensus is reached about the more complex and less covered issue of IPE.

Seven Steps for Preparing a Systemic IPE

Making the institutional environment IPE conducive, or at least not IPE destructive, requires meticulous preparatory work and persistence. In some cases, it may take continuous incremental efforts over the course of several years, if not a decade. Underestimating the need and importance of such preparatory work can easily compromise the intended IPE and its further use, eroding the overall evaluation credibility.

The seven steps outlined below assume an IPE that is led by the organization's independent evaluation unit, backed by the use of external expertise to ensure the rigor and credibility of the process. However, these steps are also applicable in situations in which there is no internal independent evaluation unit. In such cases, it is recommended that to ensure a certain degree of independence, the process be led by an internal unit (for example, an internal audit or risk management department) that is sufficiently close to upper levels of management but not directly involved in operational matters and related decision making.

The organizational assessment framework (Universalia 1985) involves five phases: planning, identification of strategic issues, development of a work plan, data collection and analysis, and reporting. The focus below is on the first three phases, as preparatory work is considered instrumental for the effective and systemic use of IPEs.

Before even starting with the first phase (planning), it is natural to define what is meant by institutional performance (that is, the object of assessment). This process should ideally reach beyond the widely accepted concepts of relevance, effectiveness, efficiency, and sustainability and cover a balanced set of indicators, as opposed to a simplistic measure of (for example, financial or output) performance. Before diving into the actual IPE, it is also important to distinguish the notions of performance from the points of view of the key stakeholders (which often differ substantially) and to agree on some basic benchmarks of success, preferably in comparison with relevant peer institutions.

Before drafting a specific IPE plan, it is essential to assess and improve, if possible, the conduciveness of the institutional environment (culture, motivation, policies, leadership), so that the minimum preplanning prerequisites are in place. A number of activities have to be performed, often in parallel (figure 3.2).

Step 1: Identify Future Developments that Justify and Facilitate an IPE

A forward-looking review of the institution's development should reveal envisaged and potential events that could be associated with the demand for, promotion of, and sustainable use of an IPE. A well-chosen opportunity and timing are essential to a pioneering and replicable corporate-level evaluation. Events and phases of the institutional development may include a new business planning cycle or system, formulation of a new strategy, a major change in leadership, a crisis response, a reorganization, and a change in credit rating, as well as a combination of such events. One possible approach is to use the IPE in support of preparing or updating a multiannual business strategy that involves all levels within the organization and requires the approval and support of the highest authority, with relevant revisiting of performance.

The reviewed experiences suggest that it is better to wait for the right set of events or opportunities and strong leadership support than to prematurely attempt an IPE. It is particularly important that the pioneering

Figure 3.2 Activities to Be Performed to Plan IPE

- 1. Identify key developments that would justify a systemic IPE.
- 2. Assess IPE feasibility (institutional framework).
- 3. Amend institutional framework toward IPE.
- 4. Define the scope and focus of the IPE.
- 5. Create a work plan: timing, resources
- 6. Employ leadership involvement and process management
- 7. Ensure follow-up and replication.

Center: Planning of IPE: toward a conducive, sustainable environment

Source: Author.

institutional evaluation proves to be timely, useful, and cost-effective, as otherwise its shortcomings may be used to challenge any follow-up or attempt at institutionalization.

Once an adequate event or process is chosen, the need for and benefits of a first IPE have to be promoted in the context of the event or process to gain substantial support from leadership as well as other levels within the institution. Consequently, key issues should be identified; timing, resource allocation, and a work plan established; and awareness activities and ownership building begun, all in an ongoing coordinated process.

The nature of the event or process should identify at least one member of the leadership who would remain seriously committed to make the event or process successful. That leader should be consulted, encouraged, and enabled to build broader support and positive expectations and attitudes within the institution toward the event and the need for the IPE.

The combination of leadership-led and participatory management of the process should be assessed and steered very carefully to balance the necessary top-down signals with the bottom-up incentives and expectations to achieve a cooperative and constructive attitude, as well as define possible centers of "sabotage" (UNDP 1994). A good combination of top-down and bottom-up approaches is essential, with strong leadership and policy commitment representing the top-down part and broad consultation and involvement of all lower levels constituting a solid base for realism and overall support from the bottom up.

In this combination of approaches, a distinctive participatory character is recommended, both as a goal and as a means (Goulet 1989). A certain degree of participation is needed to ensure adequate data collection and analysis. Such participation may act as the key ingredient of an empowerment process that could become one of the IPE–suggested improvements (Guba and Lincoln 1989). After all, it is often the case that the evaluation process is as important as its findings, as it may itself inspire or constitute a desired institutional change. For example, the teamwork on institutional vision, mandate, and performance may release the inherent potential of a major cultural and organizational change.

Step 2: Assess IPE Feasibility

Before conducting an IPE, the evaluator must determine the extent to which the organization's culture, climate, resources, and motivation allow for a comprehensive IPE to take place (IDB 1995). In addition to reviewing the overall situation, it is important to assess and eventually improve the framework and perceptions toward sharing and disclosing information, within and outside the institution. The main challenge, from the evaluator's perspective, is to reveal common denominators toward a shared willingness to learn and change, as well as to mitigate the natural sense of a threat that such processes imply. Doing so requires a good understanding of unresolved issues and prevailing opinions and interests, as well as the existence of specific cultural characteristics of the institution's personnel (one of the reasons for preferring an internally led and owned IPE, as argued below). Once main areas of suspicion and lack of cooperativeness are identified, the evaluator, in cooperation with senior management, should seek to mitigate them to build a common interest toward learning and self-improvement and to demonstrate the risks a substandard institutional performance implies.

It is very important to conduct a realistic assessment of the human and financial resources that could be used in the course of the IPE, with a focus on strategy formulation and data analysis toward a common vision. Such resources are often not obvious and require an effort to be fully revealed and understood.

Step 3: Amend the Evaluation Framework

To allow for an effective and ongoing evaluation process, the regulatory and policy framework should be reviewed and amended to the extent possible, with appropriate peer institutions' good practice as references, to facilitate a higher-level evaluation and its follow-up. This effort may be useful as a stand-alone result, even if the IPE ends up being downsized, delayed, or canceled.

The effort to lay out the framework for a smooth IPE may cause resistance. However, if well managed and articulated, it may increase interest and awareness in the evaluation function and its broader use, with a new focus on learning and strategy development. In that context, the eventual amendment of an ongoing evaluation routine or a modification to an existing evaluation role could be a very valuable side effect or even a main goal itself.

Step 4: Define the Focus and Scope of the IPE

Observing the typical minimum evaluation standards and quality already in place is necessary. However, to kick-start and institutionalize the IPE process, one may need to make certain trade-offs and compromises may need to be made. For instance, it is a good strategy to keep both the scope and the depth within reasonable limits, for two main reasons. First, any cost overrun would empower resistance, both before and after the evaluation, and may challenge any further reuse. Second, if the scope and depth are too great, the evaluation will cover too many sensitive issues at once, making the issues difficult or impossible to resolve in the follow-up phase. If the actual costs and sensitivities involved will not be matched by proportionate measures to improve performance, the usefulness and repeatability of the IPE will be seriously challenged, if not repudiated at the outset.

In identification of the strategic evaluation questions, it is important to involve most, if not all, levels in the organization and to develop a sense of broader trust and ownership across the institution, especially among the leadership. Typically, a few rounds of consultations and workshops are required, backed by a clearly articulated ongoing management commitment. These rounds should serve the dual purpose of sustaining a participative process from the start and promoting the goals and benefits of the evaluation through selected incentives, such as self-assessment trainings and first-time speak-out opportunities.

The strategic questions should be derived through a simplified diagnostic process focused on the main obvious and expected areas of underperformance relative to peer institutions (relevant research should be prepared in advance). Once such areas are identified and prioritized, a consultation on possible causes should be conducted, in the context of the evaluation framework and resource limitations.

Step 5: Create a Work Plan and Allocate Time and Resources

The IPE will require dedicated resources and time. Constraints and practices often result in the expectation or unintended use of a rapid assessment approach, on a very tight budget. A key task is to ensure sufficient resources and time to perform a meaningful IPE.

As with most of the above considerations, "the great is the enemy of good." If the scope and depth of the IPE are limited, relatively modest resources should be sufficient. In many cases, the need for substantial resources (that is, significantly above the usual annual evaluation budget) is the sole reason why an IPE is impossible, unused, or unreplicable.

The planning of resources should cover both the human and financial aspects at the appropriate time (budget preparation); ideally, preparation of the IPE should be facilitated by a decrease in the use of traditional evaluation resources and time in the given budget period. It is also important to determine the combination of the required staff, time, and funding for the IPE, as well as the eventual implementation of recommendations. A typical trap is to underestimate the second (follow-up) resource component, thereby rendering the IPE useless.

Many evaluation units operate on very tight budgets. Even if they are sufficiently independent and credible to launch an IPE, their lack of resources is an obstacle that prevents the IPE from being conducted or compromises its quality, follow-up, or both.

As the pioneering IPE and its institutionalization and demonstration or replication effects are of primary importance and a goal per se, it may be worthwhile mobilizing all possible resources, including some voluntary external peer contributions. Such contributions, even if symbolic, could be of make-or-break importance and, therefore, must be seriously explored. In addition to covering specific areas of expertise and experience, an external peer evaluator or expert may provide a critical mass of credibility and arm's-length view, which are often essential to provide the momentum for overcoming internal skepticism and resistance. Ideally, an external peer should play a moderating role and provide a second opinion as well as a convincing reference on how others used and benefited from such evaluations. In addition, the external peer could attest that pre-agreed quality standards are met for the evaluation to be credible and, hence, resilient to political and other pressures.

Timing and resources are translated into a work plan commensurate with the identified strategic issues. The work plan should cover the phases of data collection, analysis, dissemination and discussion, and follow-up implementation, ensuring a certain level of institutional commitment for implementation. Ideally, the work plan (or the event to which the IPE is attached) should also include a reevaluation round, launched after the recommended improvements are expected to be operational. Without being overprescriptive, the plan should address the main data sources on each issue, the most appropriate methodology to collect the data, the key indicators of performance on the main themes, and the time frame for each phase.

Step 6: Communicate the Purpose of the IPE and Involve Leadership

Once geared to the chosen institutional development event, the IPE process has to be outlined and communicated at the outset, with a clear purpose and users. It is useful to hold several rounds of dissemination and discussion, as doing so mitigates tensions and ambiguity associated with the process.

It is self-evident that leadership commitment is instrumental in making the process feasible, as well as adequately used in the follow-up stage. Such commitment is also important for mitigating inherent resistance from affected areas within and outside the institution. Although the leadership's direct involvement may be minimal, its role in ensuring that important stakeholders cooperate is crucial. Strong leadership support and a sense of ownership are essential to back efforts to sustain and institutionalize the process—yet another argument in favor of an internal rather than an external IPE.

At the right moment, in association with the preparatory work on the selected key institutional events, the evaluation unit has to articulate the role and merits of the intended evaluation, with convincing illustrations of good practice elsewhere. Reference to professional standards already embraced by the institution or reputable peers is generally very helpful, as is the clear presentation of the estimated costs and benefits of the IPE.

Although the use of external evaluators is typically limited by the considerations addressed under step 5, an appropriate balance can be found in consultation with the leadership and in recognition of the cost implications. In principle, the arguments favoring self-assessment prevail. A self-assessment plan ensures better leadership support, because of the cost and sensitivity or exposure implications. It also appears to allow for a wider range of participatory commitment in experimenting with assessment and enhancement techniques, as long as the process is internally controlled and owned (IDRC 1991). Supporters of an in-house evaluation should make it clear to management and staff how an internal evaluation could empower the institution with respect to its stakeholders (Universalia 1991). One practical model is to conduct an internal IPE led by the in-house independent evaluation unit (whenever available) but backed by the use of external peers and consultants as moderators and assurers of quality.

There is often concern that internally led evaluations may not be rigorous, independent, or open enough or that their recommendations may not be implemented. In fact, practice suggests that such evaluations can be very critical and straightforward, as well as used effectively. Properly conducted internal evaluations are able to raise and address the most difficult issues, resulting in major cultural and mission changes throughout an institution. They work because of the active involvement of all levels within the institution, opening up room for previously suppressed perspectives and issues. In addition, internal recommendations and action plans can be more realistic than those coming from outside, reflecting the complexity, culture, and resources of the institution.

Last but not least, detecting and mitigating the main sources of skepticism—and sometimes open sabotage—should take place at all stages. To this end, it is essential to distinguish the IPE from other activities, such as project evaluations or audits.

Step 7: Ensure Follow-up and Replication

The ultimate goal of an IPE is to lead to a strategic planning exercise based on its findings and recommendations, with provisions for reassessments in the future (box 3.1). The IPE can also establish a new type of corporate governance and board relationships, moving from the project plane toward a broader mandate, although this can be a slow and incremental process.

Follow-up and replication are typically challenged when the IPE is not geared to a major strategic event and fails to produce a specific implementation plan and reassessment commitment. Therefore, it is essential to ensure that the IPE process is closely aligned with strategy planning and reviews on a regular basis.

Box 3.1 The First IPE of the Black Sea Trade and Development Bank

Various evaluations conducted by the independent evaluation unit of the Black Sea Trade and Development Bank revealed the need for an IPE to reflect and mitigate a number of obstacles toward achieving better mandate compliance and overall efficiency. Two key issues were the "approval culture," driven by a simplistic incentives system based exclusively on lending volumes, and the high drop-out of projects before they reached completion. Having learned from the analysis of its own development, the institution was preparing a new multiannual business strategy and plan and its first capital increase. These events called for a comprehensive and institutionalized IPE, to reveal and mitigate the roots of detected issues.

- Step 1: The identification of the business strategy and plan for 2007–10 was the launching event that the IPE was to be geared to, followed by a multilevel communication of the costs and benefits, to achieve strong leadership commitment for a combination of top-down and bottom-up approaches.
- Step 2: The evaluation and strategy frameworks were analyzed; the sources and incentives for resistance were identified; and measures to mitigate resistance, including the focused use of an experienced former staff member of the World Bank Evaluation Unit in a capacity of quality control and intermediation on critical issues, were developed to ensure methodological rigor and overall credibility of the process and its outcomes.
- Step 3: The institutional framework was amended to incorporate the systemic use of the IPE as a key input to the design of new strategies and business plans, with a commitment to use the IPE outputs within the strategies and plans.
- Step 4: A synthesis of evaluation reports and studies was used to define the most critical areas and likely causes of underperformance, to streamline the scope and depth of the IPE. The relatively high project abandonment rates and associated incentives were placed at the core of the IPE focus. The methodological framework of the Universalia consultants was chosen, followed by training on its application within the existing evaluation framework and standards. Workshops for management and staff were conducted to ensure broader understanding and commitment, as well as to justify a relatively modest budget.
- Step 5: A work plan was developed in line with the budgetary process, assuming a modest (10 percent) increase in the typical evaluation budget, combined with counterbalancing the IPE costs with reduced and

(continued)

> **Box 3.1** *continued*
>
> postponed routine evaluations. For critical inputs, external references, and assurance of rigor, the plan envisaged the use of an external expert, a former member of the World Bank's Evaluation Unit.
> - Step 6: The IPE process was outlined and communicated at the outset, with a clear purpose, identified users, and top management support. Strong leadership support and a sense of ownership were essential for sustaining and institutionalizing the process, backed by the external expert but entirely managed by the internal evaluation unit. Several presentations of the IPE merits and quality assurance with reference to good practice in other institutions (for example, the International Fund for Agricultural Development) were made across the institution. Continuous monitoring and mitigation of sources of skepticism and resistance took place at all stages.
> - Step 7: The ultimate goal of the IPE based on strategic planning was incorporated into IPE–related decisions, as well as the business plan itself, with a reference to midterm reviews and subsequent business-planning activities. All the key outputs of the IPE, such as the recommendations on adopting a balanced scorecard management system and various measures to increase overall efficiency by changing the incentives for the high levels of project abandonment, became a key part of the new business plan and were implemented and reassessed by the 2009 midterm review.

Conclusion

A timely IPE can enhance the strategic management of a development institution through a process that creates a shared vision and motivation within the organization and harnesses teamwork to achieve new dimensions of performance. Crafting an IPE requires substantial preparation and the careful selection of a strategic development and appropriate timing.

The key in this challenging endeavor is to create a critical mass of preconditions and leadership support to ensure a credible and irreversible process of learning and change. The evaluation framework and approach used should be tailored to the organization being evaluated and allowed to evolve after the IPE has been institutionalized and reused.

Once successfully conducted, an IPE can gradually be institutionalized and replicated by incorporating it within the context of major strategic development in the organization. To ensure that the learning and results are used, the IPE should become an integral part of a relevant strategy design and implementation process. The IPE should not be seen as a one-time external exercise. It should go beyond a simple diagnosis to stimulate an ongoing learning process with solid internal ownership.

Notes

1. The annual COMPAS (ADB 2006) report was used for the first time as an input into the 2006 report coordinated by the World Bank and International Monetary Fund. It provides a framework for gathering information and, potentially, improving harmonization among institutions. COMPAS is based on seven categories of data: country-level capacity development; performance-based concessional financing; results-based country strategies; projects and programs; monitoring and evaluation; learning and incentives; and interagency harmonization.
2. Notable exceptions include the Global Environment Facility, which performs institutional evaluation studies every four years; the Food and Agriculture Organization; the Consultative Group on International Agricultural Research; and the International Fund for Agricultural Development.
3. IDRC and Universalia Management Group have worked in this area since 1993, making pioneering contributions in development-oriented organizational performance. Originally, they focused on the IDRC–supported centers, to improve funding management and organizational learning.
4. Multilateral development banks are subject to an ongoing harmonization process of postevaluation and impact assessment, but such efforts are recent and uncompleted. The use of different postevaluation methods, rating scales, and systems in general made it difficult to directly compare the evaluation outcomes (and ratings) of some of these institutions. The degree of direct comparability was also constrained by the different levels of disclosure of evaluation findings, as pressure for greater transparency, accountability, and intrainstitutional cooperation in postevaluation are relatively recent phenomena.

Bibliography

ADB (Asian Development Bank). 2006. *The Multilateral Development Bank Common Performance Assessment System (COMPAS) 2005 Report*. Manila: ADB.

Anderson, G., and D. Gilsig. 1995. "Issues in Participatory Evaluation: A Case Study of the SEOMEO/Canada Program of Cooperation in Human Resource Development." In *Participatory Evaluation in International Development: Theory, Practice and Prospects*, ed. E. T. Jackson and Y. Kassam. Ottawa: Mapleview Press.

Bajaj, M. 1997. "Revisiting Evaluation: A Study of the Process, Role and Contribution of Donor-Funded Evaluations to Development Organizations in South Asia." International Development Research Centre, Ottawa.

Bernard, A. 1996. *IDRC Networks: An Ethnographic Perspective*. Ottawa: International Development Research Centre.

Campbell, J. P. 1970. *Managerial Behavior, Performance and Effectiveness*. New York: McGraw-Hill.

Caplow, T. 1976. *How to Run Any Organization*. Hinsdale, IL: Dryden Press.

CIRDAP (Centre for Integrated Rural Development for Asia and the Pacific). 1996. "Institutional Self-Assessment of CIRDAP." Dhaka, Bangladesh.

CODESRIA (Council for the Development of Social Science Research in Africa). 1997. "Report of the Auto-Evaluation 1996." Dakar, Senegal.

Drucker, F. 1990. *Managing the Nonprofit Organization*. New York: Harper-Collins.

———. 1995. *Managing in a Time of Great Change*. New York: Penguin.

Etzioni, A. 1964. *Modern Organizations*. Englewood Cliffs, NJ: Prentice-Hall.

Found, Wm C. 1995. *Participatory Research and Development: An Assessment of IDRC's Experience and Prospects*. Ottawa: International Development Research Centre.

Fowler, A. 1997. *Striking a Balance: A Guide to Enhancing the Effectiveness of Non-Governmental Organisations in International Development*. London: Earthscan Publications.

Goulet, D. 1989. "Participation in Development: New Avenues." *World Development* 17 (2): 165–78.

Government of Canada. 2003. *The Managing for Results Self-Assessment Tool*. Ottawa.

Grindle, M. S., and M. E. Hilderbrand. 1995. "Building Sustainable Capacity in the Public Sector: What Can Be Done?" *Public Administration and Development* 15: 441–63.

Guba, E. G., and Y. S. Lincoln. 1989. *Fourth-Generation Evaluation*. Thousand Oaks, CA: Sage.

Harrison, M. I. 1987. *Diagnosing Organizations: Methods, Models, and Processes*. Thousand Oaks, CA: Sage.

House, E. R. 1993. *Professional Evaluation: Social Impact and Political Consequences*. Thousand Oaks, CA: Sage.

IDB (Inter-American Development Bank). 1995. *Resource Book on Participation*. Washington, DC: IDB.

IDRC (International Development Research Centre). 1991. *Empowerment through Knowledge: The Strategy of the International Development Research Centre*. Ottawa: IDRC.

Kilmann, R., and I. Kilmann. 1989. *Managing beyond the Quick Fix: A Completely Integrated Program for Creating and Maintaining Organizational Success*. San Francisco: Jossey-Bass.

Lee-Smith, D. 1997. *Evaluation as a Tool for Institutional Strengthening*. Nairobi: Mazingira Institute.

Levinson, H. 1972. *Organizational Diagnosis*. Cambridge, MA: Harvard University Press.

Likert, R. 1958. "Measuring Organizational Performance." *Harvard Business Review* 36 (2): 41–50.

Lusthaus, C., M. Adrien, G. Anderson, and F. Carden. 1999. *Enhancing Organizational Performance: A Toolbox for Self-Assessment*. Ottawa: International Development Research Centre.

Lusthaus, C., G. Anderson, and E. Murphy. 1995. *Institutional Assessment: A Framework for Strengthening Organizational Capacity for IDRC'S Research Partners*. Ottawa: International Development Research Centre.

Mackay, R., S. Debela, T. Smutylo, J. Borges-Andrade, and C. Lusthaus. 1998. *ISNAR's Achievements, Impacts, and Constraints: An Assessment of Organizational Performance and Institutional Impact*. The Hague: International Service for National Agricultural Research.

Meyer, J. W., and W. R. Scott. 1992. *Organizational Environments: Ritual and Rationality*. Thousand Oaks, CA: Sage.

Patton, M. Q. 2008. *Utilization-Focused Evaluation*, 4th ed. Thousand Oaks, CA: Sage.

Quinn, R. E., and J. Rohrbaugh. n.d. "A Spatial Model of Effectiveness Criteria: Towards a Competing Values Approach to Organizational Analysis." *Management Science* 29 (3): 363–77.

Scott, W. R. 1995. *Institutions and Organizations*. Thousand Oaks, CA: Sage.

Scriven, M. S. 1991. *Evaluation Thesaurus*, 4th ed. Thousand Oaks, CA: Sage.

Selznick, P. 1957. *Leadership in Administration: A Sociological Interpretation*. New York: Harper and Row.

Steers, R. M. 1975. "Problems in the Measurement of Organizational Effectiveness." *Administrative Science Quarterly* 20 (4): 546–58.

UNDP (United Nations Development Programme). 1994. *Capacity Development: Lessons of Experience and Guiding Principles*. New York: United Nations Development Programme.

Universalia. 1985. *Manager's Guide to Institutional Evaluations*. Hull, Quebec: Canadian International Development Agency.

———. 1995. *A Guide to Organizational Self-Assessment for IDRC–Funded Organizations*. Ottawa: International Development Research Centre.

———. 1991. "A Study of Utilization of NGO Evaluations." Unpublished manuscript.

World Bank. 1994. *Governance: The World Bank's Experience*. Washington, DC: World Bank.

CHAPTER 4

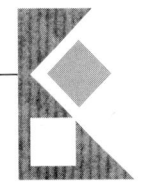

Evaluation Systems as Strategy Management Tools: Building Dubai's Institutional Learning Capacity

Mohammad A. Jaljouli

This chapter aims at opening a dialogue between evaluation practices in the area of development aid on the one hand and strategy management in both the public and private sectors on the other. Both practices rely on the flow of information that enhances the decision-making process, but the two concepts differ significantly in terms of the ownership and values driving them, the main focuses, processes, internal dynamics, and utilization.

This chapter compares the two practices. It highlights the areas of interaction and indicates how development aid can benefit from the lessons learned in the strategy management field. It also sheds light on Dubai's experience in developing a government-wide strategy management system.

It is not the intention of this chapter to assess evaluation practices in the field of development aid or to generalize judgments of its practices. The intention is to highlight areas in which each discipline can benefit from the other in enhancing the institutional learning practices for the benefit of international development.

Strategy Management Concept and Processes

The concept of strategy management stems from the pioneering work of Kaplan and Norton (2001) of Harvard Business School on the balanced scorecard and the strategy-focused organization. Strategy management is the framework by which an organization systematically manages its strategy to ensure that it is properly formulated and executed and that the whole organization is aligned to it. It is a set of processes and tools that ensure the systematic flow of information and the ability to use that information in making the right decisions to achieve the organization's strategic objectives. In broad terms, a large component of strategy management is a systematic monitoring and evaluation process.

Strategy management is based on five main principles (Kaplan and Norton 2001):

- Mobilize change through executive leadership.
- Translate strategy into operational terms.
- Align the organization to the strategy.
- Motivate to make strategy everyone's job.
- Govern to make strategy a continual process.

These principles are translated into a set of processes that include both top-down and bottom-up flows of information, change management, people management, and process management.

Mapping the Strategy

Mapping is a process through which an organization's strategy is translated into operational terms (Kaplan and Norton 2004). The map is a visual representation of an organization's strategy that demonstrates how the organization intends to create value added for its customers and stakeholders and achieve its outcomes in a logical cause-and-effect relationship. In a public sector organization, the map's logic is built up throughout different perspectives in top-down sequence, as shown in figure 4.1.

The map is guided by the outcomes and mission as a final destination. Outcomes are achieved through interaction with groups of customers

Figure 4.1 Generic Strategy Map Structure for a Public Organization

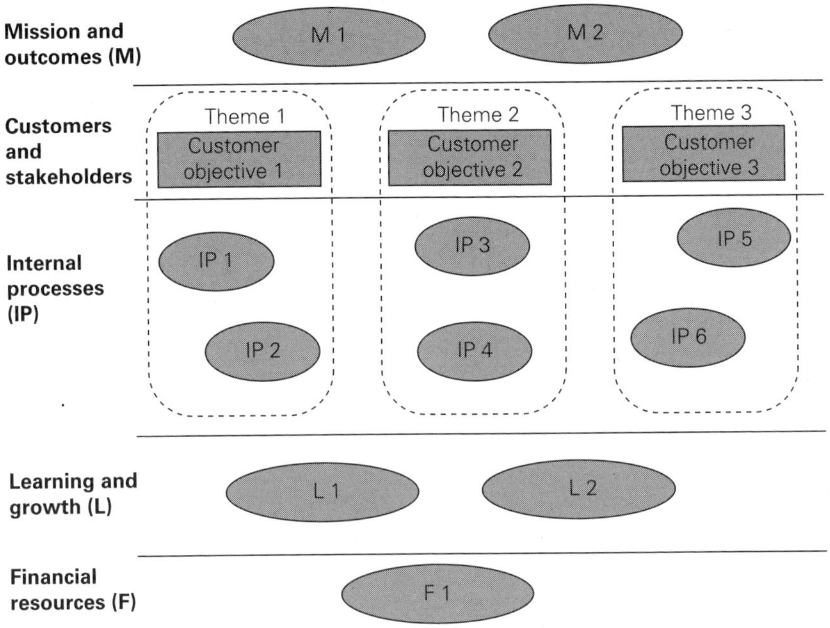

Mission and outcomes (M)	M 1, M 2
Customers and stakeholders	Theme 1: Customer objective 1 / Theme 2: Customer objective 2 / Theme 3: Customer objective 3
Internal processes (IP)	IP 1, IP 2 (Theme 1); IP 3, IP 4 (Theme 2); IP 5, IP 6 (Theme 3)
Learning and growth (L)	L 1, L 2
Financial resources (F)	F 1

Source: Kaplan and Norton 2004.

and stakeholders, each having its own values. For the organization to be able to serve its constituencies, a number of internal processes have to be introduced and supported by learning, growth, and financial enablers. The map also identifies the themes that cut across perspectives, based on the specific value added that is guided by a specific group of customers and stakeholders.

A strategy map is very useful as a management tool that dominates the management team's agenda toward introducing change. For the map to be a powerful tool, two main features have to be identified.

The first feature is the identification of cross-functional themes. Strategic themes should not represent different functions of the organization; they should represent different value added streams, to which all, or most, organizational functions contribute. Developing the strategy map around cross-functional themes helps the management team manage the organization's strategy with joint responsibility. Functional division of the strategy would deepen silo-driven management habits.

The second feature is the introduction of a new "ownership" structure. Depending on the type and size of the organization's owners, responsibility can be assigned by objectives, themes, or both. In principle, owners should be identified among the management team members. The ownership structure should promote a culture of shared responsibility and accountability, as no objective can be achieved solely as a result of a functional effort. An objective owner has the responsibility to coordinate different efforts within the organization to achieve the identified objective. The owner should also ensure proper reporting on performance with respect to the objective and act as an objective voice during strategic reviews.

Measuring the Strategy

Each objective identified on the map has to be profiled. The profile includes the identification of a strategic measure through which performance will be measured. Strategic measures can be either "lead," measuring the effort undertaken to achieve the objective, or "lag," measuring the final outcome.

Evaluators must develop a full profile for each measure. Each profile consists of information on the objective to be measured, the objective owner, the measure intent, the formula, the reporter, the measuring unit, and the frequency of measurement. It also includes information on the target and the baseline. The objective owner should develop or endorse the measure to be used and ensure the quality of data reported on it.

In some cases, the strategy is measured on a theme basis. A theme team agrees to measure the value added generated from a theme directly, through a set of measures or indexes identified for this purpose.

Managing Initiatives

In some cases—including both the internal processes and learning and growth perspectives—the objectives identified have to be supported by specific initiatives or projects to drive performance and close a performance gap. Strategic initiatives are not daily operations or projects. They are projects that drive structural change; in most cases, they have a cross-functional nature. Each initiative is profiled by describing it and identifying its relation to the objective or set of objectives. The profile should also provide information on the milestones, time line, deliverables, and initiative manager and team. The objective owner should endorse the initiative and build its logical link with the objective.

Reporting Performance

Reporting performance is the part of the process in which management of the strategy is practiced. The quality of performance reporting depends on the quality of all of the abovementioned processes. This process engages three integrated parts, in which the objective owner plays a major role:

- *Preparation of performance report.* A report is compiled based on data collected on both measures and milestones. The report analyzes performance with respect to the objective and recommends actions to be taken by the management team. The report should fully reflect the strategy map. Objective owners should review the report before it is submitted to the strategy team for discussion.
- *Strategic review.* During the strategy review meeting, it is important that owners be the ones who speak on behalf of the objectives. It is also crucial that what is discussed at these meetings is the strategy itself, represented by the strategy map, the strategic themes, and the strategic objectives. Information on the measures and initiatives supports rather than replaces the discussion of the strategy, themes, and objectives.
- *Communication.* Strategy reviews must act as communication tools, to reflect strategy performance on strategy execution through the alignment of the whole organization around common goals. Briefs summarizing overall performance and management decisions should be prepared and communicated widely throughout the organization.

Cascading the Strategy

One main objective of strategy management is to ensure alignment within the organization regarding achieving the organization's vision, mission, and objectives (box 4.1). One way to ensure alignment is by cascading the strategic themes and objectives to both core and supporting business units. It is crucial to ensure that all business units commit themselves to the same strategy to which management has committed.

Depending on the type, size, and nature of the organization, cascading can be identical, contributory, or new. In identical cascading, all business units adopt the same themes and objectives as the corporate body. In contributory cascading, the business units identify their contribution to the corporate strategy. In new cascading, business units are given room to identify their own objectives in some areas in which they have distinctive

> **Box 4.1 Where Does the Strategy Management Concept Apply?**
>
> Strategy management has many applications for public sector institutions. Many government organizations are customizing the strategy management processes and set-up to serve their needs. For example, private sector organizations place the financial perspective on the top of a strategy map as the final outcome of a business. In contrast, public sector organizations are replacing it with the outcome or mission perspective, placing the financial perspective at the bottom of the map to reflect its role as an enabler.
>
> Strategy management can also be used as an evaluation tool for major government interventions and programs. One example of such application is the Enhanced Productivity Program, a major donor-funded program in Jordan (for information, see http://www.mop.gov.jo).
>
> *Source:* Author.

business requirements that lie outside the scope of the corporate level (Kaplan and Jackson 2007).

Evaluation versus Strategy Management

The evaluation logic represents a major part of the strategy management process. Both the evaluation and strategy management processes are based on the simple plan-do-check-act logic. This section compares practices that take place in two arenas (development aid and public strategy management) from six perspectives. The comparison may not be fully systematic, because, in principle, an evaluation is a measurement tool based on social sciences research methods whereas strategy management is mainly a management framework that can use different tools of management and measurement methods, including those of the evaluation.

Ownership and Main Drivers for Change

Historically, evaluation functions related to donor-funded programs have been owned largely by donor agencies. Even where they were not fully owned by the aid agencies, donors could influence, or sometimes impose, the areas to be measured, the measures to be used, the type of information to be reported, and the frequency of reports. Evaluation practices used to be promoted by international donor organizations, which became the main drivers for more evidence-based results. Currently, the most advanced evaluation practices are promoted by international institutions such as the World Bank, and bilateral aid agencies, such as the Canadian International Development Agency (CIDA), the Danish International Development Agency (DANIDA), and the Swedish International Development Cooperation Agency (Sida).

Acknowledging the ownership challenge, both donors and partner countries realized the need to change the approach to enhance aid effectiveness, moving from a position in which evaluation is conducted based on the donor's need to one in which the developing partner practices significant ownership over the development process and its evaluation. Such realization was expressed at two important events on aid effectiveness. The High Level Forum on Aid Effectiveness, held in Paris in 2005, resulted in the Paris Declaration on Aid Effectiveness; the Third High Level Forum on Aid Effectiveness, held in Accra in 2008, resulted in the Accra Agenda for Action. Both documents stress the importance of transferring ownership, so that "partner countries exercise effective leadership over their development policies and strategies and coordinate development actions" (OECD 2005). The two documents also stress the mutual accountability for development results of both donors and partners.

As for strategy management, which developed from a corporate culture, the need was obvious to have the full function owned by the leadership and management team of the organization subject to evaluation. Strategy management usually comes from a need recognized by an organization's management team, which struggles in both planning and executing the organization's strategy. The first principle of a strategy-focused organization is to mobilize change through executive leadership. A 2007 survey conducted by Palladium, a leading strategy management firm, shows that among organizations with breakthrough results, 52 percent had leadership teams that owned the strategy, agreed on the direction, and demonstrated commitment; in 43 percent of firms, commitment was shared throughout the broader management team (Russell 2007). Anecdotal evidence suggests that unless the need for establishing a strategy management function is fully recognized by the leadership team, the system will usually fail.

Values Driving the Concept and the Practice

The main value used to drive the evaluation processes in the field of development aid evaluation was ensuring the best utilization of the funds provided by donors. Organizational learning and accountability for development results have also started to emerge as main values driving evaluation practices in development aid. However, in light of the fact that the evaluation is usually performed by a third party, the practice itself does not necessarily support translating the evaluation results into lessons reflected in management practice. Unless the evaluation process becomes an integral part of the management processes and is fully owned by the management team, evaluation will still be perceived as an outsider's interference in the organization's business or as an artificial accessory.

A number of development evaluation practices provide values that may not be captured by conventional aid evaluation practices. Enhancing program theories is a main result of theory-based evaluations that are based on challenging the assumptions embedded in theories of change. Different participatory practices in evaluation produce a wide range of benefits, not the least of which is the promotion of ownership and participation. Self-evaluation approaches in general lead to greater understanding of the institutional environment, leading to more systemic learning and the promotion of a culture of accountability.

The main values that drive strategy management are systematic learning and alignment. All strategy management processes support these values. The mapping and measuring exercises have to be conducted by a core team representing the organization and approved by the management team. The ownership structure represents the new joint management thinking, taking the organization away from the silo mentality and stressing the fact that the team needs to jointly drive performance without jeopardizing the accountability factor. In fact, accountability by the management team is extended to include, in addition to direct responsibility of functions within each team member's area, the indirect corporate responsibility that each member of the organization's team contributes to. The strategy reviews are well-organized forums at which all performance information that is brought is discussed openly by the owners themselves. Ultimately, resource alignment improves the way people perform their day-to-day jobs.

The Main Focus

An area of strength for evaluation practices is that they focus on the quality of data reported and on the evidence such data provide through the analysis. All evaluation processes and features—the key performance indicator identification, the evaluation matrix development, the data triangulation and verification, the impartiality of the third party conducting the evaluation, and the different methods of analyzing and reporting the data—support this focus.

Both evaluators and policy makers have long addressed the issue of utilization of evaluation results. In many cases, evaluators complain that their evidence-based evaluation results are not being fully utilized, often because of the lack of political will, especially when evaluations address relevance issues in cultures that do not pay much attention to contextual frameworks. Another reason behind low levels of utilization may be the fact that evaluation studies are often conducted by outsiders, making it easy for managers and executives to ignore or reject their recommendations.

Although the quality of data and analysis is acknowledged in strategy management practices, the main share of attention is given to the management process and the utilization of the data in ensuring organizational learning and alignment. All strategy management processes—including mapping the strategy, measuring the strategy, managing the initiatives, and reporting performance, all of which need to be tested against the management cycle of the organization to ensure that they support achieving the mission—support this concept.

In the public sector, practitioners of strategy management may not pay enough attention to the quality and depth of analysis typical of evaluation studies, possibly because strategy management is practiced mostly outside the boundaries of the social sciences and is not based on the research tools used by evaluators. Another reason may be the desire of strategy managers to monitor a certain number of indicators with numerical values that are easy to absorb in the systems built, which limits their ability to use the wide range of research methods practiced by evaluators.

Process Systemization

Evaluation studies are vertical assessments; they are usually conducted to assess and analyze the root causes of a certain level of performance, in particular, projects or programs within an identified period of time. Verticality does not support systematic recurrence very much. Moreover, projects and programs subject to evaluations may not necessarily be tied into well-defined integrated multidimensional strategic contexts. The nature of both analytical studies and development projects makes it necessary to call for consistent systematic contexts that can be translated into systems.

Recent trends in evaluation suggest moving from studies to streams (Kuzek and Rist 2004). A number of governments around the world are already adopting this approach. Governments in Australia, Canada, and the United States have adopted different models for evaluation systems (Mayne, Divorski, and Lemaire 1999). Some anchor their evaluation processes to the executive body, some to the legislature, and others to both.[1]

In contrast, strategy management is a systemic framework. It stems from the core strategic processes of organizations. The concept of strategy management started as a measurement system based on a balanced scorecard to measure organizational performance recurrently and systematically. It then transformed into a framework to manage the strategy execution at the corporate level and ensure resource alignment. Recently, it became a framework that ensures the alignment of the operational management cycle with the strategy management cycle. Strategy management is thus not only the nerve system of an organization but also its heart and brain.

Process Custodianship and Governance

Driven by a legitimate call for impartiality, the body responsible for the evaluation function in the development field is usually an independent body, in most cases detached from operations. A natural issue linked to this positioning is that this body be perceived largely as a control body that collects data on others' performance and reports to a third party (a board of directors in some cases, an aid agency in others). This positioning does not fully support the utilization of the evaluation results, which are not systematically reflected in operations management (as in the discussion of the process systemization above). In many cases, a blame game between those who report and those who are reported on begins. The object of the evaluation spends enormous energy defending and justifying its actions.

Other approaches to evaluations, such as participatory ones, overcome such issues by making the evaluation process a partnership of evaluators, evaluatees, and constituencies. However, using evaluation results systemically may remain an issue until institutional arrangements in this regard are put in place.

For strategy management, because the process is part of the core strategic processes of an organization, a strategy or performance management body manages the entire process. This body undertakes three important roles, those of architect, process owner, and integrator. The architect defines and clarifies the philosophy of performance management and the processes required to execute it. The process owner defines, develops, and oversees the execution of processes required to manage the strategy. The integrator ensures that the processes owned and run by other functional executives are linked to the strategy (Kaplan and Norton 2008). The office of strategy management is part of the organizational structure; its head is a member of the management team that reports directly to the chief executive officer. Reporting to the chief executive officer is natural, as strategy is owned by the executive leadership; other constituencies, mainly shareholders, are concerned mainly about results. When it comes to measuring the strategy, functional executives report on their own performance; it is the responsibility of the office of strategy management to coordinate the measurement and reporting processes and verify the results through an independent process that entails surveying customer and stakeholder voice.

The constituencies of not-for-profit organizations and government structures are wider than those of the private sector. They include management teams and boards, citizens, parliaments, civil society, the media, and independent audit bureaus. One way to respect the values of impartiality and practicality is to establish different contexts, each owned, managed, and measured by a different party (figure 4.2).

The high-level context, which governs national development, must be owned by all constituents. Although managed by government, the high-end outcomes of the national agenda should be measured by impartial bodies

Figure 4.2 Process Custodianship and Governance in Different Contexts

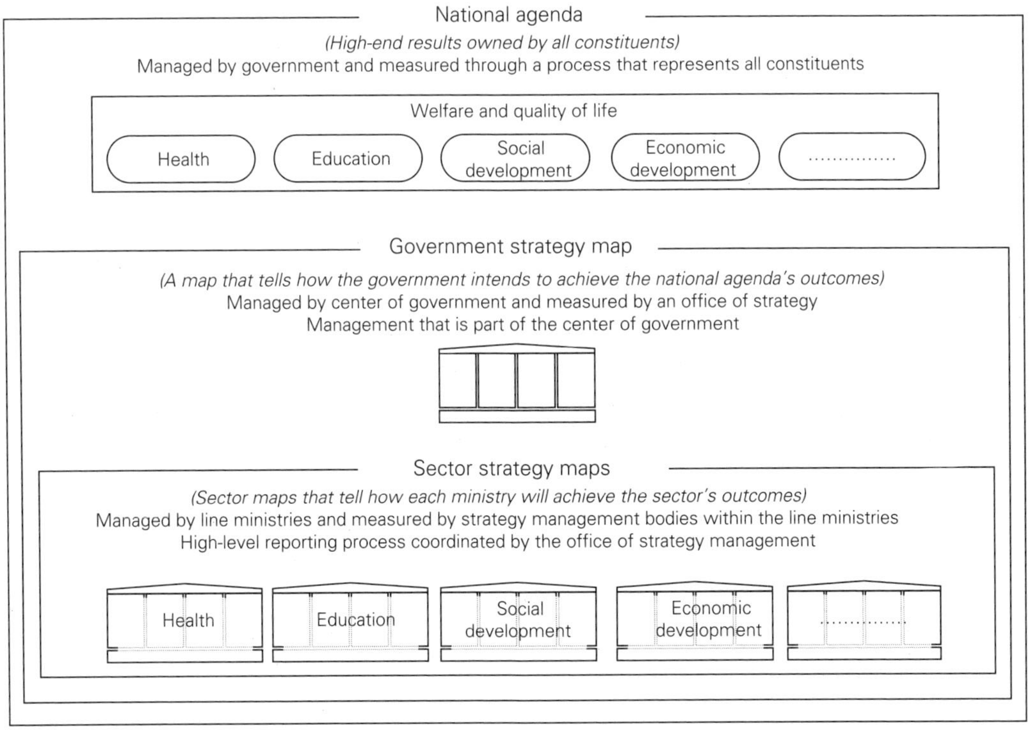

National agenda
(High-end results owned by all constituents)
Managed by government and measured through a process that represents all constituents

Welfare and quality of life
- Health
- Education
- Social development
- Economic development
- ....

Government strategy map
(A map that tells how the government intends to achieve the national agenda's outcomes)
Managed by center of government and measured by an office of strategy Management that is part of the center of government

Sector strategy maps
(Sector maps that tell how each ministry will achieve the sector's outcomes)
Managed by line ministries and measured by strategy management bodies within the line ministries
High-level reporting process coordinated by the office of strategy management
- Health
- Education
- Social development
- Economic development
- ....

Source: Author.

representing all constituencies. Evaluation processes play a major role in this regard. Once the national context is agreed on, it becomes the government's role to introduce its strategy—its plans for achieving high-level outcomes. At this stage, the context could be owned by the executive; strategy management would play the major role in framing the institutional learning system through its strategy development and execution processes. Evaluation would also play a main role in assessing the strategy outcomes, within the agreed-upon strategic context and the strategy management framework. The same logic applies to the sectoral context, where the executive owns both the context and the measurement framework. Different ministries would manage their strategies in a process coordinated by the center of government. Evaluation also has a key role to play in assessing the sector outcomes on different levels.

In conclusion, whatever the context, it is important to differentiate three roles when building institutional learning capacity:

- The context owner is the ultimate constituency, which should receive the results. Depending on the context, it could be the society as a whole, the people's representatives, the board, or another entity.
- The process custodian is the body that orchestrates the management and measurement process. Depending on the context, it could be the office of strategy management, the performance management unit, the strategy department, or another entity.
- The measurement expert is the technical body responsible for conducting the assessment. Depending on the context, it could be an evaluator, a performance management expert, a subject matter expert, or another entity.

This chapter does not suggest that evaluation results within the government and sector contexts not be reported to other constituencies; on the contrary, such systems should always be built on full transparency, and results should always be available to constituencies. What this section argues is that the strategy management framework, including the evaluation component, on these two levels should be built in to serve the operation's needs and the executives in managing their strategy.

The Processes

Evaluation and strategy management share some core processes, but a number of differences can also be highlighted. Each concept has its own advantages. Evaluation processes are powerful tools for analyzing data and drilling down to the root causes of weak performance, especially in areas where a single measure or key performance indicator cannot measure a high-level outcome objective. Strategy management is a powerful system to ensure proper utilization and reflection of the performance data on the way organizations do their businesses. It ensures alignment of all resources, functions, and policies toward achieving the ultimate goals. Both concepts can align their processes to ensure the highest degree of data accuracy and the most effective utilization of the information reported. Table 4.1 compares the processes related to the two concepts.

How Can Strategy Management and Evaluation Processes Be Integrated?

Strategy management and evaluation share similar processes, and each has its own advantages. To best utilize the advantages of both concepts, this section suggests an integrated framework that combines the contextual advantage of strategy management with the depth of analysis of evaluation. The process map shown in figure 4.3 departs from the assumption that all evaluation studies should come within a context. This context is defined by the strategy in place; the strategic success is identified by the achievement accomplished with respect to certain objectives. The focus of the strategy performance should be directed toward the objectives themselves rather than the programs, projects, or initiatives undertaken to support them.

Managing strategic performance starts with a scoping exercise conducted by the context owners and managed by the process custodian, to create a context or a logic model that shows how value is being created and how change is being introduced. One tool suggested is the strategy map, which demonstrates value creation through a group of integrated and complementary themes, each with its own theory of change.

Once the scope is clear and the objectives are identified, a process for developing the right measures to measure success commences. This process entails, in addition to the context owner and the process custodian, the measurement experts. Some objectives can be measured through direct or proxy indicators listed in a scorecard; these objectives are mostly in the area of measuring the internal processes and enablers. Other objectives—especially in the areas of the high-end results of the value propositions of customers and stakeholders and the mission—probably require more than a single indicator to be measured. Evaluation studies are designed and conducted by the measurement experts at this stage to assess the strategic outcomes. The evaluation studies need to create certain parameters that can be monitored systematically over time. Creating such parameters supports the

Table 4.1 Evaluation, Strategy Management, and Potential Areas of Integration

Dimension	Evaluation in development aid	Strategy management	Potential areas of integration
Where are we now and where do we want to be in the future?	Identifying outputs and outcomes	Formulating a strategy based on analyzing the internal and external environment; identifying core competencies; and identifying the mission, vision, and high-level outcomes	
How will we get there?	Developing a theory of change (the theory through which a program intends to bring about change, based on assumptions) Developing a program or project logical framework (liner logical thinking that captures inputs, activities, and outputs)	Introducing strategic themes (directed by the voice of customers and stakeholders); demonstrating the value added through which the organization intends to achieve its mission and vision (strategy mapping); assigning ownership (a new concept of joint responsibility and extended accountability); and identifying strategic initiatives that drive change toward achieving an objective, theme, or value added	Evaluation processes could use strategy mapping techniques, especially in designing nonlinear theories of change. The idea of having a strategy map is not only to represent the theory of change visually but also to use the map as a management tool and an agenda for the management team.
How do we measure our success?	Developing the evaluation matrix on the five evaluation criteria (relevance, effectiveness, efficiency, impact, and sustainability) and the methods of measurement; collecting the data; analyzing the data	Identifying strategic measures, including descriptions, formulas, units of measurement, frequency of measurement, measurement owners, sources of data, target information, and baseline information (if available); collecting the data; and analyzing the data	Strategy management processes can make use of development evaluation methods, especially in measuring strategic themes, customer propositions, and high-level outcomes, where single measures may be insufficient.
How will the information be used?	Reporting performance	Reporting performance, conducting strategy reviews, and communicating performance results to strategy management	
How do we ensure alignment?		Cascading, linking human resources to strategy, and linking budget to strategic priorities	

Source: Author.

Figure 4.3 High-Level Integrated Strategy Management and Evaluation Process

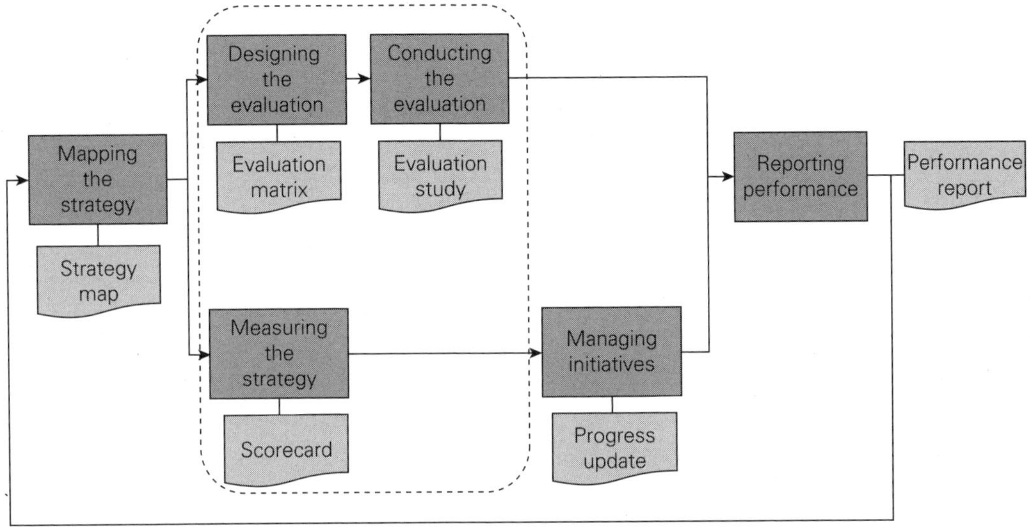

[Flowchart: Mapping the strategy → Strategy map; Designing the evaluation → Evaluation matrix; Conducting the evaluation → Evaluation study; Measuring the strategy → Scorecard; Managing initiatives → Progress update; Reporting performance → Performance report]

Source: Author.

evaluation's integration into the strategy management context, ending up with periodic performance reports and strategic reviews.

Based on the performance gaps identified by the measurement process, strategic initiatives to bridge the gaps are identified in a process that involves the three parties and is orchestrated by the process custodian. Information on both performance and initiatives is then consolidated by the process custodian in comprehensive reports, analyzing overall strategic performance. Reports are then discussed by the context owners in strategy review sessions. Performance reports and the strategic reviews are then communicated back to the strategic scope.

Building Dubai's Institutional Learning Capacity

Dubai is one of the fastest-growing economies in the world and one of the most dynamic cities in the Middle East. Since 2000, it has maintained double-digit gross domestic product (GDP) growth, effectively utilizing its core competencies as an international logistics hub, an attractive destination for international tourists, and a preferred place for living and doing business.

In 2005, Dubai announced its 10-year strategic plan, the Dubai Strategic Plan (DSP). The comprehensive 300-page document covers 12 sectors divided into 5 main streams: economic development; social development; security, safety, and justice; infrastructure, land, and environment; and public sector excellence.

In 2008, the center of government and the whole government body were still struggling to execute the strategy and report on progress toward achieving the DSP's objectives. Coordinating efforts by stakeholders to get things done was difficult, given the scope of the strategy.

Since mid-2008, efforts have been made to build the institutional learning capacity of Dubai's government by building an overall strategy management system that would enable the center of government (the Executive Council) to ensure proper execution of the DSP. The suggested system is a powerful tool not only for ensuring systematic reporting on the strategy execution but also for providing a platform for the leadership team to share joint responsibility in managing their city and sharing accountability for its prosperity.

Getting Started

Between 2003 and 2008, Dubai's center of government measured institutions' performance according to a set of key policy indicators. Some of these indicators were shared across government, especially in the fields of human resource development, financial resources, and customer satisfaction. Other indicators addressed the specific area of business of each department. Targets were identified based on international best practices or as an increment to the previous level of performance. No single strategic reference for Dubai existed: some departments had their own strategies, others had simple business or operational plans. There was lack of clear ownership of the system, which line departments perceived as a burdensome exercise to fulfill the center of government's needs rather than to manage their own performance. The system put emphasis on measurement and was unable to provide a strategic direction. All of these factors resulted in the lack of solid recognition of the system by government departments.

In early 2008, a new concept of strategy management was introduced and a communication effort made to start disseminating awareness of the urgency of change. The challenge was to execute the recently published DSP and to provide the Executive Council with a better information and management system to help it do so.

Overall System Architecture

The architecture of the new strategy management system is based on two main processes, cascading and reporting (figure 4.4). The cascading

Figure 4.4 Architecture of Dubai's Strategy Management Framework

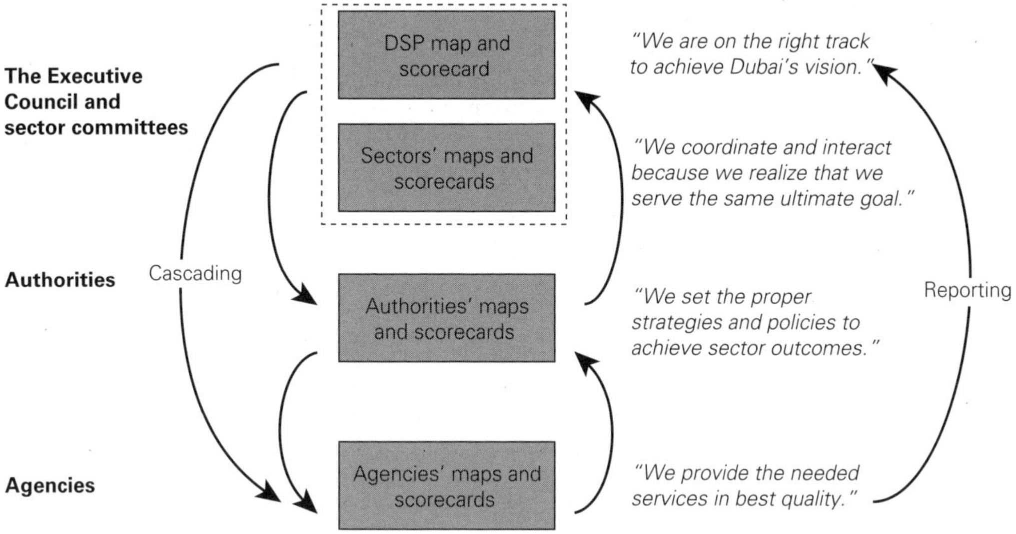

Sources: Government of Dubai 2005 and author.

processes ensure that the DSP is disseminated to the sector, authority, and agency levels and that each of these layers commits to achieving the DSP objectives within the cross-sectoral strategic themes.

As shown in figure 4.4, the first two layers are managed by the Executive Council and the sector committees (permanent committees that existed before the introduction of the new system). The sector committees are composed of Executive Council members representing various sectors. Each committee is responsible for coordinating efforts among the government bodies that operate within the sector, avoiding overlaps, and ensuring efficient execution of cross-sectoral policies. The committees are not decision-making bodies; they make recommendations to the Executive Council, the ultimate decision-making body at the executive level.

The second layer represents the departments and authorities. These bodies are responsible for making policies governing different economic, social, and legal sectors.[2] The authorities are not supposed to deliver direct services to the public (that function is within the agencies' jurisdiction). Each authority has its own strategy, which is cascaded from the DSP. Each authority also has its own strategy management system, which ensures proper execution of the authority's strategy in alignment with the DSP. Information is solicited from the authorities' strategy management systems to feed into the DSP management system.

At the third layer, agencies are responsible for direct service delivery to the public. Agencies report to the authorities within a specific sector, but authorities remain the sole accountable bodies of the sector's performance before the Executive Council; agencies are accountable to the authorities. To ensure synergy and alignment within sectors, agencies should have their own strategy maps cascaded down from the authorities' maps.

The system is managed at the Executive Council level by ensuring the appropriate mapping of the DSP and the development of a scorecard and reporting system. Once the system is developed at the DSP level, the cascading process begins at the authority and agency levels and reporting starts to happen from the bottom layers to feed into the areas of performance on the DSP level. With regard to strategy execution, no reporting except the DSP map and scorecard is required from the authorities to the Executive Council. Similarly, no reporting is required from the agency to the authority other than the DSP and authority maps.

Through this framework, Dubai is not only promoting systematic reporting and accountability culture, but also trying to introduce a consistent dynamic dialogue on overall growth trends, priorities, and objectives.

Mapping the Dubai Strategic Plan: Introducing a Shared Framework for Better Strategy Management

A DSP map was developed to provide a comprehensive understanding of Dubai's strategic priorities through 2015. The map is based on the DSP document and on one-on-one interviews with Executive Council members and directors general of government departments and authorities. The map consists of four vertical themes, representing the value added expected by the four groups of customers: Dubai's people, the business sector, the Emiratis, and federal and international institutions (figure 4.5). In addition, the map includes three horizontal (cross-cutting) themes: ensuring a conducive environment, excellent government machinery, and sustainable financial resources.

Mapping the DSP is not just the projection of the DSP objectives onto a map. The value added behind introducing DSP's map is twofold.

Moving from sectors to cross-sectoral themes
The DSP structure is based on five main groups of sectors, each managed by a sector committee. Based on such structure, it is not possible to draw a comprehensive picture describing Dubai in 2015 irrespective of what

Figure 4.5 Dubai's Strategy Map

	To enhance Dubai's sustainable development, promote its international position, and make it a financial, business, and tourism center
Mission	
Customers and stakeholders	**Dubai's people** *(To enhance the quality of life)* — "We look forward to a safe and just city that provides its people and residents with advanced living standards and world class services, along with a rich social life in a tolerant society. A city that is a preferred place for living" • **Business sector** *(To maintain a sustainable economic growth)* — "We look forward to a city that provides attractive and continuous business opportunities, an a conducive business environment. A city that is a preferred place for investment" • **Emiratis** *(To promote citizenship and participation)* — "We look forward to a city that promotes a citizenship based on equal rights and duties. A city that enables its citizens to lead its development and promotes their national loyalty" • **Federal and international institutions** *(To support the federation and to positively interact with the world)* — "We look forward to a city that supports the federation's ties with integrated and synergized frameworks. A city that is active on the international arena with its pioneering model to support the international development"
Internal processes	A set of objectives that describe how Dubai intends to meet the customers and stakeholders' needs in light of its mission above, especially with regard to good policies and excellent services
Conducive environment	A set of objectives that describe what kind of conducive environment Dubai needs to support its strategy, especially with regard to competent human capital, developed legislative framework, enabling information capital, and physical infrastructure along with macroeconomic stability
Excellent government machinery	A set of objectives that describe what kind of government machinery should be in place to support the strategy execution, especially with regard to good governance, competent government human resources, effective communication, quality services, and performance excellence
Sustainable financial resources	A set of objectives that describe what kind of government financial management should be in place to support the strategy execution, especially with regard to good financial planning, updated financial legislations, enhanced efficiency, proper budget preparation and execution process along with financial discipline

Source: Author.

different sectors would look like. From the average individual's point of view, what matters is not whether there is good infrastructure, sufficient energy, or competent social services; what matters is whether an individual enjoys a life with high quality standards, to which all the aforementioned sectors contribute. During the mapping exercise, it was important to think of an overarching level above the sectors to represent the real value added from the customers' perspective, which led to the emergence of the strategic themes.

Moving from sector management to theme management

Managing the DSP will be based on the strategic themes rather than the sectors. At the national level, ownership of the themes will be assigned to the committees, which will execute a different agenda from what they already manage on the sector level. The head of each committee will be responsible for managing a specific theme, irrespective of his or her area of responsibility at the sector level. The same will apply to the sector committees: each committee will have to manage its sector in a way that fully supports the themes committed to at the DSP level. The DSP map will be cascaded to all sectors and authorities. Each sector and authority will adopt the same five themes identified at Dubai's level, with stakeholder voices spelled out in each theme, and will define its contribution toward achieving the objectives in the DSP themes.

Measuring the DSP

The DSP will be measured using two methods (box 4.2). The first method is to directly measure the objectives identified. This method is expected to be used at the sector level, where specific objectives have already been identified. The second method is to measure the themes with a profile of measures or index for each theme. This measure is expected to be used at the upper part of the system related to Dubai's map. Development evaluation methods can be used in measuring the themes.

Six teams, representing government departments and authorities, will work jointly to develop the themes and objective profiles. Part of this exercise will be to identify and profile the strategic measures. Once this exercise is complete, the data collection process will commence. The first report is to be produced in mid-2010 and will be the baseline report. Performance data will be captured in two ways: by compiling data solicited from various sectors and authorities' performance reports generated from their strategy management systems and by conducting surveys to capture customer value propositions and high-level outcomes.

> **Box 4.2 How Is Public Value Created and Measured in This Model?**
>
> Strategy management is a framework that draws on different concepts and values within its boundaries. The outline of a strategy map does not impose the content; it provides the framework through which value is created within the strategic context, providing the decision maker with an opportunity to focus on the main priorities when developing a strategy. It also helps a management team manage a strategy in a comprehensive and integrated manner.
>
> That said, the concept of public value, explored by Moore (1995), is a value that can be represented and measured using the strategy management framework. In Dubai's map, the ultimate goal is reflected in its mission—"to enhance Dubai's sustainable development"—which is translated into a number of value propositions demonstrated in the four vertical themes. For the city's multicultural society, the public value is spilled out as follows: "We look forward to a safe and just city that provides its people and residents with advanced living standards and world-class services, along with a rich social life in a tolerant society, a city that is a preferred place for living." A proposition that represents a public value would be the base for the measurement process as well. When surveying Dubai's people in an attempt to measure the extent to which the city has achieved its values, success will not be about only individuals' satisfaction but more about the city's ability to achieve the public value identified and agreed upon by different constituencies and their representatives.
>
> The same logic applies to the third theme, the Emiratis. Citizenship and participation are not subject to the interpretation of individuals but to the public value articulated in the people's voice: "We look forward to a city that promotes a citizenship based on equal rights and duties, a city that enables its citizens to lead its development and promotes their national loyalty."

Reporting Performance and Managing Strategic Reviews

The process of performance reporting and system review is designed to ensure timely reporting and review meetings. It consists of three steps:

- *Preparation of performance report.* Performance data are compiled based on authority performance reports, which come out quarterly. Specific surveys are also conducted to capture data that are outside the authority-level scorecards. Both measurement and initiative teams work on each measure and initiative to analyze and interpret the data and propose corrective actions. Each objective report is reviewed by the concerned owner, and a full report is presented to the chair before the meeting.

- *Review meeting.* Following each semiannual report, a strategy review meeting is conducted. During the meeting, the theme and objective owners present the performance reports. Each owner acts as an objective voice. The owner describes the current performance using both the measure and initiative information, analyzes the root causes of the performance, and recommends any corrective action.
- *Communication of performance to strategy execution.* Following the review meeting, all Executive Council decisions are articulated and communicated to all stakeholders. A process to follow up on compliance with Executive Council decisions takes place, and the level of compliance is reported back to the Executive Council. The main performance messages are articulated and communicated across the government.

Dubai's Strategy Management Challenges

The challenges of introducing a strategy management system to Dubai do not differ from those associated with introducing change in any context. Three main challenges are most important.

Dealing with scale and complexity

Dubai is a city-state, with government machinery of more than 20 departments and authorities as well as many other agencies and statutory bodies. Among the 133 members of Palladium's Hall of Fame, only five cities are listed, none of which has the variety of Dubai's governmental functions. With such a huge structure, it is a challenge to apply the concept and processes of strategy management, which until now had been applied mostly to single private and public organizations. Dubai's government structure is not only spread out horizontally, it also runs vertically, with the Executive Council at the top, under which are the five sector committees, the departments and authorities, and, finally, the agencies and other statutory bodies.

The approach adopted to confront such a challenge was to go gradually. The development process started by piloting the application on one of the newly established authorities. The pilot backed the experience with lessons learned, after which it was decided to adopt a top-down approach. The main themes of Dubai's map were then identified and cascaded down to the five sector committees. The plan is to have the first reporting cycle at both the Dubai and the committees' levels completed before cascading the system to the department and authority level.

Moving from silos to integration

As in other governments, departments and authorities in Dubai own specific development portfolios (health, education, social development). Each owner drives the development of a specific development field and is held accountable for the results. Strategy maps include themes, value propositions, and other objectives that do not fall under a specific area of ownership, with the maps based on cross-sectoral value creation theory. Accordingly, there was a need for a strategy management ownership structure with theme and objective owners to manage the strategy in an integrated manner. Introducing a new strategy management governance structure was not easy; departments could realize only their own shares of responsibility. Moreover, the new structure was perceived as a new hierarchy.

The approach to this challenge was to stick to the theme-based integrated management model, insisting on having all themes at all levels. To overcome the ownership issue, it was agreed that theme ownership would be assigned to the heads of sector committees. They are currently wearing another hat and managing another integrated agenda that differs from that of the sectors. At the sector level, ownership is assigned to the objectives, not the themes, with the shared objectives to be assigned to the head of the committee. Once experience is developed, theme ownership can be introduced at this level.

In an attempt to deepen integration among government sectors and departments, strategy execution support teams were formed (figure 4.6).

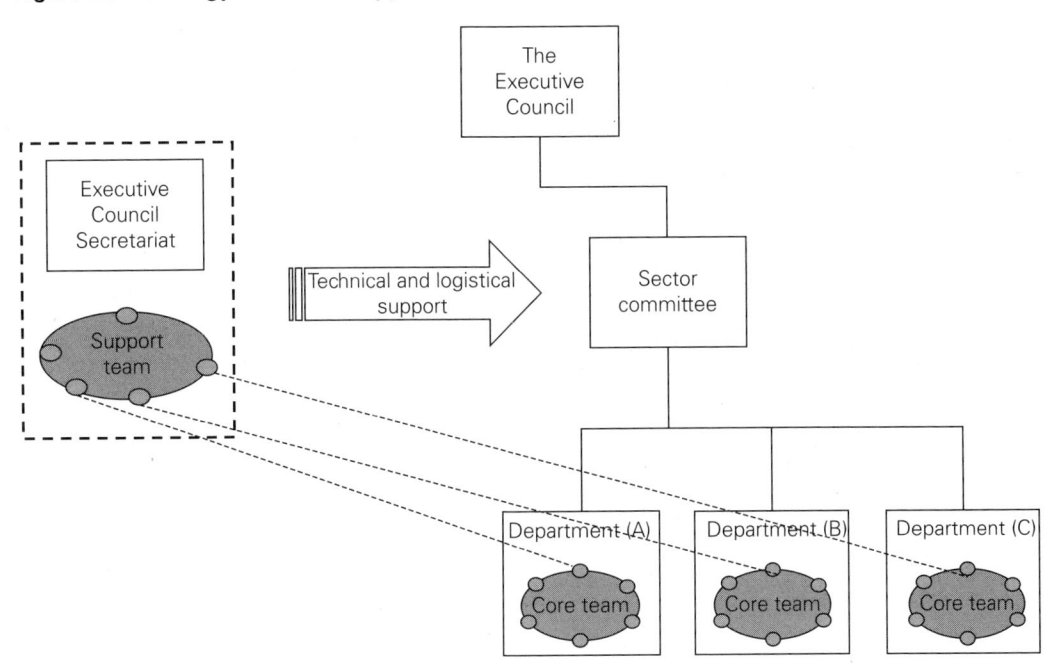

Figure 4.6 Strategy Execution Support Team

Source: Author.

These teams comprise professionals and subject matter experts (heads of strategy and performance units) representing different government bodies. The objective of the support teams is to support the development and integration of Dubai's strategy management system at the sector level and introduce integration between different government bodies at the middle-management level.

Meeting the measurement challenge

The information infrastructure within the Dubai government is not yet mature enough to support operating the strategy management system. There is no clear picture on the quality of the data already collected and reported, although anecdotal evidence suggests variance in the quality of data collection, documentation, and reporting processes across the government. Consistent with the gradual approach adopted, the decision was made to run the system with whatever data and information are available, acknowledging that there will be many gaps in reporting while at the same time continuing to work on data and information production process at all levels.

The plan is to use the strategy mapping exercise and the policy agenda development process as a scoping exercise to identify the data and

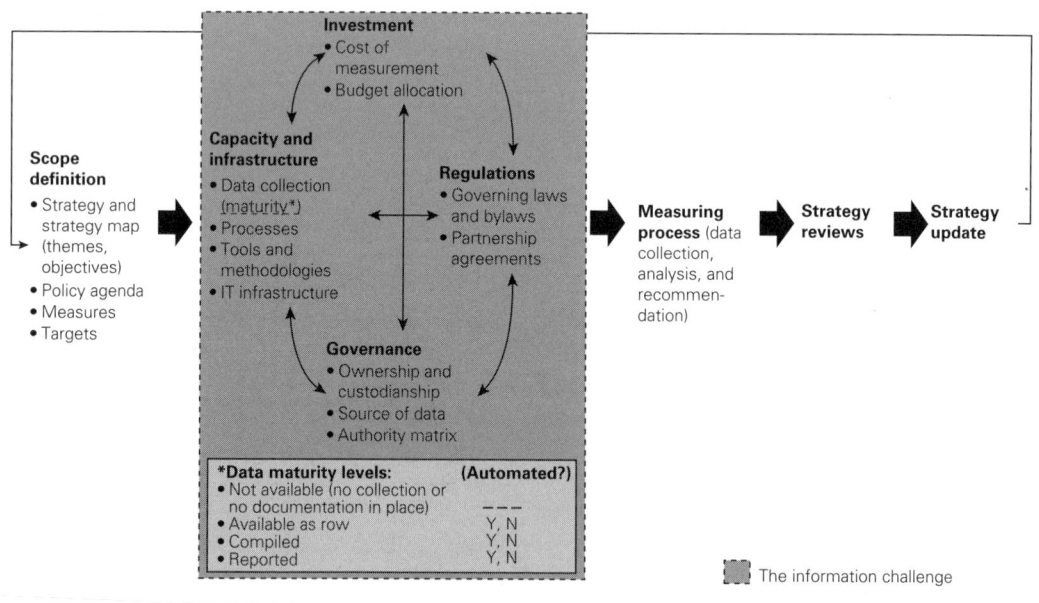

Figure 4.7 Dubai's Strategy Execution Measurement Challenge

```
                                    Investment
                                  • Cost of
                                    measurement
                                  • Budget allocation

                          Capacity and
Scope                     infrastructure
definition                • Data collection       Regulations
• Strategy and              (maturity*)           • Governing laws    Measuring          Strategy         Strategy
  strategy map            • Processes               and bylaws        process (data      reviews          update
  (themes,                • Tools and             • Partnership       collection,
  objectives)               methodologies           agreements        analysis, and
• Policy agenda           • IT infrastructure                         recommen-
• Measures                                                            dation)
• Targets
                            Governance
                          • Ownership and
                            custodianship
                          • Source of data
                          • Authority matrix

*Data maturity levels:            (Automated?)
• Not available (no collection or
  no documentation in place)          ---
• Available as row                    Y, N
• Compiled                            Y, N
• Reported                            Y, N
```

▓▓ The information challenge

Source: Author.

Note: — = not available, N = No, Y = Yes.

information needed for the decision-making process (figure 4.7). A comprehensive assessment process is to take place to identify the gaps associated in the data and information environment in four main areas: capacity and infrastructure (the maturity of data collection, processes, tools and methodologies, and information technology infrastructure); the investment needed (the cost of measurement and budget locations); the governance definition (ownerships, sources of data, and authority matrix); and regulations required to govern the data collection process (laws and bylaws, partnerships, and agreements).

Notes

1. See chapter 1 of this book for a description of a very important effort to build a monitoring and evaluation system in Sri Lanka by gradually integrating evaluation studies into the mainstream institutional learning system. Such a system is positioned within the executive; efforts are made to establish institutional links to the legislature.
2. In 2007, the Dubai government introduced a new typology to the government structure by which departments are transformed into authorities responsible for policy making, while the service delivery is transferred to agencies. This typology has not fully been implemented; the current structure includes departments, authorities, and agencies.

Bibliography

Bastoe, P. O. 1999. "Linking Evaluation with Strategic Planning, Budgeting, Monitoring, and Auditing." In *Building Effective Evaluation Capacity: Lessons from Practice*, ed. R. Boyle and D. Lemaire. Piscataway, NJ: Transaction Publishers.

Government of Dubai. 2005. "Dubai Strategic Plan." Dubai.

Kaplan, R., and C. Jackson. 2007. "Managing by Strategic Themes." *Balanced Scorecard Report* 9 (5).

Kaplan, R., and D. Norton. 2001. *Strategy Focused Organization*. Boston: Harvard Business School Press.

———. 2004. *Strategy Maps: Converting Intangible Assets into Tangible Outcomes*. Boston: Harvard Business School Press.

———. 2006. *Alignment*. Boston: Harvard Business School Press.

———. 2008. *The Execution Premium: Linking Strategy to Operations for Competitive Advantage*. Boston: Harvard Business School Press.

Kuzek, J., and R. Rist. 2004. *Ten Steps to a Results-Based Monitoring and Evaluation Systems*. Washington, DC: World Bank.

Mayne, J., S. Divorski, and D. Lemaire. 1999. "Locating Evaluation: Anchoring Evaluation in the Executive or the Legislature, or Both, or Elsewhere?"

In *Building Effective Evaluation Capacity: Lessons from Practice*, ed. R. Boyle and D. Lemaire. Piscataway, NJ: Transaction Publishers.

Moore, M. 1995. *Creating Public Value: Strategic Management in the Public Sector*. Cambridge, MA: Harvard University Press.

OECD (Organisation for Economic Co-operation and Development). 2005. *Paris Declaration*. Paris: OECD.

———. 2008. *Accra Agenda for Action*. Accra: OECD.

Palladium Group. 2009. *Hall of Fame Organizations*. http://www.thepalladiumgroup.com/about/hof/Pages/HofViewer.aspx.

Russell, R. 2007. "Make It Breakthrough: Findings from the 2007 Global SFO Survey." *Balanced Scorecard Report* 9 (6).

CHAPTER 5

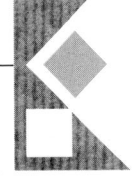

A Conceptual Framework for Developing Evaluation Capacities: Building on Good Practice

Caroline Heider

The purpose of this chapter is to contribute to a better understanding of the complexities of evaluation capacity development and suggest ways of approaching them within an institutional context or at the national level. The chapter applies good practice in capacity development to attain good practice in evaluation, so that it can serve its purposes of accountability and learning. It builds on established good practice in these two professions and on the experience of evaluating capacity development.

Both evaluation and capacity development are multifaceted and evolving. This chapter therefore captures only a segment of the whole at a particular point in time.[1] Capacity development practitioners continue to develop and refine concepts and practices; "The Challenge of Capacity Development" (OECD/DAC 2006) is subtitled "Working towards Good Practice" in full recognition of the challenges still ahead. In a similar way, the evaluation profession continues to grow.

This chapter comes at an important time. The demand for evaluation is high, but clients are increasingly critical of evaluation practices that are not demonstrating independence, credibility, and utility. In addition, following the Paris Declaration and the Accra Agenda for Action, there has been increasing demand for evaluation capacities in partner countries. For instance, the evaluations of the "Delivering as One" initiative of the United Nations will be country led. Therefore, developing evaluation capacities is important for a range of stakeholders in the development and humanitarian communities. This chapter aims to provide these stakeholders with a conceptual framework to support their efforts.

The chapter is divided into five main sections. The first section describes the principles of evaluation. The second section discusses evaluation capacities at three levels, which overlay the evaluation principles with capacity development ideas. The third section discusses the capabilities and processes to instill them. The fourth section discusses examples and provides some suggestions for stakeholders working on evaluation capacity development. The last section briefly summarizes the chapter.

Evaluation Principles

The evaluation principles used here date back to those defined at a meeting of evaluation professionals in 1991 and probably to before then.[2] The terms, defined in the annex to this chapter, have become integral to the evaluation profession.[3] The principle of *independence* took central stage at multilateral development banks when, in the mid-1990s, the evaluation function at the World Bank started reporting to the executive board rather than the president, a change that was replicated in regional development banks and stimulated discussions in the United Nations and elsewhere.

In 2008, the framework for peer reviews of evaluation functions in the United Nations (UN) system identified three principles as central to evaluation: independence, credibility, and utility (DAC/UNEG 2007).

- *Independence* forms the bedrock of good evaluation practice.[4] It is fundamental to the credibility and utility of evaluation. It should lead to impartiality, reflected in, for instance, the choice of subjects of evaluation and the evaluation method. Independence is achieved at the structural, institutional, and individual levels.
- The *credibility* of evaluation is enhanced with greater independence, but it needs to be accompanied by the competence of the evaluators, the transparency of the evaluation process, and the impartiality of the evaluators and the process.

- The *utility* of evaluation is not guaranteed by independence and credibility. Utility requires that commissioners and evaluators undertake the evaluation with the intention to use its results, that they undertake the evaluation at a time when the results can meaningfully inform decision-making processes, and that evaluations be accessible. This principle exists to ensure that evaluations are conducted to influence change that enables governments and organizations to achieve their objectives and achieve them better.

Together these principles are markers of high-quality evaluation and ensure good practice in evaluation. Independence, credibility, and utility are three equal sides of the triangle at the center of which the quality of evaluation rests. Their interrelationship, including inherent complementarities and tensions, is illustrated in figure 5.1. Each of the central evaluation principles supports the others.

Complementarities exist between these principles: an evaluation that is biased toward the perspective of one stakeholder (that is, not independent or impartial) tends not to be credible to others. If an evaluation lacks credibility, it is unlikely that stakeholders will pay attention to it, let alone use it; as a result, its utility diminishes. Ignoring stakeholders, their interests, or time lines will reduce both the utility of an evaluation and the credibility of its process. By maintaining a good balance between independence, credibility, and utility, these three principles reinforce one another and enhance the quality of the evaluation.

Tensions may also exist between evaluation principles. For instance, independence can lead to isolation of the evaluation function, which reduces its utility. Some stakeholders may perceive evaluations to be useful

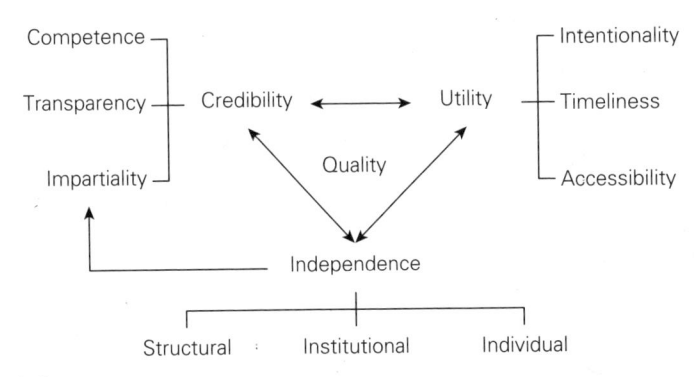

Figure 5.1 Evaluation Principles

```
Competence ┐                              ┌ Intentionality
Transparency ┼─ Credibility ←───→ Utility ┼ Timeliness
Impartiality ┘         ╲ Quality ╱        └ Accessibility
                        ╲      ╱
                       Independence
                    ┌──────┼──────┐
                 Structural Institutional Individual
```

Source: Author.

A Conceptual Framework for Developing Evaluation Capacities: Building on Good Practice solely when they report only successes (and omit information about failures) or serve fundraising or publicity purposes. Policy makers may want to pursue a certain course of action that could be derailed by evidence. However, evaluations that report only positive results have little credibility with other, well-informed stakeholders.[5] Equally important, they are of little, if any, use in resolving problems. When problems remain unknown or are covered up, solutions cannot be found to them, hampering stakeholders in achieving their objectives.

Stakeholders often believe that credibility can derive exclusively from close familiarity with the subject under evaluation. They ignore the fact that such close links eliminate independence and reduce the chance that the evaluation will produce an impartial and credible evaluation that provides insights.

All evaluators must act in line with these evaluation principles.[6] Measures are needed to ensure that adherence to them does not depend on individuals alone, however. Evaluators may be subjective. They may lack an understanding that independence is granted to ensure impartiality and not for other reasons. They may be under pressure from stakeholders who want to influence evaluation findings. Therefore, it is important to have an institutional framework that holds evaluators accountable and protects them from undue influence as well as an enabling environment that supports evaluation, learning, and accountability.

Developing Capacity at Three Levels

Capacity development is central to development and progress. The Accra Agenda for Action is the latest commitment to strengthening capacities in support of ownership of development processes. Investments in developing capacities have been made for many years, supported by many different actors, many of whom struggle with similar challenges.

The concept of capacity development began with a focus on training individuals.[7] It evolved into institutional development when it was recognized that individuals worked within the context of their organizations and that more than training was therefore needed for them to be successful (UNIDO 1990).[8] It further evolved into capacity development, acknowledging that organizations do not work in isolation but require an enabling environment that consists of, among other components, policies, networks, and an attitude of engagement.[9] Capacity therefore goes beyond an individual or an organization. Evaluation principles need to be integrated with measures

Figure 5.2 The Three Levels of Capacity

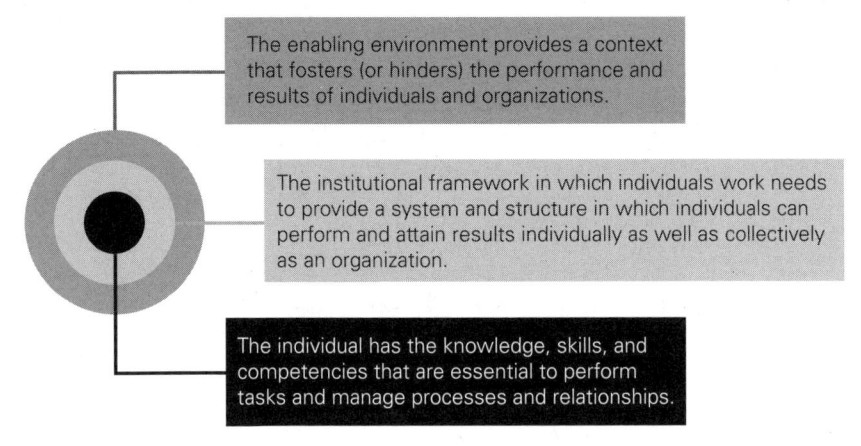

The enabling environment provides a context that fosters (or hinders) the performance and results of individuals and organizations.

The institutional framework in which individuals work needs to provide a system and structure in which individuals can perform and attain results individually as well as collectively as an organization.

The individual has the knowledge, skills, and competencies that are essential to perform tasks and manage processes and relationships.

Source: Author.

that go beyond the individual to span the institutional framework and the enabling environment for evaluation (figure 5.2).

The Enabling Environment

The enabling environment for evaluation is determined by a culture of learning and accountability—that is, the degree to which information about past performance is sought and the extent to which there is a drive to continuously improve and hold people responsible for actions taken, resources spent, and results achieved. In such an environment, evaluation is understood to help decision makers and implementers achieve common goals more efficiently and effectively. Such a culture is embedded in tacit norms of behavior: the understanding of what can and should (and should not) be done.[10] Behaviors are often modeled by leaders. These norms should be codified in government legislation or an evaluation policy that expresses the commitment of leadership or the organization to learning, accountability, and evaluation principles.

An enabling environment is also supported by or created through governance structures that demand independent evaluation, be it through parliaments or governing bodies, and enhanced through professional associations and networks that set standards and strive toward greater professionalism in evaluation (box 5.1). The structural independence of an evaluation function is important to create an enabling environment: the

> **Box 5.1 Ensuring Evaluators' Structural Independence**
>
> Structural independence requires that an evaluation function or office not report to the individual responsible for the issue being evaluated. If this is not the case, the evaluation function may be under political or organizational pressure that interferes with the independent and impartial planning, conduct, and reporting of evaluation findings. Examples of structural independence include the following:
>
> - national systems in which evaluators report directly to Parliament to ensure the highest degree of independence and ensure that it benefits from impartial evaluation insights
> - evaluation functions in many development banks, including the World Bank, where evaluation units report directly to the executive board
> - the UN system, in which evaluation norms suggest that a reporting line to the governing body or the head of the organization is adequate to ensure structural independence
> - the practices of the Food and Agriculture Organization or the United Nations Development Programme, which introduced dual reporting lines (a functional line to the governing body and an administrative line to the head of the organization).
>
> Of course, structural independence does not guarantee impartiality. Impartiality depends on the evaluators and institutional measures that help safeguard independence.

evaluation function should not report to the person or function responsible for the policies, strategies, or operations being evaluated. Ideally, the enabling environment is such that decision makers proactively demand impartial evaluations to inform their debates and choices, which increases the usefulness of evaluations.[11]

The Institutional Framework

The institutional framework for evaluation ensures that a system exists to implement and safeguard the independence, credibility, and utility of the evaluation. Such a framework reduces the risk that declared commitments to independence are revoked by making systems more difficult to reverse without the agreement of all stakeholders. It also reduces the risk inherent in depending on individuals and their behavior. Creating a system of checks and balances helps ensure accountability and protect individuals.

A good institutional framework has the following characteristics:

- It includes a system of peer review that ensures that the evaluation function is set up to safeguard and implement the principles of independence, credibility, and utility.
- It establishes safeguards to protect individual evaluators (evaluators, evaluation managers, and heads of evaluation functions) when exercising their independence, including through transparent and credible processes for selecting, appointing, renewing, and terminating the evaluator and assurances that evaluation staff will not suffer in any way as a result of the findings they report.
- It ensures the creation of a multidisciplinary evaluation team, which increases the credibility of the evaluation by providing technical competence and knowledge of multiple dimensions of the issues.
- It secures the independence of funding of evaluations at an adequate level, to ensure that evaluations are carried out and that budget holders do not influence what is evaluated and how. Funding should be under the direct control of the head of the evaluation function and should be sufficient for an adequate work program.
- It combines measures for impartial or purposive selection of evaluation subjects to ensure impartiality and increased utility by making deliberate choices linked to decision-making processes.
- It uses objective criteria in the selection of subjects for evaluation, to ensure that the evaluation sample is representative of the whole; there is no bias to select only good performers or problem cases. To ensure the utility of the evaluation, subjects may be chosen purposively to link the conduct of the evaluation to the information needs and decision-making processes of those using evaluation findings. In these cases, a consultation process to determine what the most important and strategic topics are for evaluation is important to ensure that various stakeholders' needs are considered.
- It sets out a system to plan, undertake, and report evaluation findings in an independent, credible, and useful way. To increase objectivity in the planning and conduct of evaluation, systems are needed to increase the rigor, transparency, and predictability of evaluation processes and products. Such systems can include more or less detailed process descriptions or guidelines for the design of evaluations, preparatory work, and reporting. The processes should have built-in steps for communication, consultation, and quality assurance, which should be communicated to stakeholders to enhance transparency and secure their willingness to share information.

- It institutes measures that increase the usefulness of evaluations, including the sharing of findings and lessons that can be applied to other subjects. Evaluations should be undertaken with the intention that stakeholders and evaluators will use their results. The findings of evaluations can be used to understand the performance of an organization, with the intention of replicating positive aspects and rectifying systemic problems. The timeliness of evaluations and the presentation of their findings are also critical to ensure utility. Evaluations must also be accessible, meaning that they are available to the public; can be retrieved (through, for example, a user-friendly Web site); are written in clear language, with limited jargon; and are distributed to a wide group of relevant stakeholders.

Even with structures and systems in place, the independence and impartiality of evaluation depends on the integrity and professionalism of individuals. The profession requires limiting personal biases to the extent possible. In some circumstances, external evaluators are believed to exercise greater independence than those who work in an organization, because they are less exposed to institutional or peer pressures or have not absorbed the institutional culture in an unquestioning way.[12] However, individual or intellectual independence depends on individuals, whose behavior demonstrates adherence to and practice of the following evaluation principles: avoiding conflict of interest, acting with integrity and independence of mind, engaging in evaluations for which they are competent, acting impartially, and undertaking evaluations with a clear understanding of the clients and their decision-making process. Many evaluation associations and evaluation functions of national and international organizations have adopted codes of conduct for evaluators; the UN Evaluation Group has developed ethical guidelines (UNEG 2008b). Debates about professional standards and accreditation of evaluators and evaluation managers have been ongoing within professional forums for years.

Table 5.1 provides an overview of the points discussed in this section. It illustrates the intersections between the three levels of capacities and the three evaluation principles.

From Capacities to Capabilities

The above discussion centers on individuals and entities, such as governing bodies, management structures, evaluation units, or evaluators, and how they collectively form an evaluation capacity of mutually reinforcing ingredients.[13] To be effective, evaluators need to be capable of delivering independent, credible, and useful evaluations and much more. Without such ability,

Table 5.1 Evaluation Principles and the Three Levels of Capacity

Level	Independence	Credibility	Utility
Enabling environment	• Culture of accountability and learning • Government legislation or evaluation policy • Community of practice, networks, and associations for evaluation		
	• Governing or oversight body that seeks independent credible advice • Structural independence	• Provision of access to information that facilitates credible evaluation	• Attitude that entails intention to use evaluation findings and recommendations • Willingness to change
Institutional framework	• Institutionalized process of peer review to assess independence, credibility, and utility of the evaluation function		
	• Independent budget • Impartial selection of evaluation subjects • Independent planning and conduct • Noninterference in reporting of findings • Measures to protect evaluators from repercussions	• Evaluation quality assurance system to ensure credibility, transparency, and impartiality • Multidisciplinary evaluation team that works well together	• Understanding of the value of evaluation • Consultation processes • Timeliness of the evaluation • Accessibility of the evaluation • Active sharing of lessons from evaluation • Utility of the evaluation, demonstrated by implementation of recommendations
	• Ethics guidelines • Code of conduct		
Individual	• Avoidance of conflict of interest • Behavioral independence • Integrity	• Competence (technical knowledge and evaluation skills) • Impartiality	• Client orientation • Communication • Coordination with different stakeholders and ongoing processes

Source: Author.

evaluators can produce reports whose recommendations are not acted upon or are implemented only mechanically.

A five-year project on capacity development (ECDPM 2008) concluded that the following capacities needed to be developed:

- committing and engaging: developing volition, empowerment, motivation, attitude, and confidence

- carrying out technical, service delivery, and logistical tasks: performing core functions directed at the implementation of mandated goals
- relating to stakeholders and attracting resources and support: managing relationships, mobilizing resources, engaging in networking, building legitimacy, and protecting space
- adapting and engaging in self-renewal: learning, strategizing, adapting, repositioning, and managing change
- balancing coherence and diversity: encouraging innovation and stability, controlling fragmentation, managing complexity, and balancing the capability mix.

The distinction between capacities and capabilities is important. A written evaluation policy (capacity) means little if it is not backed by capabilities to commit to and deliver its promises. An evaluation unit may exist and carry out evaluations, but it may lack the capability to relate to stakeholders and attract resources or to adapt and self-renew by learning to provide new evaluation types in response to changing needs.

Capabilities need to be interpreted differently depending on the stakeholders concerned. For instance, the commitment and engagement of stakeholders in the enabling environment will set the culture for learning and accountability. The capability to commit and engage for an evaluation unit requires it to set and abide by evaluation principles. The evaluator must adopt an attitude of behavioral independence. The application of these capabilities to the three levels at which evaluation capacities need to be established is summarized in table 5.2.

The enabling environment for evaluation needs to be committed to a culture of learning and accountability; to adopt an evaluation policy that is in line with the evaluation principles and legitimizes evaluation; and to use evaluation findings and insights in policy making, performance improvements, and organizational renewal. Such an environment accepts that the independence of evaluation, including its funding, needs to be safeguarded. In a national context, doing so could entail embedding evaluation into legislation and government policy. Within an organization, the institutional culture, evaluation policy, and resources for evaluation form the context in which an evaluation function operates.

The evaluation function should be committed to the evaluation principles, protect them and evaluators from pressures, and have the motivation to implement them in daily practice. It should have a system that safeguards and institutionalizes independence, credibility, and utility. In its relationships with others, it needs to demonstrate legitimacy, based on impartiality and credibility (including technical competence). It needs to contribute to

Table 5.2 Evaluation Capabilities at the Three Levels of Capacity

Capability	Enabling environment for evaluation	Institutional framework for evaluation	Evaluators, evaluation managers, and heads of evaluations units
Commit and engage	Culture of learning and accountability that empowers individuals and organizations to reflect on their practice, take stock of what works and what does not, and take necessary action	Commitment to evaluation principles and the motivation and attitude to follow through on them in daily practice	Commitment to evaluation principles, ethical guidelines, and code of conduct; attitude of independence and impartiality; motivation to conduct evaluations in a credible and useful way
Carry out technical, service delivery, and logistical tasks	Evaluation policy that codifies evaluation principles and good practice	Ability to conduct independent, credible, and utilizable evaluations to support organizational adaptation and renewal	Competence, from both an evaluation and a technical point of view, to conduct evaluations
Relate to stakeholders and attract resources and support	Legitimization of evaluation through evaluation policy and actions and recognition of need to ensure adequate and independent funding	Ability to demonstrate legitimacy based on impartiality and credibility, to protect evaluation principles and standards and evaluators, and to generate adequate funding	Ability to conduct evaluations transparently and credibly and to relate to and communicate with stakeholders
Adapt and self-renew	Recognition that evaluation plays a role in adaptation and self-renewal	Ability to make strategic choices about evaluation's engagement in organizational renewal and to relate evaluation findings to stakeholders to ensure learning; ability to frequently adapt and update evaluation methods and approaches	Ability to learn new evaluation skills
Balance coherence and diversity	Management of change, using evaluation evidence and recommendations when available; avoidance of fragmentation of systems for learning and accountability	Ability to ensure evaluation processes and approaches are systematic but flexible, to balance capabilities on the team, and to employ a mix of approaches to develop an evaluation culture	Ability to find the right balance between systematically applying evaluation guidelines and seeking opportunities for innovation

Source: Author.

the adaptation and renewal of the context within which it works (an organization or a reform that affects more than one organization). It has to have the capability to work systematically (to ensure transparency) but flexibly (to ensure credibility and utility), use a mix of tools to foster an evaluation culture, and keep its methods and approaches updated. The evaluation team needs to include evaluators with a mix of capabilities, and it has to have the capacity to determine and negotiate adequate funding.

Individual evaluators have to be committed to the evaluation principles, ethical guidelines, and the code of conduct. They must demonstrate independence and impartiality and conduct evaluations in a credible and useful way. Evaluators are expected to be technically competent as evaluators or in the field that is being evaluated, capable of delivering the evaluation service in question, and up to date in their knowledge of evaluation methods and techniques. Evaluators should have the ability to follow guidelines but seek possibilities for innovation.

The Importance of the Process of Capacity Development

The process of capacity development is an important part of the outcome, because capacities and capabilities are developed through a process of interaction and dialogue, mixed with specific initiatives to set up systems, install hardware, and train people. The process combines parts that are well planned (based on participatory diagnostics of capacities and their weaknesses) with others that are flexible and opportunistic.

The sheer number of stakeholders and range of capacities and capabilities discussed above illustrate the complexities of capacity development and flag the need for planning and implementation tools that address complexity—something blueprints tend not to be good at (OECD/DAC 2006). Space needs to be created for analyzing capacity gaps in a participatory way, agreeing on common goals, and translating them into a joint strategy while at the same time maintaining the flexibility and capability to grasp opportunities as they arise, learn from experience, and change tactics and work at various levels of capacity at the same time.

Capacity development practitioners, such as the European Centre for Development Policy Management, concluded that 10 process matters are important for success in capacity development. These issues have been regrouped here around three themes: the drive from within, developing and agreeing on clear expectations, and "ordered chaos" (or combining high degrees of flexibility with systematic approaches).

The Drive from Within

Capacity development needs to come from within or have strong internal champions. If an idea is imposed from the outside, capacity development is not likely to succeed. The drive from within relates to the capability to commit and engage. It includes the following elements:

- *Ownership.* Ownership manifests itself in local or internal champions, resource allocations, and engagement. It is difficult to measure, is not homogenous across internal stakeholders, and is not constant over time.
- *Leadership.* Leadership is important for setting the culture of learning and accountability, but it must fit with the context and its culture
- *Collective action, motivation, and commitment.* Capacity development will not occur if it involves one person writing documents. It requires engaging various stakeholders whose capacities and capabilities will be developed.

Developing and Agreeing on Clear Expectations

The process of developing and agreeing on clear expectations in capacity development is, in itself, part of the capacity development process. Developing a common understanding of capacity weaknesses through a participatory, structured diagnostic can serve as an analytical framework with which to move attention from resource gaps to broader issues. A shared vision of needed capacities is important for channeling resources toward clear objectives. Very often the many actors in capacity development have tacit understandings of what capacity is and how it should be developed. Few actors have explicit strategies, which makes it difficult to find common ground and work in the same direction. A diagnosis of existing capacities is necessary to find entry points to start capacity development. This diagnosis benefits when it is developed in a participatory way that develops ownership at the same time.

Ordered Chaos

"Ordered chaos"—combining flexibility with systematic approaches—entails the recognition that capacity development does not (always) follow an ordered process. This approach includes planned as well as incremental and emergent approaches. For instance, when developing specific skills, a well-structured process, such as the 10 steps proposed by Kusek and Rist (2004), would be appropriate. In contrast, when trying to influence culture to become more supportive of learning and accountability, opportunities such as informal conversations with a key stakeholder may arise unexpectedly. In these contexts, capacity development initiatives would be incremental and emergent in response to opportunities as they arise.

Capacity development also requires recognizing the less tangible aspects of capacities and combining small and large initiatives, depending on the context and opportunities. It requires finding the right balance between an operating space that allows capacities to evolve and accountability for capacity development results. Because capacity development takes time, it is necessary to stay the course (even through adverse times) but build quick wins into the process (to keep up motivation and build on success) as well as time to reflect and evaluate whether progress is being made.

Where to Start?

There is no one-size-fits-all prescription for where an evaluation should start. Depending on the situation, a diagnostic could be the best entry point to understand where the strengths, weaknesses, and gaps are. Sometimes, however, it may be necessary to first have a champion within, who provides ownership and leadership of the process and generates interest in developing evaluation capacities. In other situations, the quality and credibility of evaluation has to be improved or the incentives for accountability and learning need to be improved before anything else can happen. In many cases, a mix of all of these components is needed to develop capacities.

One entry point for developing institutional capacities is a diagnostic, which can be done using the conceptual framework suggested here and through peer reviews. Expert review can support a diagnostic process and lend it credibility, but the evaluation unit needs to be involved in and own the diagnostic process. The diagnosis could lead to a revision of policy, as has happened in the case of the United Nations Development Programme, or to the formulation of a strategy to develop evaluation capacities.

Very few organizations have articulated an evaluation strategy, much less one that explains how evaluation capacities will be developed. Yet good practice in capacity development argues for articulating such strategy, to establish a common vision and bring stakeholders together to work toward a common goal. Such a strategy would employ linear planning approaches (when implementing a training program, as discussed in chapter 10, for instance); incremental approaches (when gradually expanding the evaluation requirements in a national system, as discussed in chapter 1, for instance); and emergent approaches, in which a number of flexible, informal initiatives are needed to, for instance, respond to opportunities when possible and necessary (see chapter 9).

The following subsections provide examples of ways to draw out suggestions from stakeholders and develop evaluation capacities. The discussion is structured around the three levels (the enabling environment, the institutional framework, and the individual), because they relate to identifiable stakeholders. At all of these levels, it is advisable to understand existing capacities, capabilities, and reluctance to adopting certain standards to develop a corresponding and relevant capacity development strategy.

Placing Evaluation Capacities in the Context of Good Governance

The relationship between governance and evaluation is interdependent: good governance creates an enabling environment for evaluation, and evaluation reinforces good governance. The Sri Lanka case study presented in chapter 1 provides a good example of how commitment from the highest political level (the prime minister) created an enabling environment for evaluation. By demanding reports on results, stakeholders in ministries were enabled, even required, to record and reflect on performance. This strong leadership was combined with a strong champion to translate political commitment into practical action.

Ideally, governments or chief executives of organizations seek independent, credible, and utilizable advice through an evaluation. In chapter 2, Wiesner argues that demand for evaluation creates a strong enabling environment for evaluation. In this case, decision makers demand feedback on the use of resources and the results achieved; through their demand for such information, they create an environment that enables evaluative thinking and practice. Wiesner suggests that political and institutional power structures can limit the environment in which evaluations are conducted, especially if vested interests resist evidence that might demonstrate the weaknesses of political choices. In these cases, it is important to counterbalance political power structures with other stakeholders and establish legislation or an evaluation policy that legitimizes and commits the country or organization to the evaluation principles.[14]

An environment that is unresponsive to, or even fearful of, evaluation may reflect lack of understanding of how evaluation can improve decision making. In these cases, the evaluation function needs to deliver credible, high-quality evaluations to demonstrate the value added of evaluation. In addition, it will be necessary to explain the role and usefulness of evaluation in the context of governance and performance of the organization as a whole. Chapter 4, on building Dubai's institutional learning capacity, is an example in which evaluation is embedded in the strategic management processes to increase the usefulness of evaluation and decrease negative perceptions. Chapter 3, on the evaluation of institutional performance, illustrates the incremental approaches to gaining confidence and creating an environment that eventually believes in the value of evaluation. Table 5.3 summarizes tips for various stakeholders on reinforcing the enabling environment for evaluation.

Delivering Evaluation Services that Are Independent, Credible, and Utilizable

The importance of developing an institutional framework for evaluation—rather than using ad hoc arrangements—lies in the safeguarding of the evaluation principles, the provision of a framework that protects and holds

Table 5.3   Tips for Reinforcing an Enabling Environment for Evaluation

Stakeholders	Tips
Governing bodies (parliaments, executive boards, and so forth)	• Be aware of the threats to the independence, credibility, and utility of evaluation, and look for measures to safeguard these principles. • Adopt and oversee the implementation of legislation or policies that institutionalize the independence, credibility, and utility of evaluation. • Exercise oversight over the quality of evaluation. • Request the evaluation and demonstrated use of evaluation findings and recommendations.
Heads of state, ministers, policy makers, chief executives	• Demonstrate leadership in setting a culture of learning and accountability. • Seek and use evidence from evaluations to validate the attainment of goals and objectives and to improve performance whenever possible. • Understand evaluation as part of good governance that aims to use public resources effectively and efficiently to achieve the goals that governments or organizations aim to achieve.
Evaluation function	• Demonstrate value added of independent, credible, and utilizable evaluations. • Raise stakeholders' awareness of the role and importance of evaluation and evaluation principles. • Contribute to evaluative thinking through awareness building, dialogue, and training.
Professional evaluation networks, associations, and similar groups	• Set standards as benchmarks that can be used to convince other stakeholders about the importance of the evaluation principles and measures to safeguard them.

Source: Author.

evaluators accountable, and the predictability and transparency of the framework for all stakeholders. Such a system needs to be built so that it has the capability to adapt and self-renew, to respond to new challenges with, for instance, a focus on new issues or by introducing new types of evaluations that address information gaps.

Generally, the evaluation function needs to lead efforts to develop the institutional framework for evaluation, setting up systems, processes, and guidelines that are in line with evaluation principles and fit with the work of the organization or country. Table 5.4 summarizes dimensions that an institutional framework for evaluation could or should entail and the rationale for including them.

These systems may include human resource management measures that ensure the selection of an independent and qualified head of the office

Table 5.4 Tips for Developing an Institutional Framework for Evaluation

Stakeholders	Tips
Governing bodies (parliaments, executive boards, and so forth)	• Get briefed about the evaluation system to understand whether the institutional framework includes adequate checks and balances and to become a discerning reader of evaluation reports. • Request that due process be followed for the selection, appointment, and termination of the contract of the head of the evaluation function.
Heads of state, ministers, policy makers, chief executives	• Get briefed about the evaluation system to understand whether the institutional framework includes adequate checks and balances and to become a discerning reader of evaluation reports. • Introduce processes for the selection of the head of evaluation that ensure the person's independence. • Provide secure, separate, and adequate funding for the evaluation.
Evaluation function	• Develop and document systems for the selection, design, conduct, and reporting of evaluations. • Provide briefings on these standards to increase transparency and confidence in the process and products, which enhances credibility. • Develop mechanisms to ensure that lessons from evaluation are systematically shared and integrated into debates and decision-making processes.
Professional evaluation networks, associations, and similar groups	• Set professional standards and good practice standards. • Develop and implement professionalization, accreditation, and credentialing systems.

Source: Author.

of evaluation. The best systems cannot ignore the human factor, which highlights the importance of selecting and appointing heads of evaluation functions that are capable of safeguarding the evaluation principles and managing the evaluation function so that it delivers independent, credible, and utilizable evaluations (box 5.2). The process should assure governing or oversight bodies and chief executives alike that an impartial candidate has been chosen. Evaluators should have contractual arrangements that protect them from repercussions, should critical evaluations be unwelcome. In addition, it is important that a system be set up that holds evaluators accountable for their actions through a code of conduct or ethics guidelines, such as those established by the United Nations Evaluation Group.

To set up a planning system that is representative for evaluations of operations, the Office of Evaluation at the World Food Programme analyzed its portfolio to identify factors that should be used to ensure that the sample is representative of operations. Its analysis resulted in a system that combines the size and number of operations to reflect the considerable variation in these factors (a small number of operations represent a large proportion of the financial value of the portfolio, with the rest spread over a large number of small operations). Treating each operation, regardless of size, equally

---

Box 5.2   Selecting the Head of Evaluation

A good process for selecting heads of evaluation offices includes the following steps:

1. The process should be agreed on by key stakeholders.
2. The process should be documented and publicized for reasons of transparency.
3. The composition of the panel should ensure credibility in the eyes of key stakeholders (doing so requires representation of stakeholder groups and the profession).
4. The panel should have clear terms of reference that specify whether the panel "chooses" or "suggests" and identifies who has the final decision-making power.
5. The panel should be involved in the entire process, including agreeing on the vacancy announcement, setting the selection criteria, agreeing on interview questions and criteria for assessing answers, and so forth.
6. Appointment should be made for a fixed period and a contract written for the same duration.
7. The renewal of the contract should follow a process that involves the panel to ensure that is based on performance and not on the production of biased evaluations.
8. The termination process should involve the panel to ensure that cancellation of the contract is based on performance issues rather than critical evaluations.

Source: Author.

would have overemphasized the smaller operations in the sample; selecting the sample by size would have underrepresented the smaller operations in the overall sample. The weighted numbers are applied to determine how many operations in each geographical region should be selected for evaluation. By contrast, a different system was needed for the strategic evaluations, to ensure that they addressed issues important to key decision makers in the governing body and management. It involved consultations with these stakeholders. The utility of all evaluations is enhanced by linking them to decision-making processes.

An example of a system that ensures complete independence of finance is that of the International Fund for Agriculture Development. Its evaluation policy determines that the budget is prepared independently of the institution's secretariat. The process is managed by the evaluation office and involves discussions and approval of the evaluation committee. The work program and budget of the evaluation office appear as a separate, clearly identifiable section in the Fund's overall work program and budget.[15] This example can be contrasted with others, in which funding of evaluations depends on the approval of project managers, who may or may not accept an independent evaluation.

Another system that is important to develop is one that governs evaluation processes and sets standards for evaluation products, which often take the form of guidelines or handbooks. Putting information about the process into the public domain increases the transparency of evaluation processes. The production of guidance materials often needs to go hand in hand with briefings (between the evaluation manager and the evaluation team and between evaluators and the managers of operations), to clarify expectations in evaluation quality and process. The process also needs to include formal feedback processes, quality standards, and assurance mechanisms. If evaluations are conducted in a decentralized way (that is, not managed by a central evaluation office), training will be needed to ensure that standards are understood and implemented.

Evaluation functions need to have the capacity to provide feedback on findings and recommendations into decision-making processes as well as to share lessons from evaluations. Efforts can include creating search engines on Web sites of repositories of lessons from evaluations, incorporating evaluation lessons into guidance materials that program managers use, and more proactive efforts to share evaluation lessons throughout the evaluation process. Many of these dissemination systems struggle with the challenge of providing lessons from evaluations to the communities in which projects take place and evaluators collect information. Table 5.4 summarizes tips for various stakeholders on creating an institutional framework for evaluation.

Table 5.5 Tips for Developing Evaluators' Skills and Knowledge

Stakeholder	Tips
Evaluation function	• Invest in training.
	• Build teams that are multidisciplinary.
	• Encourage team work and cross-fertilization.
Providers of evaluation training	• Continue to develop and offer training courses.
	• Increasingly move toward university courses to build a professional tradition.
Professional evaluation networks, associations, and similar groups	• Provide opportunities for professional exchanges and networking.

Source: Author.

Impartiality, Knowledge, and Skills of Individuals

The best enabling environment and institutional arrangements will not replace the individuals involved in evaluation. Their integrity to plan, undertake, and report evaluation findings in an impartial way is essential (table 5.5). They determine whether an evaluation is credible and useful. Their professional competencies and their ability to listen, understand, and weigh the views of different stakeholders are central to the quality of evaluation.

The importance of training as a tool for one part of the capacity development process is well understood. Chapter 10, on capacity building in monitoring and evaluation (M&E) through the design and implementation of results-based M&E systems, illustrates the importance of a structured training program that is based on specific training needs and training goals. It is important to coach and mentor evaluation managers and evaluators, as Porter notes in chapter 9, especially when they are working for the first time in a field or work in an environment that is not enabling or supportive.

Conclusion

This chapter demonstrates the synergies that exist between the evaluation profession and that of capacity development practitioners. A combination of good practice from both sides promises to result in greater effectiveness in developing capacities that will safeguard and apply the evaluation principles of independence, credibility, and utility as well as higher returns on investments in evaluation capacity development. The chapter comes at an important time, when evaluation needs to professionalize and demand for evaluation and for developing evaluation capacities is high.

Consideration of three levels of capacity (the enabling environment, the institutional framework, and the individual) is important to institutionalize evaluation capacities in ways that support and protect individuals while holding them accountable. The three levels, together with the capabilities needed, provide a conceptual framework that moves the debate from improving the skills of individuals or attracting resources to a more sophisticated set of ingredients that promises to mutually reinforce capacities. Applying the conceptual framework to specific examples provides a number of pointers for stakeholders who want to build evaluation capacity.

Annex 5.A   Definitions

Accessibility means that stakeholders have unrestricted access to evaluations that can be retrieved easily from their storage place. It also requires that evaluations be written in ways that are easily understandable and that findings be shared with stakeholders and interested parties.

Accountability is the obligation to account for (and report on) work carried out and results achieved.

Competence of evaluators means that they have—and can demonstrate—a good understanding of the subject under evaluation, evaluation principles, and rigorous data collection and analysis, including ethical principles, for evaluation.

Credibility is the extent to which evaluation findings and conclusions are believable and trustworthy. Credibility is determined by objective factors, such as the transparency of the evaluation process and the accuracy of the evaluation report, and subjective factors, such as the perceived or demonstrated impartiality and competence of the evaluators.

Impartiality is the absence of bias. It entails due process, methodological rigor, and the consideration and presentation of achievements, challenges, successes, and failures.

Independence means that the evaluation is free from influences—political or organizational pressures or personal preferences—that would bias its conduct, findings, conclusions, or recommendations. It implies that evaluations are typically carried out or managed by entities and individuals who are free of the control of those responsible for the design and implementation of the subject of evaluation.

Intentionality is a clear intent to use evaluation findings. In the context of limited resources, the planning and selection of evaluation work has to be carefully done.

Learning means that lessons are drawn from experience and accepted and internalized in practice, thereby building on success and avoiding past mistakes.

(continued)

Annex 5.A *continued*

Timeliness means that evaluations are chosen and completed so that their findings and recommendations are available in time to inform decision-making processes.

Transparency means that consultation with the major stakeholders is an essential feature at all stages of the evaluation process. Transparency improves the credibility and quality of the evaluation. It can facilitate consensus building and ownership of the findings, conclusions, and recommendations

Utility means that evaluations aim to and do affect decision making. Evaluations must be perceived as relevant and useful and be presented in a clear and concise way. Evaluations are valuable to the extent that they serve the information and decision-making needs of intended users, including answering the questions raised about the evaluation by the people who commissioned it.

Source: Author, based on European Commission n.d.; OECD/DAC 2002; UNEG 2005a, 2005b; DAC/UNEG 2007; UNEG 2008b; World Food Programme 2008.

Notes

1. Morgan (2006) suggests that capacity development is not well defined, no courses are given, and practitioners do not form a coherent group. Professionalization of capacity development practitioners is much needed.
2. The meeting was held by the evaluation network of the Development Assistance Committee of the Organisation of Economic Co-operation and Development. The evaluation principles were included in *DAC Principles for Effective Aid,* published in 1992.
3. Many of the principles discussed then had been discussed at and were later integrated into international and regional evaluation associations, such as the American and African Evaluation Associations, the Evaluation Cooperation Group of the multilateral development banks, and in the norms of the United Nations Evaluation Group. The terms used are not always identical, but the underlying principles are.
4. Chelimsky (2008), among others, discusses how the lack of independence affects the choice, design, and methodologies used in an evaluation, all of which adversely affect the impartiality of the evaluation.
5. As Boyle and Lemaire (1999, 39) note, "Educated consumers can help create an evaluation 'ethos' where evaluation is valued as an integral part of the government decision-making process."
6. Self-evaluations are a valid evaluation tool, but they are not as independent as evaluations undertaken or managed by a party not directly involved in the design, implementation, or management of the operation.
7. Many evaluations still observe that capacity development places a heavy emphasis on training, with limited understanding of the needs for other measures.

8. The UNIDO report defines *institutional capability* to include services to be performed; demand for these services; capabilities (skills in necessary quantity and quality) to meet demand; hardware (including facilities, premises, and instruments); methodology; legislation; and management and coordination functions. These features, considered necessary for an institution to function, were integrated into project design training and the annual evaluation reports of UNIDO at the time.
9. The need for an enabling environment has been noted in the work of the European Centre for Development and Policy Management.
10. As Toulemonde (1999, 167) notes, "Once this culture is well established, evaluation is deeply rooted in the administrative values, is seen as an undisputed duty, and becomes one of the fundamentals of the governing system. The culture provides the collective pressure that makes decision makers overcome their reluctance, even when evaluation deeply contradicts their self-interest."
11. Mayne, Divorski, and Lemaire (1999, 39) suggest that "to ensure utility of evaluations to various interests, structure and controls are not sufficient. Where they can have an influence, institutional users of evaluation must be proactive and assume responsibility for getting the kinds of evaluations they want others to produce."
12. Sonnichsen (1999) discusses the advantages and disadvantages of internal and external evaluators and of centralized and decentralized evaluation units.
13. The term *capability* in this context does not refer to Amartya Sen's *capability approach*, which focuses on the capabilities of the individual. Instead, it is used in the sense of the ability to do or accomplish something.
14. A growing number of UN organizations are adopting evaluation policies. At the World Food Programme, the evaluation policy establishes the commitment to the evaluation principles and explains measures to safeguard them.
15. The work program and budget can be found at http://www.ifad.org/evaluation/whatwedo/wp/index.htm.

Bibliography

ADB (Asian Development Bank). 1997. "Special Study of the Effectiveness and Impact of Training in Education Projects in Indonesia." Asian Development Bank, Manila.

———. 2000. "Special Evaluation Study on the Effectiveness and Impact of Asian Development Bank Assistance to the Reform of Public Expenditure Management in Bhutan, India, Kiribati, and Lao People's Democratic Republic." Asian Development Bank, Manila.

———. 2002. *Country Assistance Program Evaluation in Mongolia*. Manila: Asian Development Bank.

———. 2003. "Special Evaluation Study on Asian Development Bank Capacity Building Assistance for Managing Water Supply and Sanitation to Republic of the Fiji Islands, Kiribati, Papua New Guinea, and Republic of the Marshall Islands." Asian Development Bank, Manila.

———. 2004. *Special Evaluation Study on Capacity Development Assistance of the Asian Development Bank to the Lao People's Democratic Republic.* Manila: Asian Development Bank.

Arnold, M. 2006. "Developing Evaluation Capacity in Extension 4-H Field Faculty: A Framework for Success." *American Journal of Evaluation* 27 (2): 257–69

AusAID. 2006. "A Staged Approach to Assess, Plan and Monitor Capacity Building." Canberra.

Blagescu, M., and J. Young. 2006. "Capacity Development for Policy Advocacy: Current Thinking and Approaches among Agencies Supporting Civil Society Organisations." ODI Working Paper 260, Overseas Development Institute, London.

Boesen, N., and O. Therkildsen. 2005. *A Results-Oriented Approach to Capacity Change.* Danish International Development Agency (DANIDA), Copenhagen.

Bolger, J. 2000. "Capacity Development: Why, What and How." CIDA Policy Branch, Canadian International Development Agency Capacity Development Occasional Series 1 (1).

Boyle, R., and D. Lemaire, eds. 1999. *Building Effective Evaluation Capacity: Lessons from Practice.* Piscataway, NJ: Transaction Publishers.

Chelimsky, E. 2008. "A Clash of Cultures: Improving the 'Fit' between Evaluative Independence and the Political Requirements of a Democratic Society." *American Journal of Evaluation* 29 (4): 400–15.

Constantinou, N. 2007. "Capacity Development in the World Bank Group: A Review of Nonlending Approaches." *Capacity Development Briefs* 23, World Bank Institute, Washington, DC.

DAC (Development Assistance Committee) and UNEG (United Nations Evaluation Group). 2007. *Framework for Professional Peer Reviews.* DAC/UNEG Joint Task Force on Professional Peer Reviews of Evaluation Functions in Multilateral Organizations, January.

DANIDA (Danish International Development Agency). 2002. *Capacity Development Evaluation Step 1: Contributions to an Analytical Framework.* Evaluation Cooperation Group, Copenhagen.

ECDPM (European Centre for Development Policy Management). 2000. "Informing the Capacity Debate: Operational Experiences." *Capacity.org* 4 (January).

———. 2001. "Tools of the Trade: Capacity Assessment." *Capacity.org* 8 (January).

———. 2002. "Capacity for Development: Insights and Innovation." *Capacity.org* 14 (July).

———. 2003. "Capacity Development: The Why's and How's." *Capacity.org* 19 (October).

———. 2004a. "Meso-Level Capacity Development." *Capacity.org* 22 (July).

———. 2004b. "Renewing Approaches to Institutional Development." *Capacity.org* 20 (January).

———. 2005. "Exploring the Soft Side of Capacity Development." *Capacity.org* 24 (January).

———. 2008. *Capacity Change and Performance: Insights and Implications for Development Cooperation*. Policy Brief 21, European Centre for Development Policy Management, Maastricht, the Netherlands.

European Commission. n.d. *EC Evaluation Glossary*. http://ec.europa.eu/regional_policy/sources/docgener/evaluation/evalsed/glossary/index_en.htm.

Evaluation Cooperation Group. 2007. "Template for Assessing the Independence of Evaluation Organizations." http://siteresources.worldbank.org/EXTGLOREGPARPROG/Resources/ECG_AssessingIndependence.pdf.

———. 2009. *Review Framework for the Evaluation Function in Multilateral Development Banks* 2009.

IASC (Inter-Agency Standing Committee). 2007. *Capacity Building for Emergency Responses*. Geneva.

Kusek, J. Z., and R. C. Rist. 2004. *Ten Steps to a Results-Based Monitoring and Evaluation System: A Handbook for Development Practitioners*. Washington, DC: World Bank.

Land, T., V. Hauck, and H. Baser. 2009. "Capacity Development: Between Planned Interventions and Emergent Processes." ECDPM Policy Brief 22, European Centre for Development Policy Management, Maastricht, the Netherlands.

Mayne, J., S. Divorski, and D. Lemaire. 1999. "Locating Evaluation: Anchoring Evaluation in the Executive or the Legislature, or Both or Elsewhere?" In *Building Evaluation Capacity: Lessons from Practice*, ed. R. Boyle and D. Lemaire, 23–52. Piscataway, NJ: Transaction Publishers.

Missika-Wierzba, B., and M. Nelson. 2006. "A Revolution in Capacity Development? Africans Ask Tough Questions." *Capacity Development Brief* 16, World Bank Institute, Washington, DC.

Morgan, P. 2006. *The Concept of Capacity*. Maastricht, the Netherlands: European Centre for Development Policy Management.

OECD/DAC (Organisation for Economic Co-operation and Development/Development Assistance Committee). 1992. *DAC Principles for Effective Aid*. Paris: OECD/DAC.

———. 2002. *DAC Glossary of Key Terms in Evaluation and Results-Based Management*. Paris: OECD/DAC.

———. 2006. "The Challenge of Capacity Development: Working towards Good Practice." Paris. http://www.oecd.org/dataoecd/4/36/36326495.pdf.

Sonnischen, R. C. 1999. "Building Evaluation Capacity with Organizations." In *Building Effective Evaluation Capacity: Lessons from Practice*, ed. R. Boyle and D. Lemaire, 53–74. Piscataway, NJ: Transaction Publishers.

Teskey, G. 2005. "Capacity Development and State Building: Issues, Evidence and Implications for DfID." Department for International Development, London.

Toulemonde, J. 1999. "Incentives, Constraints and Culture-Building as Instruments for the Development of Evaluation Demand." In *Building Effective Evaluation Capacity*, ed. R. Boyle and D. Lemaire, 153–75. New Brunswick, NJ: Transaction Publishers.

UNDP (United Nations Development Programme). 2005. "Measuring Capacities: An Illustrative Catalogue to Benchmarks and Indicators." Capacity Development Action Brief, New York.

———. 2007. "Capacity Development Practice Note." New York

UNEG (United Nations Evaluation Group). 2005a. *Norms for Evaluation in the UN System*. New York: UNEG.

———. 2005b. *Standards for Evaluation in the UN System*. New York: UNEG.

———. 2008a. *UNEG Code of Conduct for Evaluation in the UN System*. New York: UNEG.

———. 2008b. *UNEG Ethical Guidelines for Evaluation*. New York: UNEG.

UNICEF (United Nations Children's Fund). 2002. "Capacity Building for UNICEF Humanitarian Response in Review." Working Paper, Evaluation Office, New York.

UNIDO (United Nations Industrial Development Organization). 1990. *Report on the Evaluation of UNDP–Financed and UNIDO–Executed Projects of Technical Assistance in Metrology*. Vienna: UNIDO.

World Bank. 2005. *Capacity Building in Africa: An OED Evaluation of World Bank Support*, Washington, DC: Operations Evaluation Department, World Bank.

———. 2006. *Evaluation Capacity Development Working Paper Series*. Washington, DC: World Bank.

World Food Programme. 2008. *Evaluation of WFP's Capacity Development Policy and Operations*. Rome: World Food Programme, Office of Evaluation.

Zinke, J. 2006. *ECPDM Study on Capacity, Change and Performance: Final Workshop Report*. Maastricht, the Netherlands: European Centre for Development Policy Management.

CHAPTER 6

Supporting Evaluation Capacity on Environment and Development

Rob D. van den Berg

The IDEAS conference in 2009 focused on evaluation capacity development. Several chapters in this book provide excellent examples of how evaluation capacity was supported, strengthened, and empowered in recent years. The GEF Evaluation Office presented a unique international initiative to create a community of practice in Johannesburg and reviews the origins of this initiative and its current status in this article.

Upgrading Evaluation of Sustainable Development: How to Identify Best International Practices

In 2003, the Council of the Global Environment Facility (GEF) decided to upgrade the monitoring and evaluation (M&E) unit of the GEF Secretariat

---

The author would like to thank Margaret Spearman for her contribution to this article and Sandra Romboli for her presentation at the IDEAS conference. Elements of this article are based on *Evaluating Climate Change and Development*, ed. Rob D. van den Berg and Osvaldo Feinstein, World Bank Series on Development, vol. 8, 2009.

into an independent office for M&E, which would report directly to the council. This office would have as one of its aims to ensure that evaluation in the GEF would take place according to best international practices and standards. Between 2003 and 2006, the office gradually turned into an internationally recognized evaluation unit. Monitoring as a management concern was turned over to the secretariat in 2005 and confirmed in the M&E policy the GEF adopted in February 2006.

Part of the challenge of adopting best international standards and practices is to identify what those practices are. The GEF Evaluation Office faced a tough challenge in this regard, because it focuses on environmental issues. Its objectives include reducing the threat of climate change, reducing the loss of biodiversity, tackling environmental problems of international water bodies, eliminating threats to the ozone layer, taking persistent organic pollutants out of the environment, and preventing land degradation. A large body of literature exists on evaluation in various public sectors (health, education, international cooperation, and development). There was an important gap in the literature on how to evaluate interventions in all of the areas covered by the GEF, however.

The GEF and its partner agencies—the World Bank, the United Nations Development Programme (UNDP), and the United Nations Environment Programme (UNEP)—had evaluated many of its interventions; other institutions active on these issues also conducted evaluations. A 2004–05 inventory of evaluations revealed that methods were mainly adapted from standard practices in international development evaluation. In many evaluations, scientists handled the specific challenges of environmental issues.

Several reasons seemed to be behind the lack of international standards in environmental evaluation. One was the fact that many evaluation units did not have the critical mass to build up a track record in environmental evaluation. In many cases, just one or two professionals would take care of all the environmental evaluations an organization needed. As these professionals could not be jacks of all trades in the evaluation business, they had to rely on expertise from scientists and evaluation consultants.

A second problem seemed to be the fragmented nature of the community. Many evaluators in nongovernmental organizations had not met and did not know their colleagues in international organizations. Every evaluation seemed to lead to another wild search on the Internet and in country offices to identify potential candidates for inclusion in the evaluation team.

An underlying cause of the fragmented nature of the community seemed to be that no recent international evaluation gathering had focused on environmental issues. Many meetings included environmental streams or environmental sessions, but they often presented a specific evaluation or methodology rather than aiming to achieve a greater level of understanding of the state of the art. In 2005, the GEF Evaluation Office undertook a second inventory of international evaluators' meetings and concluded there was a gap on environmental issues.

The big three international evaluator networks—the Evaluation Network (for bilateral donors), the Evaluation Cooperation Group (for international financial institutions), and the UN Evaluation Group—organized several international conferences on various topics. Evaluation capacity development was discussed several times, but environmental evaluation, especially in relation to development, was never the exclusive topic of an international gathering of ex post evaluators.

There is a vibrant community of ex ante environmental impact assessment evaluators. These experts meet regularly to discuss and identify international best practices and new developments in environmental impact assessments that are undertaken before a new infrastructure or development project starts. These impact assessments had become obligatory in many organizations and in many nations and consequently had led to an active market of consultants, scientists, and experts to conduct them. These professionals were not involved in and did not discuss ex post evaluations, however, and the ex post evaluation community did not join these meetings. Ex post evaluators tend to keep their distance from ex ante evaluations, because they do not want to enter into a conflict of interest later on, when they need to evaluate ex post what they would have evaluated ex ante.

Once the new GEF M&E policy was approved, the office realized that one way to start up the process of connecting the dots in the environmental evaluation community and identify emerging best practices would be to organize an international meeting of evaluators on these issues. The GEF Council agreed that doing so would help the office identify international best practices and provided an initial grant, with the understanding that voluntary contributions from other partners would fund the main costs of the international meeting that would be organized.

Partnering and Preparatory Work for the International Conference

Throughout 2006 and 2007, the GEF Evaluation Office built an impressive partnership to organize an international meeting of evaluators on the environment and sustainable development. Early collaborators included the Agence Française de Développement (AFD) and the Fonds Français pour l'Environnement Mondial (FFEM), the World Conservation Union (IUCN), the Independent Evaluation Group of the World Bank, the Bibliotheca Alexandrina in the Arab Republic of Egypt, and the International Development Evaluation Association (IDEAS). In 2007, the special program for building research capacity on adaptation in Africa, based in Dakar, Senegal, and sponsored by the Department for International Development (DfID) of the United Kingdom and the International Development Research Centre (IDRC) of Canada, also joined the organizing committee.

Given the wide variety of technical issues in environmental protection and sustainable development, the steering committee decided early on to focus the meeting on climate change rather than to tackle other global issues, such as biodiversity, ozone layer depletion, persistent organic pollutants, and the like. However, it was decided not to focus only on mitigation of climate change, which would focus on reduction of greenhouse gas emissions, but also to look at the relatively new subject of adaptation to climate change. Although humanity has adapted to climate change throughout history, the rate and extent of climate change is now increasing dramatically. This called for special action, which required special M&E.

The steering committee prepared a concept note and a preliminary budget to facilitate fund raising. Grants were received from many donors, notably the Arab Republic of Egypt, Switzerland, Norway, Denmark, the Netherlands, the United Kingdom, the United States, France, and Germany. Although contributions were relatively small, they enabled the organizing committee to set the necessary preparations in motion. Grants were also small, because the envisaged size of the meeting was less than 100 dedicated professional evaluators, perhaps with a number of policy makers or environmental experts and scientists attending as well.

From the beginning, the aim was to gather evaluators from all regions. It was hoped that this could be done by mobilizing regional evaluators' associations. For this purpose, representatives of the GEF Evaluation Office attended regional conferences in Latin America (organized by Red latinoamericana de monitoreo y evaluación [REDLAC]), Africa (organized by the African Evaluation Association [Afrea]), Europe (organized by the European Evaluation Society), and Asia and Oceania (organized by the Australasian Evaluation Society). A special grant from Switzerland made it possible to organize a preliminary meeting in Kazakhstan to mobilize evaluation capacity in the Central Asian countries.

The IDEAS member in the steering committee, Doha Abdelhamid, together with Professor Salah A. Soliman, of the Bibliotheca Alexandrina, played a crucial role in ensuring generous support from the government of Egypt for hosting the meeting in the Bibliotheca Alexandrina. They also managed to convince the U.S. Agency for International Development (USAID) office in Cairo to become a sponsor of the meeting and gained support from several Egyptian ministries for an Egyptian side event at the opening of the conference.

A call for registration of participants went out in the second half of 2007. The response was overwhelming, with more than 200 submissions to participate and present. This meant that the funding, which was aimed at organizing a relatively small international expert gathering, was no longer adequate, despite efforts by the steering committee to find ways to reduce the budget for the meeting, which was now turning into an international conference. A special effort was made to raise funds for travel and per diem costs of participants, which led to a generous contribution by the IDRC- and DFID-funded Program for Building Adaptation Capacity in Dakar for 30 African participants.

Building Up an Inventory of Evaluations

One element of the preparation of the conference was an invitation to evaluation units, evaluators, and development and conservation agencies and institutions to send in evaluations that could be considered relevant to climate change mitigation and adaptation. More than 400 evaluations were received. As could be expected, most of them dealt with climate change mitigation; only a few were on adaptation. The evaluations were put into a Web-based library and analyzed on methodological issues, scope, and coverage. It was hoped that this would lead to an early identification of best practices that could be discussed at the conference.

A first perusal of the material indicated that there appeared to be a preponderance of "reports" and "studies," some of which were ex ante in nature. They also seemed to be limited in findings and scope, often focusing on a very specific institutional perspective. Many focused on a project, with little sense of larger-scale programmatic approaches; policy frameworks; or economic, regional, or other considerations and drivers of sustainability.

Nevertheless, an effort was made to draw initial conclusions from the material, especially on methodological issues. Time and funding were not sufficient to conduct an in-depth analysis of the material. However, even if it was not possible to draw any quick conclusions regarding best international practices, some conclusions could be drawn on the emerging picture. One of the key presentations at the conference was based on the evaluations on mitigation issues.

The International Conference on Evaluating Climate Change and Development

In May 2008, the conference took place in Alexandria, in the wonderful facilities of the Bibliotheca Alexandrina. On May 10, the international conference was opened by a statement from the First Lady of Egypt, Mrs. Suzanne Mubarak, followed by speeches from the director of the Bibliotheca Alexandrina, Dr. Ismail Serageldin, and the chief executive officer of the GEF, Mrs. Monique Barbut. The opening session of the conference highlighted the experience of Egypt in addressing mitigation to climate change and discussed how Egypt should tackle adaptation issues, which had become a priority of the Egyptian government in the early months of 2008.

On May 11, the international part of the conference started, with a keynote address by Robert Picciotto, the former director general of the World Bank's evaluation unit. He placed environmental evaluation firmly in the broader context of human rights and security. His point of departure was that climate change is part of the overall development challenge, which is characterized by insecurity globally, regionally, nationally, and locally. He proposed integrating climate change issues into a general framework of human security to create a new development paradigm that could provide the inspiration for evaluators to link climate change to development.

Picciotto called for evaluations of the global policies and collaborative initiatives that shape the international response to climate change and other global threats to peace and prosperity. Cognizant of the fact that no evaluation office is mandated to undertake this kind of evaluation, he challenged evaluation offices to collaborate in independent multipartner evaluations of international efforts to tackle climate change and development. He argued that development evaluation has to break through the current asymmetrical attention to assessing the performance of recipients rather than the neglect of actions of the donors.[1]

Three strands of presentations had been identified before the conference: mitigation, adaptation, and vulnerability. Other keynote speeches were presented over the two days. Sessions took place on how evaluation capacity on these issues could be supported, strengthened, and empowered by regional and global evaluation associations. IDEAS participated actively in these interactions. At the end of the conference, several conclusions could be drawn from the material presented and the discussions held.

On reduction of greenhouse gases—or mitigation of climate change, as it is more technically known—conference papers showed that project and program interventions are generally successful. Internationally, a success rate of 75 percent is deemed acceptable in development cooperation; the meta-evaluation of mitigation evaluations showed that more than 80 percent of climate change mitigation efforts are successful. On energy efficiency efforts, also aimed at reducing greenhouse gas emissions, examples were shown of interventions that have permanently changed the markets for specific products, such as more energy efficient lightbulbs.

The new emerging issue was how to adapt to climate change, something that is already happening. How will developing countries face the onslaught of higher temperatures, rising sea levels, changing waterfall patterns, and increasingly frequent natural disasters? Societies will have to reduce their vulnerability to these changes. Papers presented at the conference demonstrated a richness of efforts to address vulnerability in a systematic manner, in a way that governments and local communities will better understand what is happening. Societies can then cope with these changes by adapting to them. For them to be able to do so, capacity to deal with these issues, not only through monitoring but also through actively managing these situations, is of crucial importance.

The conference presented a rich variety of approaches to frameworks for understanding and tackling the links and trade-offs between mitigation, adaptation, and development issues. Picciotto proposed human security as a framework for evaluation, including an appeal for international collaboration in the evaluation community to tackle global issues. Other approaches and frameworks presented included a life cycle approach, asset-based approaches, ecosystem services methodology, and risk screening.

Publication of Conference Papers and Further Studies Envisaged

The immediate concern of the GEF Evaluation Office was to ensure that the most interesting and promising chapters presented at the conference would be published and become available to a wider audience. The editor of the World Bank Series on Development, Osvaldo Feinstein, of Transaction Publishers, who was also a member of the steering committee of the conference, offered to publish them in his series. Rather than publish proceedings, it was decided to ask authors to rework their presentations into chapters for the book. The publication, *Evaluating Climate Change and Development* (van den Berg and Feinstein 2010), came out one year after the conference.

It was also expressed at the end of the conference that there were several areas in which further work could be done. First, it was felt that the analysis of mitigation evaluations had been cursory and could be improved upon if taken up with sufficient time and inputs from practitioners. It was recognized that sufficient material should be available to draw conclusions on best practices in several areas of mitigation work. For example, many evaluations of energy alternatives for local communities have been conducted. It should be possible to look into methodological issues and identify a best practice framework for evaluations that tackle this issue. Evaluations of changes in management and planning in the energy sector and in energy policies would be another potential subject for which a best practice framework could be identified. Other areas include innovation and technology transfer, market transformations, and renewable energy issues.

These best practices, or frameworks, could, in parallel or consecutively, be translated into guidelines for mitigation evaluations. Given the fact that climate change and development evaluators had met, often for the first time, at the conference, they could be challenged to continue to collaborate to establish these guidelines as professional standards.

On adaptation issues, the many promising approaches highlighted at the conference and included in this book pointed to the need to continue an exchange of lessons learned and discussion of experiences. This, in turn, could lead to improved frameworks or concepts through which adaptation can be monitored and evaluated. A repository could be built that would include promising avenues to explore and innovative ways to set up M&E frameworks on adaptation, as well as guidelines and best practices.

Adaptation is a relatively new area of work for many governments, agencies, and local communities. Many are struggling to identify indicators that provide information on whether a country, region, or community is actually adapting to climate change. The conference saw examples of adaptation indicators at the community level. It was thought that evaluators would be able to collaborate with scientists and policy makers to think through whether similar indicators could work at other levels. A related issue would be to develop approaches to mainstreaming into regular development work or sector policies of countries. These four areas of work—meta-evaluation of mitigation experiences, development of guidelines for mitigation evaluations, identification of common lessons in adaptation, and indicators for adaptation—would be starting points for a voyage of discovery that an ongoing community of practice could undertake after the conference, building on the chapters, evaluations, and studies presented in *Evaluating Climate Change and Development*.

A Virtual Community of Practice

One of the most critical issues raised by the conference was that of knowledge sharing and regional networking. With the highest rate of attendance, and animated discussions, the evaluation and regional networking sessions sparked fruitful exchanges on the strengths and weaknesses of various associations and partnerships. A common sentiment was that there are significant challenges to overcome in laying the groundwork for sharing results and developing best practices.

To better focus on follow-up activities, the GEF Evaluation Office conducted a postconference survey, which collected data from more than 500 professionals, including members of dozens of regional and international networking associations. More than 350 people expressed interest in joining a community of practice that would fulfill the networking and knowledge-sharing potential presented at the conference.

On the basis of this survey, a two-tiered response to build on the momentum of the conference was developed. The first avenue was to continue to update and improve the electronic repository of climate change and development evaluations and studies that had been assembled for the conference. The second road proposed the building of a virtual community of practices that would interact through social interactive software.

Building such a community of practice will present a series of challenges. The first would be to ensure active participation from evaluators other than those in Organisation for Economic Co-operation and Development (OECD) countries: as Agrawal and Rao show for India in chapter 7, even in a country with a strong evaluation tradition, environmental evaluation does not have strong roots. The good news was that 40 percent of survey respondents came from developing countries. This high level was no doubt reached through the active support of regional evaluation associations and IDEAS. It should be possible to build on this interest and achieve an active participation in the community of practice.

The second challenge relates to the professional community of evaluators, among whom there is little experience with or confidence in new forms of interactive software. The survey showed high levels of confidence in relatively old-fashioned and trusted modes of communication: a group e-mail list-serve scored highest, followed by a Web site and an old-fashioned newsletter. New modalities such as a wiki or an electronic repository, were not high on the list of instruments that survey respondents used much.

Few evaluators have contributed to Wikipedia or other wiki-based exchange mechanisms. After consultation with experts on knowledge sharing and interactive software, the GEF Evaluation Office gradually realized that a community of practice on its own will not achieve much unless a moderator helps keep discussions and contributions organized and provides support to new initiatives that need to be accommodated. Furthermore, it was pointed out that a community of practice in itself is often not capable of undertaking analytic studies or synthetic work that needs to be done; support is needed, through research analysts, consultants, or senior experts who can provide substantive input into discussions.

The GEF Evaluation Office decided that external funding was needed for the four studies envisaged at the end of the Alexandria conference, which require substantial preparatory work. The community of practice will deliver a substantial contribution to this work by interacting on the approach, reacting to specific terms of reference, peer reviewing intermediate products, and contributing actively to discussing guidelines, frameworks, and indicators that will enrich and validate the reports coming out of these studies. Through active participation of evaluators from the South, capacity on evaluating climate change and development will be further supported and developed.

Funding this work also ensures that discussions in the community of practice will be actively moderated, with due attention to capacity-building issues, by a moderator who will ensure that support is provided to evaluators from the South. This moderator will also initiate and manage meta-evaluations, synthetic studies, and the development of guidelines, benchmarks, and indicators from the existing and new material gathered in the electronic repository. Products will be delivered to the community of practice (thus directly benefiting evaluators in the South) and to donors.

Collaboration with IDEAS and Other Evaluation Associations

It is envisaged that the community of practice will become part of a larger community of evaluators and others involved in evaluating environmentally sustainable development. The community will be supported by partners such as IDEAS and other evaluation associations, which will contribute by opening up their networks and activities (seminars, conferences, and so forth) to support the community of practice. Several steps have already been taken in this direction. The efforts to create a community of practice were presented at the IDEAS conference in Johannesburg in March 2009. In June 2009, a follow-up meeting was held in Almaty with a group of evaluators from Central Asia for possible input into the International Program

Evaluation Network (IPEN) in the Kyrgyz Republic in September 2010. (Unfortunately, due to political events in the Kyrgyz Republic, the conference was not held.) Links to other evaluation associations with roots in the developing world, such as the initiatives noted by Agrawal and Rao in chapter 7, will be explored.

The challenge is to start up and manage a viable community of practice that will provide support to evaluators on climate change and development issues. Later on, such a community could also address other environmental issues, such as the conservation of biodiversity, the removal of dangerous chemicals, and the preservation of ecological services. The GEF Evaluation Office will coordinate these efforts in collaboration with associations such as IDEAS and IPEN, supported by donors such as Sweden and Switzerland. In this way, substantive work can be combined with support to evaluation capacity development all over the world. The community will focus on supporting the emerging capacity in partner countries on issues of credibility and utility (see chapter 5), helping enable countries to better tackle the challenges of sustainable development in a changing climate.

Note

1. At the IDEAS conference in Johannesburg, Picciotto returned to the issue of climate change as one of the new challenges evaluators are facing (see chapter 11).

Reference

van den Berg, Rob D., and Osvaldo Feinstein, eds. 2010. *Evaluating Climate Change and Development*. World Bank Series on Development, vol. 8. Piscataway, NJ: World Bank.

CHAPTER 7

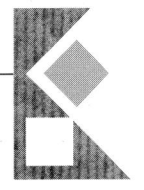

Capacity Building: The Indian Experience

Rashmi Agrawal and Banda V L N Rao

Over the past half a century, development evaluation has rapidly evolved as a discipline with its own conceptual framework, body of methods, standards of practice, and corresponding sets of requisite competencies among practitioners. In several countries, both developed and developing, the process of development evaluation has been institutionalized, with both public and private sectors participating in the process. The private sector is increasingly playing a greater role. Professional bodies of evaluators have emerged, at national and international levels, contributing to the exchange of experience and conceptual and methodological refinements. Most bilateral and international financial or technical aid programs have long made evaluations—formative, midterm, summative, or prospective—an essential component of the aid approval process. International agreements, such as the Paris Declaration on Aid Effectiveness (2005) and the follow-up Accra Agenda for Action (2008) focus on, among other things, managing the utilization of aid for delivery of results, accountability, and transparency, recognizing that development evaluation is a means toward these ends.

Although the practice of conducting evaluation studies has taken firm root in the field of economic and social development, the extent of utilization of the results of such studies varies considerably from case-to-case, ranging from nonuse to maximum utilization. Evaluation of any development policy, program, or individual project can be viewed as a project itself. It uses up resources, with attendant opportunity costs. Its quality, benefits, and impact have to be demonstrated through its own evaluation. Patton (1999) cites an example used by UNICEF to drive home this point: every $20 used in evaluation is $20 not available to immunize a child. As he notes, "Evaluation cannot, therefore, afford to become wasteful. Evaluators bear the burden of demonstrating that their contributions ultimately increase the number of children who are immunized, hungry people who are fed, productivity of farmers, and more (7)." Patton, who advocates the use of "utilization-focused evaluations (1997)," argues that "the value of an evaluation has to be at least equal its cost and should be evaluated according to its utilization ... no matter how rigorous the methods of data collection, design, and reporting are in evaluation, if it does not get used it is a bad evaluation" (1999, 16). Weiss (2004) notes that unused evaluation is a waste of resources.

Evaluators are not always the ones exclusively, if at all, responsible for the nonutilization of evaluation results. Even when evaluators conduct an evaluation that provides practical information to intended users, the results fail to be used. Greater methodological rigor, as noted by Patton, has not contributed to "solving the use problem" (Patton 1997, 16). The utilization rate, even for methodologically sound evaluations, is very low. Bamberger, Rugh, and Mabry (2006, 156) also agree that the low utilization rate of evaluations is a matter of concern. This point of view prima facie appears to be true, but it is important to understand how the concept of utilization is approached.

Utilization of Evaluations: Various Viewpoints

Utilization of evaluation results leading to enhancement of the quality and impact of the development intervention may be considered the ultimate test of an evaluation. It is not always easy, however, to infer the fact or identify the shape of such use, because determine whether an evaluation was used, because utilization can take a variety of forms. The commissioners of evaluation may consider the evaluation results very carefully and come to the conclusion that none of the recommendations can be implemented because of some policy or practical reasons. The evaluation may find that everything is fine with the project and no remedial action is called for. Alternatively, some or all of the results and recommendations may be found useful and put to use for possible improved results. The results of evaluation may not be used in reshaping the program, but they may find application elsewhere in the planning or implementation of some other program or be taken into account in the formulation of policy at a future date. If nothing else, the evaluation study and its results may develop evaluative thinking among policy planners, program implementers, and project managers, which itself may be considered a positive impact of the study, leading to evaluation capacity building. The utilization of an evaluation may thus be at the micro, or individual project, level or at the macro, or policy, level; its assessment is analogous to assessing overall impact rather than the results of a specific development project.

Thus there can be different viewpoints about whether the results of an evaluation study have been utilized. Even with reference to the project evaluated, the utilization may be total, partial, or not at all. Rist (1999, 111–112) points out that "evaluation utilization is . . . an area of strong passions, disagreements, and widely varying perspectives" and that "what do we mean by 'utilization' and how would we know it when we see it are but two of the points of discussion in the evaluation community now for more than 25 years." As Patton (1986) notes, conclusions regarding non-utilization of evaluation results are to a substantial degree the result of too narrow a definition of utilization, with emphasis on direct and immediate impact on program decisions.

Henry and Mark (2003) elaborate a model indicating the "pathways" through which evaluation results can be utilized. They distinguish three levels of influence of evaluation results: individual, interpersonal, and collective. At all three levels, they list specific changes that take place as a result of evaluation results. At the individual level, the list includes attitudinal change, skill acquisition, and behavioral change. Changes at the interpersonal level include changes in justification, persuasion, and social norms. At the collective level, the changes are in setting the agenda and modifying policy. This model thus postulates that evaluations not only have impact on individuals, they also affect interactions they have with others as well as collective actions of organizations and groups.

Many researchers have worked on the utilization of evaluations, as it is understood in practice. Patton's *Utilization-Focused Evaluation* (1997) cites examples of useful evaluations. Garrett (1999) provides examples of policy evaluations conducted by the International Food Policy Research Institute and indicates their utility in terms of resource utilization and policy formulation. Ingram and Feinstein (2001) report that user-friendly evaluation products were produced after a World Bank evaluation. These are positive aspects of the utilization of evaluations. In contrast, some evaluations have resulted in reports that are either not usable (because of poor quality) or not acceptable to the commissioners of evaluation (for other reasons).

Researchers have discussed various problems in the effective utilization of evaluation results. In a review of studies conducted on the use of evaluations up to the 1980s, Thompson (1994) notes that evaluation results were often disregarded. Fitzpatrick, Sanders, and Worthen (2003) find that utilization of evaluation results increased after the mid-1980s and 1990s. Patton (1986) opines that if results are produced in a presentable form, evaluation findings will be used. His argument indicates that there could be some genuine reasons for the use or nonuse of evaluation findings.

Owen and Rogers (1999) classify such factors into two groups. The first relates to the characteristics of the evaluation—that is, the way it is conducted. This group includes the quality of evaluation and the credibility of the evaluators, the relevance of the evaluation, the communication between evaluator and stakeholders, the political climate, the user's commitment, and other factors. The second group of factors includes characteristics of the settings in which the findings are to be utilized, such as the relevance of the evaluation to the decision maker's needs and the overall policy environment in which the program evaluated is being operated. For instance, a recommendation emanating purely from considerations of operational efficiency may not be found acceptable in a rights-based environment.

Utilization thus depends on a number of factors, which can be situational or related to resources, context, quality, or some other factor. This chapter skirts controversies and makes an attempt at studying the extent of the utilization of development evaluations with reference to some evaluations of major development programs in India. It identifies the factors that impede or facilitate utilization of evaluation results and looks at the possibilities for enhancing the extent of utilization through capacity building among evaluators and evaluation commissioners. It also elaborates how evaluations have made their impact at the micro as well as the macro level, ranging from immediate utilization to utility at a later date, directly or indirectly. As the context is India, a brief digression into the institutional mechanism for evaluation of developmental interventions is relevant before these issues are discussed.

Institutional Mechanism for Development Evaluation in India

Governmental institutional mechanisms for evaluation evolved in several developed countries during the 1960s (Canada, Germany, Sweden, the United States) and 1970s (Denmark, Finland, France, the Netherlands, Norway, the United Kingdom). In India, the government's institutions for program monitoring and evaluation have been in place ever since the initiation of the process of planned development in the early 1950s (figure 7.1).

The Program Evaluation Organisation (PEO) was set up in the national Planning Commission in 1952. It now operates through seven regional offices and eight field offices. These institutions conduct evaluation studies on the development programs of various ministries in the central government, usually at the request of the government and, on occasion, on the initiative of the national Planning Commission itself. Similar institutions emerged within the planning departments of most state governments during the 1960s and early 1970s.

A Development Evaluation Advisory Committee (DEAC) advises PEO on prioritization of areas of research, methodologies to be adopted, establishment of linkages between PEO and various evaluation research organizations and academic institutions, and follow-up action on evaluation results. In addition to these permanent arrangements for evaluation at the national and state levels, several ministries in the central government implementing large-scale programs (such as rural development programs or special schemes in employment, health, and education) have their own arrangements for evaluating programs independently on a regular basis. In recent years, evaluation of development projects of the government has increasingly being conducted by independent research organizations, particularly in the voluntary sector.

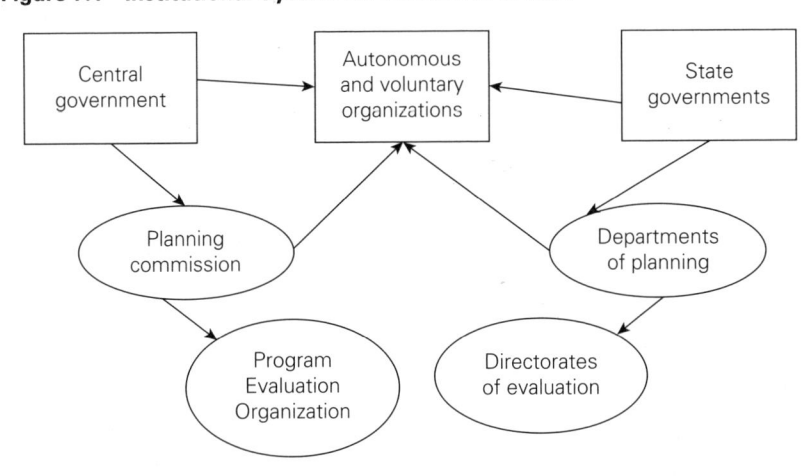

Figure 7.1 Institutional System for Evaluation in India

Source: Authors.

Factors Influencing Utilization of Evaluation Results: The Indian Experience

Over the years, monitoring and evaluation has become a standard component of development programs and projects in India; a budget for these activities is allocated. A large proportion of the evaluation work is done by independent research organizations, small and large. Although there has been a substantial step-up in development evaluation activity in India, it is not certain that these evaluations have always, or even in most cases, made a contribution toward enhancing the development process.

It is not that evaluations have not been useful at all. Several examples of how evaluation helped shape development projects can be cited. For instance, the Mahila Samriddhi Yojana scheme, which inculcates the habit of saving among rural women, had been in operation from 1993. After a PEO evaluation, the scheme was dropped as an independent scheme and merged with Indira Mahila Yojana, another women's empowerment scheme, to optimize resource use. The Employment Assurance Scheme, operated during the 1990s to ensure a minimum of 100 days of manual work to the rural unemployed in extremely backward areas of the country, was evaluated by PEO in 2000. Based on the findings, a restructured scheme, Sampoorna Grameen Rozgar Yojana, was initiated in 2001–02 that incorporated many of the recommendations of the evaluation report. Based on a 2001 PEO evaluation study on the national project on biogas development, the Ministry of Nonconventional Resources formulated detailed guidelines for implementation of the program beginning in 2002–03. The nationwide program for rural poverty reduction through self-employment, Swarn Jayanti Grameen Swarozgar Yojana, is also subject to periodic evaluation and has been modified from time to time to make the program more effective, self-contained, and sustainable.

Although many such examples of evaluations successfully utilized to bring about improvements in the development projects can be cited, there are several others where the situation is different. The results are not used at all, even if they emanate from well-conducted evaluations, or they are used selectively to support the continuation of an ongoing program. Experience shows that a number of factors are responsible for the utilization or lack of utilization of evaluation results.

Need-Based or Routine Exercises

Need-based evaluations, such as those commissioned with specific objectives or to tackle specific problems, have been found to be utilization oriented. Often, however, a provision for evaluation is included in the scheme of a development project without any specific commitment to the evaluation process or intention to use the results of the evaluation to influence the shape of the program. Such evaluations are carried out in a routine and perfunctory manner. Neither valid nor accurate data are collected, and the results of the evaluation are not awaited; the program continues unaffected or is modified independently of the evaluation results. Many of the annual reports of the departments and ministries note that their programs were evaluated, but there is hardly ever any mention of the recommendations made by such evaluations or changes made in the programs as a consequence. Such evaluations are conducted only as a formality. As a case in point, mention may be made of the scheme of informal coaching and training for educated unemployed youth belonging to scheduled castes and tribes (socially deprived classes in Indian society) through reputed educational institutions. The scheme is operated every year. Every year an annual internal study is conducted to assess the impact of the training on the employability of those trained. The program continued for years, unaffected by the results of the studies.

In contrast, an evaluation of public delivery agencies in Bangalore was conducted using citizen report cards, with the aim of improving services. The evaluation found high levels of dissatisfaction with the behaviors of public servants as well as high levels of problems of citizens. These findings were discussed in the media, attracting the attention of the authorities. Repeated evaluations observed significant improvements in the performance of the public agencies. This evaluation was based on a very specific need, awareness about which was created using the media.

Evaluator's Capacities

Although evaluators' competencies in conducting evaluations are not always sufficient to ensure utilization of evaluation results, they constitute the necessary conditions. It is argued that "the evaluation through the research arm of the decision-making agency sometimes increases the likelihood that the results will be used" (OECD 1991). The case of the employment assurance scheme in India, cited earlier, supports this argument. The competencies of the PEO, which conducted the evaluation, no doubt contributed to the fact that the results were utilized.

A large number of agencies, qualified and not so qualified, are looking for consultancy activities in development evaluation. There are generally provisions stipulated to enable the sponsoring organization to verify the qualifications, experience, financial viability, and other credentials of the agencies before the evaluations are contracted out. Commissioners of evaluations assess the technical and financial aspects of the study proposals received, but there is greater emphasis on the financial aspects. Where bids are given to the organization with the lowest bid, the assigning of a job to a not so technically competent bidder cannot be ruled out. Agencies eager to undertake any possible job express their interest for undertaking a wide range of activities, even if they do not have the necessary expertise in a specific field.

Sponsors of Evaluations and Clarity of Terms of Reference

Many evaluations are conducted by external or independent agencies; the authorities responsible for formulating and implementing the projects are not really involved in the technical aspects of their evaluation. Apart from the argument that external and independent evaluations have greater objectivity and creditability, there is also a practical consideration. Although every program and project is generally required to be evaluated, not all of the agencies conceiving or implementing the developmental interventions are equipped with evaluation capabilities.

The bridge between the thinking of commissioners and evaluators are the Terms of Reference (ToR). Clarity in ToRs can prepare the ground for better understanding by sponsors and evaluators, leading to better utilization of evaluation findings. In practice, ToRs are often not discussed by the two parties; the sponsoring authority peremptorily hands them to the evaluating agency, without adequately considering what can be achieved through the evaluation given the resources committed. There is often a lack of understanding between the sponsoring agency and the evaluating agency on the specific objectives of evaluation and the instruments and manner of data collection.

At the other extreme are cases in which sponsoring authorities ask the evaluating agency to prepare the ToRs. Even where the ToRs are framed by the sponsoring agency or mutually settled and the evaluation conducted to meet the information needs as stipulated in the ToRs, the sponsoring authorities subsequently raise issues not covered by the ToR, affecting the utilization of the report.

Multiple Evaluations of a Program: Bane or Boon?

The same development program is often evaluated by more than one agency at a time. Although multiple evaluations can potentially provide findings from different perspectives, giving deeper insights into the problems, each evaluation produces its own perceptions of the problems and prescriptions for fixing them. The recommendations from one evaluation are sometimes not consistent with those of another, making it difficult to reconcile the recommendations.

An example is the evaluation of the development programs implemented in a backward region of Orissa. A number of development schemes and programs are being implemented in this region, and a number of evaluations have been conducted by various agencies at the same time as well as at different points in time. Although the results of various evaluations certainly provided useful inputs to program planners in working out a suitable development strategy for the region, action on the recommendations of evaluations was influenced by personal opinions and attitudes. The evaluations were thus not entirely a waste of effort, but they did not always lead to effective action.

Completely ignoring the recommendations of an evaluation is not common; their selective utilization is more frequent. Selective utilization is perfectly valid if the choice is objective, based on policy and practical considerations, without any hidden agenda. This is not always the case. For instance, various rural development programs are subjected to concurrent evaluation studies by reputable and independent research organizations and necessary modifications made to the programs. Village-based impact assessment studies are also conducted to assess the collective impact of all the rural development programs on the individuals, the community, and the area as a whole. Based on selective results of these studies, it was concluded that there had been a collective beneficial impact of the programs on rural incomes and social infrastructure, a conclusion used as a justification for extending the impact studies to more districts. One cannot be sure that all the results of the studies were duly weighed in reaching this decision.

Dissemination of Evaluation Findings

Dissemination of evaluation findings to a widespread audience has been found to be directly linked with utilization of evaluations. This is evident from the study of citizen report cards cited earlier, where the findings of the study were disseminated through the media, which created awareness among the public at large. The findings of evaluation reports often remain restricted, as reports are submitted only to the sponsoring agency, which may not make these reports public in their entirety. It is not clear that all the findings of all evaluations should be made publicly available, as doing so might hurt the interests of some stakeholders and violate their rights. Various views on this issue in terms of ethics, implications, and future policy actions need attention before any argument in favor or against is put forward.

Acceptance of Evaluation Reports

Delay in accepting an evaluation report may make the evaluation's findings irrelevant and ineffective. Although a time frame for completing the evaluations is indicted in the ToR, no time is fixed for the sponsoring organization for accepting or rejecting the report or indicating where it needs improvement. Queries and suggestions from the sponsoring authority and replies from the evaluating agencies often continue for a long time, resulting in delays without any useful final outcome. There are cases in which the acceptance of evaluation reports took almost two years, by which time they lost their relevance, as the data had become dated. Sometimes the people who had sponsored the evaluation had been transferred and the new incumbents showed little interest in pursuing the evaluation results. The time taken to accept or reject the findings may be related to the willingness of the sponsors to consider the evaluation and the communication process between the sponsoring and evaluating agencies.

Wherever immediate attention is paid to the evaluation results, utilization is better. In a recently conducted concurrent evaluation of a teacher recruitment drive in one of the states in India, this phenomenon was observed. In this evaluation, results were communicated to the sponsoring agency periodically, even before final submission of the report, and corrective measures were taken.

There has to be political and administrative willingness on the part of the sponsors of the evaluations to appreciate the findings and the recommendations made and to identify and use the results for quick modifications in the program. Change is resisted: departments implementing certain programs hardly desire to make amendments to existing programs. Proposals for changes in established procedures, however welcome and needed they may be from the program impact point of view, are resisted because the recommendations may not be consistent with the thinking already established in the organization.

Capacity Building for Better Utilization of Evaluations

The factors discussed above can be divided into two groups, one including those that can be directly or indirectly related to the capacities of sponsors of evaluation and another to the capacities of evaluators. For example, conceiving need-based evaluation, ensuring proper timing, preparing clear and focused ToRs, selecting a competent evaluator, and disseminating evaluation findings are related to the competencies and ethics of the sponsors. Evaluators' capacities, the objectivity of their reports, and so forth are part of the capacities and ethics of evaluators. To make evaluations utilization oriented, it is essential that the capacities of both sponsors and evaluators be of a high standard.

To enhance evaluation utilization, it is important to

- develop the capacities of program planners and implementers and evaluation sponsors to help them appreciate the importance of evaluation and think in the language of evaluation
- institutionalize monitoring and evaluation in the organization
- identify the requirements of a good-quality evaluation and good evaluators
- identify appropriate and vital evaluation questions and prepare focused ToRs
- allocate adequate human resources, time, and money to facilitate quality evaluations
- objectively assess the evaluation results and recommendations
- consider the results in reshaping the development program.

Equally important from the point of view of utilization is the availability of the relevant capacities within the evaluating agency. These capacities include not only the skills required for the conduct of a successful quantitative statistical survey but the whole range of abilities, including

- formulating appropriate evaluation questions in consultation with various stakeholders
- identifying, gathering, processing, and interpreting all relevant qualitative and quantitative data objectively and efficiently
- formulating appropriate recommendations for program modification, conveying them to the implementers of the program, and convincing them that the modifications will increase greater program impact
- observing sound ethical principles while conducting the evaluation.

Comprehensive programs for capacity building in the area of development evaluation are, therefore, of utmost importance for ensuring optimum use of investments. There are generally programs for enhancement of skills in statistics, social sciences, development economics, and management as independent streams; what is required is a capacity-building program that adopts a multidisciplinary approach that develops or augments skills in development process, quantitative and qualitative data analysis, project management, communication, and other soft skills. Different evaluation experts use different approaches and techniques, each with their own strengths and limitations.

There is a need for an institutionalized forum that facilitates interaction and exchange to enhance knowledge in the field. The International Program for Development Evaluation Training (IPDET) is one such initiative. It conducts annual training programs for practitioners of development evaluation. The International Development Evaluation Association (IDEAS) and national associations (such as the International Development Research Centre [IDRC] of Canada) in several developed countries provide a platform for exchange of knowledge in the field of evaluation.

Comparable institutions are rare in the developing world. A recent initiative is the project by the Association for Stimulating Know-How (ASK), operating as a nongovernmental organization in Delhi. A community of evaluators has been created to establish a regionally active forum for interaction among evaluation experts in South Asia. The project plans to bring together evaluation experts from Bangladesh, India, Nepal, Pakistan, and Sri Lanka who think it is important to contribute to the theory and practice of evaluation by engaging with one another in person and through seminars, trainings, and discussions and exchanges over the Internet.

In India, the national Planning Commission recently took up some initiatives to institutionalize capacity building in development evaluation. A unit for training in development evaluation was set up at the Institute of Applied Manpower Research in New Delhi. The unit organizes training programs for officials of the central and state governments as well as for the voluntary sector.

On-the-Job Capacity Building: A Case Study

In addition to capacity-building processes through institutionalized mechanisms, periodic evaluations by organizations and brainstorming sessions provide on-the-job training to evaluators and evaluation commissioners. An example is the evaluation of the Prime Minister Rojgar Yojana (PMRY) scheme in India, which promotes self-employment among unemployed educated youth in rural and urban areas.

PMRY was implemented in 1993–94. The scheme provided for financial and technical assistance and guidance to eligible applicants through loans from financial institutions, a government subsidy, and entrepreneurial training at professional training institutions for setting up small self-employment ventures. The scheme was evaluated three times, in 1996, 2001, and 2005, by the Institute of Applied Manpower Research, an independent research organization in the public sector with years of experience in the field. The objectives of the evaluation included assessing the impact of the program in terms of the extent of employment and incomes generated, studying the pattern of loan disbursement and its repayment, and examining the adequacy of the scheme's implementing units in the district industry centers (an implementation organization at the grassroots level) in terms of infrastructure, staff, and other factors. The sponsors and evaluators were the same for all three evaluations.

While 10 percent of recommendations were implemented after the first evaluation, about 30 percent of the recommendations were implemented after the second evaluation. However, a number of recommendations were repeated from one evaluation to another, indicating that they did not find favor with the sponsors for some reason or other. After the third evaluation, the scheme was overhauled on the basis of the evaluation results over the years. Although several of the recommendations made in various evaluations have not been implemented, the direction, if not the scale, of changes introduced has been consistent with the findings of the evaluations. Channels of communication developed between the two agencies over the years, fostering better understanding. The quality of the evaluation also improved in the areas of participation of stakeholders, framing of ToRs, and evaluation design, for example. After the third evaluation, the sponsors held extensive discussions about the findings and recommendations, which helped the evaluating agency understand why some of the recommendations were not implementable.

A thorough discussion between the evaluating organization and the sponsoring agency on evaluation findings is always fruitful. During the second round of evaluation, a recommendation was made that beneficiaries should have at least 10 years of schooling, as applicants who have just 8 years of schooling are unable to prepare proper project reports. The third evaluation also indicated that the ventures of beneficiaries with just 8 years of schooling were less successful than those of beneficiaries with at least 10 years of education. During discussions, the sponsoring agency argued that as the scheme is for poor people in both rural and urban areas, a number of potential beneficiaries would be excluded from the scheme if the number of years of education were raised.[1] Keeping this policy framework in mind, the third round of evaluation did not recommending raising the basic qualification but suggested that assistance to beneficiaries should come as a package including assistance in the choice of activity, preparation of the project report, technical training, financial assistance, follow-up of ventures, and so forth. Detailed deliberations between the sponsoring organization and the evaluating agency both before and after the evaluation led to acceptable and implementable recommendations.

Conclusions

India's experience of utilization of evaluations makes sense in the light of the model postulated by Henry and Mark (2003). Experience shows that the usefulness of an evaluation may or may not be scheme specific, time specific, or organization specific. Its usefulness may not be immediately apparent, but it may manifest itself in a much broader context, such as in relation to policy decisions at the macro level.

No evaluation is fruitless. Even where results have not been utilized for a particular project or program, evaluations in India have influenced public opinion and attitudes of policy makers, leading to convergence of schemes, modifications in policies, and the introduction of new interventions with better planning and implementation mechanisms. A good example is the evolution over the 1980s and 1990s of the Integrated Rural Development Program and its associated programs, such as Development of Women and Children in Rural Areas (DWACRA) and Training of Rural Youth for Self-Employment (TRYSEM), into the single holistic program Sampoorna Grameen Swarozgar Yojana (SGSY). Regular concurrent evaluation helped in periodically modifying the content of the program and eventually achieving cohesion and convergence of resources. All evaluations may not have as profound an impact. Every evaluation, however, contributes by influencing some program decisions or at least generating awareness of the drawbacks involved and stimulating thought about how they can be overcome. The very fact that a program will eventually be subject to evaluation before its extension in time or expansion in space is likely to instill a sense of purpose in planning and implementing a program.

It is, therefore, not correct to question the usefulness of an evaluation on the basis of the absence of immediate and direct application of its findings. There is a need to inculcate a sense of seriousness in conducting evaluations among both sponsoring organizations and evaluating agencies. Sponsoring organizations have to ensure that technically sound evaluations are entrusted to competent organizations that can deliver. Evaluating agencies have to be objective. The goals of conducting evaluations should be very clear to both parties.

The evaluating agency should not only make a timely presentation of its report, it should also consider its duty to follow up on the implementation of its recommendations and efforts to eliminate impediments in the way of implementation. The sponsoring authority should give adequate publicity to the evaluation report and seek comments from the public at large before making appropriate decisions. It is strongly suggested that a follow-up study be taken up to map the utilization of evaluations conducted so far. Such follow-up should be a continuous process, not a one-time effort.

There may be a need for a centralized, high-powered institution to look at various evaluation studies of developmental programs conducted from time to time, ensure proper study of the recommendations flowing out of these evaluations, and track the follow-up action taken on each recommendation. India has agencies like the Comptroller General of Accounts, but its functions fall in the sphere of audit. It may be worth redefining the roles of program evaluation organization in the Planning Commission and its counterparts in the states, particularly in the current context of outsourcing evaluation functions. This organization would not conduct evaluations itself but would oversee the implementation of the results of various evaluations.

A prerequisite for ensuring that the results of evaluation studies are fully utilized in the modification of policies, programs, and projects for improved performance and optimum utilization of investible resources is that the evaluation be of a high quality. This, in turn, requires that the agency conducting the evaluation be equipped with all essential skills, is knowledgeable about the latest theory and practice in the field of development evaluation, and is capable of applying that knowledge to the problem on hand.

Capacity-building programs at the international, national, and subnational levels are essential to generate such skills. Equally important are institutional mechanisms available to all countries to promote the spread of knowledge in the field of development evaluation through frequent interactions among practitioners in different countries and spheres of activity. Capacities are also developed through experience. But agencies cannot afford to have evaluators learn through trial and error.

Note

1. Stretching this rights-based policy formulation to its logical conclusion, the scheme as overhauled now prescribes no eligibility condition based on education for projects below a specified limit. Adequate guidance and entrepreneurial training are a part of the program.

Bibliography

Bamberger, M., J. Rugh, and L. Mabry. 2006. *Real World Evaluation: Working under Budget, Time, Data and Political Constraints*. Thousand Oaks, CA: Sage.

Brinkerhoff, R. O., D. M. Brethower, T. Hluchyj, and J. R. Nowakowski. 1983. *Program Evaluation: A Practitioner's Guide for Trainers and Evaluators*. Boston: Kluver-Nijhoff.

Cousins, J. B., and K. A. Leithwood. 1986. "Current Empirical Research on Evaluation Utilization." *Review of Educational Research* 56 (3): 331–64.

Fitzpatrick, J. L., J. R. Sanders, and B. R. Worthen. 2003. *Program Evaluation: Alternative Approaches and Practical Guidelines*. 3rd ed. Boston: Allyn & Bacon.

Garrett, J. 1999. *Research That Matters: The Impact of IFPRI's Policy Research*. Washington, DC: International Food Policy Research Institute.

Government of India. 2004. *Development Evaluation in PEO and Its Impact*. PEO Report No. 188, Planning Commission, Program Evaluation Organisation, New Delhi.

Geene, J. C. 1988. "Stakeholder Participation and Utilization in Program Evaluation." *Evaluation Review* 12 (2): 91–116.

Hatry, H. P. 1999. *Performance Measurement: Getting Results*. Washington, DC: Urban Institute Press.

Henry, G. T., and M. M. Mark. 2003. "Beyond Use: Understanding Evaluation's Influence on Attitudes and Actions." *American Journal of Evaluation* 24 (3): 293–314.

House, E. R., and K. R. Howe. 1999. *Values in Evaluation and Social Research*. Thousand Oaks, CA: Sage.

IAMR (Institute of Applied Manpower Research). 2002. *Prime Minister's Rozgar Yojana (PMRY), An Evaluation (Second Round)*. New Delhi: IAMR.

———. 2006. *Report on Evaluation of Prime Minister's Rozgar Yojana (PMRY), Third Round*. New Delhi: IAMR.

Ingram, G., and O. Feinstein. 2001. "Learning and Evaluation: World Bank's Experience." *Evaluation Insights* 3 (1): 4–6.

King, J. A. 1988. "Research on Evaluation Use and Its Implications for Evaluation Research and Practice." *Studies in Educational Evaluation* 14 (3): 285–99.

Mayne, J., S. Divorski, and D. Lemaire. 1999. "Locating Evaluation: Anchoring Evaluation in the Executive or the Legislature, or Both or Elsewhere." In *Building Effective Evaluation Capacity: Lessons from Practice,* ed. R. Boyle and D. Lemaire, 23–52. New Brunswick, N. J.: Transaction Publishers.

OECD/DAC (Organisation for Economic Co-operation and Development/Development Assistance Committee). 1991. *DAC Principles for Effective Aid*. Paris: OECD.

Owen, J. M., and P. Rogers. 1999. *Program Evaluation: Forms and Approaches*. 2nd ed. Thousand Oaks, CA: Sage.

Patton, M. Q. 1986. *Utilization-Focused Evaluation*. 2nd ed. Thousand Oaks, CA: Sage.

———. 1997. *Utilization-Focused Evaluation: The New Century Text*. 3rd ed. Thousand Oaks, CA: Sage.

———. 1999. *Utilization-Focused Evaluation in Africa: Evaluation Training Lectures Delivered to the Inaugural Conference of the African Evaluation Association,* ed. P. N. Chaiban and M. Patel. http://www.afrea.org/documents.

Picciotto R. 2002. *Development Cooperation and Performance Evaluation: The Monterrey Challenge.* Washington, DC: World Bank, Operations Evaluation Department.

Prasad, S. 2000. *Report on Evaluation of Prime Minister's Rozgar Yojana (PMRY) 1994–95.* New Delhi: Institute of Applied Manpower Research.

Rist, R. C. 1999. "Linking Evaluation Utilization and Governance: Fundamental Challenges for Countries Building Evaluation Capacity." In *Building Effective Evaluation Capacity: Lessons from Practice,* ed. R. Boyle and D. Lemaire, 111–32. New Brunswick, NJ: Transaction Publishers.

Scriven, M. 1967. "The Methodology of Evaluation." In *Curriculum Evaluation,* American Educational Research Association Monograph Series on Evaluation 1: 39–83. Chicago: Rand McNally.

Sonnichsen, R. C. 1999. "Building Evaluation Capacity within Organisations." In *Building Effective Evaluation Capacity: Lessons from Practice,* ed. R. Boyle and D. Lemaire, 53–74. New Brunswick, N. J.: Transaction Publishers.

Thompson, B. 1994. "The Revised Program Evaluation Standards and Their Correlation with the Evaluation Use Literature." Paper presented at the annual meeting of the American Educational Research Association, New Orleans, April 4–8.

Toulemonde, J. 1999. " Incentives, Constraints, and Culture-building as Instruments for the Development of Evaluation Demand." In *Building Effective Evaluation Capacity: Lessons from Practice,* ed. R. Boyle and D. Lemaire, 153–176. New Brunswick, N. J.: Transaction Publishers.

Weiss, C. 2004. "Identifying the Intended Use(s) of an Evaluation." Evaluation Guideline 6, International Development Research Centre, Ottawa. http://www.idrc.ca/uploads/user-S/115644998416Guideline.pdf.

CHAPTER 8

The Environmental/Rural Development and Food Security Program in Madagascar

Balsama Andriantseheno

The Environment/Rural Development and Food Security program of the U.S. Agency for International Development (USAID) was designed to respond to the strategic objective of conserving biologically diverse forest ecosystems by improving sustainable natural resource management and environmentally sensitive development (Program Strategic Objective SO6). The program, run by various implementing partners for four years, was expected to improve forest management systems, maintain the biological integrity of critical biodiversity habitats, reduce slash-and-burn practices, increase investment initiatives and partnerships in natural resource management, and improve environmental governance. In addition to this program, USAID/Madagascar has a robust PL 480 Title II Food for Peace program, which works to improve vulnerable people's food security in synergy with and under the common goals of the environment and rural development program area.

Regional alliances were set up to ensure collaboration and complementarity among USAID's implementing partners. The operating basis for the alliance is based on the nature, health, wealth, and power approach, an interdependent framework for understanding programmatic linkages (figure 8.1).

The framework is made up of four elements:

- *Nature*. Nature includes all types of natural resources (land, water, forests, wildlife) that are dynamic, socially embedded, economic, or political. It includes the gamut of natural resources that have economic, cultural, existence, aesthetic, biodiversity, or other value.
- *Health*. Health is a fundamental building block of human capital that is essential for human productivity. It includes both physical and mental aspects.
- *Wealth*. Natural capital is the basis of rural production and economic development systems across Africa. This component represents the economic concerns of natural resources management.
- *Power*. Governance refers to the interactions among structures, processes, rules, and traditions that determine how authority is exercised, how responsibilities are distributed, how decisions are made, and how various actors are implicated.

Links among these elements are evident when implementing activities related to water management, food security, and agriculture. For instance,

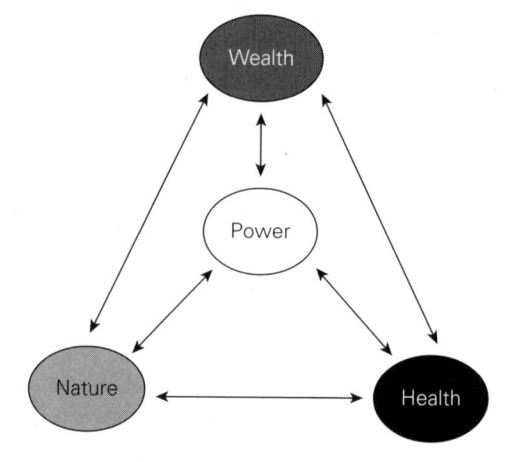

Figure 8.1 Relationship between Nature, Health, Wealth, and Power

Source: Author.

undertaking forest management activities requires that local people (that is, forest users) be in good health. Without sufficient nutrition and adequate quantities of potable water, forest management activities cannot be completed. Ill health translates into a need for cash to buy medication and, at times, premature death. This need may put pressure on forest resources, as people look for commodities to sell for money. Premature death means fewer family members to work in the fields and reduced overall family health, which contributes to the cycle of poverty. In addition, forest pressure from local populations is related to, among other factors, increases in the growth of local populations (through natural growth or migration). Good health, access to potable water, food security, and family planning activities therefore all have direct links with forest management.

As the number of households per settlement increases, the need to clear additional land for dwellings or agriculture also increases. Interventions therefore also focus on supporting farmers living near forest corridors to diversify their agricultural products and better manage their finite natural resources. Private sector firms and nongovernmental organizations work directly with rural farmers associations, producer groups, and agribusinesses to more effectively link diversified products to markets. The U.S. government's Millennium Challenge Account program complements these efforts through work on land tenure reform, improvement of financing mechanisms, and expansion of agricultural business and markets.

The Stocktaking Exercise

The purpose of the stocktaking exercise was to create an inventory of best practices and experiences of activities in Madagascar related to the environment, rural development, and food security. The exercise was intended to help USAID/Madagascar identify options, opportunities, and competitive advantages for the planning of future environment and rural development activities. Findings and recommendations were the main outputs. The stocktaking focused not only on best practices but on all lessons learned, positive and negative.

Based on the request of the USAID implementing partners, the stocktaking exercise was designed as an interactive and participatory process that would provide development practitioners responsible for the implementation of the program with the opportunity to share their experiences, knowledge, tools, and lessons learned in the form of publishable articles. These articles would also serve as a key input to the final reports as the various USAID programs come to a close. The services of a consulting firm, ADAPT, were contracted to help USAID's implementing partners fully participate in the stocktaking exercise while continuing their regular program activities.

USAID/Madagascar also established a memorandum of understanding with Translinks to further the objective of increasing social, economic, and environmental benefits through sustainable natural resources management. This partnership of the Wildlife Conservation Society, the Earth Institute of Columbia University, Enterprise Works/VITA, Forest Trends, the Land Tenure Center of the University of Wisconsin, and USAID aimed to address the linkages between nature, health, wealth, and power by identifying practical field-tested approaches that simultaneously promote resource management, rural wealth creation, and strong, equitable governance.

Roles and Responsibilities

The USAID Environment/Rural Development Team, in collaboration with the coordinator, was responsible for overseeing and facilitating the stocktaking exercise. The following services were provided:

- Communicate key information to implementing partners on the stocktaking process and time frame.
- Organize and facilitate discussions at the national level with implementing partners to develop themes and abstracts for the articles.
- Organize, facilitate, and finance initial workshops in the three eco-regions to develop themes and abstracts for the articles.
- Facilitate exchange and discussions between national and eco-regional levels.
- As needed, provide technical specialists and ghostwriters to thematic groups to draft the articles and finance thematic workshops.
- Organize, facilitate, and finance a midterm technical workshop.
- Review and critique articles.
- Organize, facilitate, and finance a final colloquium on "Knowledge, Tools, and Best Practices for Promoting Nature, Health, Wealth, and Power Linkages Based on 15 Years of USAID Experience in Supporting Environment and Rural Development Activities in Madagascar."

USAID implementing partners provided their knowledge and experiences in developing themes, analyzing approaches and tools, drawing lessons learned, and identifying best practices. They also served as the coauthors of publishable articles. USAID implementing partners were the lead authors; partners were solicited as coauthors within the context of the collaborative nature of the USAID program activities. Specific roles and responsibilities for the implementing partners were as follows:

- Participate in national, eco-regional, thematic workshops to develop themes and abstracts for the articles by sharing their knowledge and experience about the strengths and shortcomings for the different approaches and tools.
- With the assistance of technical specialists or ghostwriters, as needed, oversee or draft articles that will serve as key input for final reports (29 articles were prepared).
- Contribute knowledge and experience through dialogue and discussions on stocktaking themes developed by national and eco-regional teams.

The exercise was coordinated and managed by two people: one from USAID and one from an external consulting firm. The exercise was run for six months.

Issues Raised

The following issues were raised during the stocktaking exercise:

- Unlike a regular program evaluation output, the results did not provide a broad overview of the program. Even if a traditional evaluation had been conducted, it would have been very difficult to provide a broad overview of the program, because each project developed its own monitoring and evaluation (M&E) system without any coordination between them.
- If a classical evaluation process had been conducted on each project within the USAID program, how would the results of all project evaluations be consolidated to capture the overall achievement toward Program Strategic Objective SO6?
- If from the start there was an effort to develop a strategic and programmatic approach, why did that effort not go further and adopt a more integrated and complementary programmatic M&E system at the project level?
- What needs to be done to obtain a broad overview of the program and a realistic measurement of its efficacy in meeting SO6?

Lessons Learned

A variety of lessons were learned from the exercise:

- Involvement of regional implementing partners enriched the stocktaking exercise. The central-regional duality appeared to be very much alive from the beginning of the stocktaking process. As soon as the regional implementing partner teams heard about the launching of the exercise, in Antananarivo, all of them asked to have their own launching ceremonies as well, so that the themes and subjects would not be imposed on them by the central level. Holding regional launching ceremonies was very profitable to the exercise, as the teams from the regions brought in many themes and ideas that could not be defined or treated only at the central level. The central-level teams excelled at policy and strategy analysis; regional evaluators complemented their work by bringing in the practical side of the approaches. Each region had its own way of tackling the process and the stocktaking exercise. This diversity brought richness to the exercise.
- Many coordination problems arose from the fact that teams included representatives from more than one organization. These problems included difficulties with leadership, meeting times, work sharing, consolidation, and finalization responsibility. Coordination problems delayed work production until the article finalization process. The last article was received only on November 27, 2008.
- Despite their strong interest, most of the participants found it difficult to produce an academic article. Their capacity needs to be reinforced and built.
- Lack of motivation was a problem from the beginning. Participants needed to understand that their contribution in the stocktaking process was part of their daily work within their own organization and that USAID was not willing to pay anyone who was already working for an implementing partner or a USAID-supported project for their article. The team leader had to write a letter explaining this position to all implementing partners and USAID-supported projects. None of the implementing partners budgeted funds for this exercise, but all of them recognized that the content and quality of the next program would depend on the success of this stocktaking exercise. This was the main reason why participants agreed to contribute, although there was also very strong interest in the prospect of being published in an international scholarly journal.
- Lack of participation of actors other than the implementing partners and USAID limited the exercise. These exercises would be improved by involving other donors (with their supported projects) and local governments.

- No article was written on the need for better integration within USAID Environment/Rural Development and between it and other USAID departments. This shortcoming—particularly the coordination problem between the Environment/Rural Development and Health departments within USAID at the country level, a problem that had impacts on the field activity coordination with implementing partners—was discussed during the August seminar.

Recommendations

The following broad recommendations for the M&E process came out of the exercise:

- The format used in this version of the stocktaking exercise was very participative; it allowed project field personnel to share their views about their projects and programs and about USAID almost without restriction. The fact that their candid views were captured contributed to the richness of the products. The prospect of being published in an international journal interested many people. This format should therefore be retained as a regular periodical internal process in partnerships financed by USAID Environment/Rural Development.
- Coordination between departments inside USAID at a country's highest level is strongly recommended, because it directly affects field activities by operators.
- A more participative process—involving other field partners, other donors, decentralized structures, and local governments—would benefit future stocktaking processes. However, USAID should be careful about opening up the exercise too much, lest the USAID specificity of the products be lost.
- Within a programmatic approach, classical one-on-one M&E systems do not permit a richer consolidation at the higher level for the program. When each contractor develops its own M&E systems, no one can build a consolidated M&E matrix to measure the real results and impacts of the program as a whole.

There is a need to develop a better M&E system that should abide by the following rules:

- A single main M&E system should be developed that integrates most of the indicators identified to answer the Program Strategic Objective to allow a richer and easier consolidation of the results and impacts.

- Each project that is developed for the program can have its own internal M&E system, but it has to be closely tied to the main system. Periodic consolidation should be done on the main M&E system to make sure each project is feeding it the right way in a timely manner. Projects' M&E systems should operate like decentralized systems strongly linked to the main one but as autonomous as possible. Direct feeding of the main system by the projects is possible if a good and reliable quality control process is implemented.
- M&E human resources capacities should be built up and reinforced as needed at all project levels. This new M&E philosophy has to be shared and understood by all implementing partners' staff, especially M&E officers. An initial discussion and exchange between those officers and managers will have to build up and validate a common program theory of change/logical framework, out of which the main program indicators will come (based on USAID's and implementing partners' common understanding of SO6); all contributions and contributors to a particular indicator should be known. Once a program logical framework is validated and available, each project can build up its own M&E system to make sure it will be based on the main system. The structure that manages the main M&E system will have to give a hand to each project as needed to make sure that everything is compatible and complementary.
- As complementarities are needed between projects, the structure that manages the main M&E system should be given the power to supervise all projects' internal M&E systems. The standard to be used and followed by all M&E systems within the USAID program should come from that structure (after USAID's validation) and be internalized by all projects. The managing structure will assist each project in setting up its own M&E system, making sure that similarities and complementarities are captured. Discussions and exchanges between all projects may be needed to ensure that all M&E systems are compatible and complementary and that all project managers and M&E officers understand what is expected in their area of M&E and indicators. A program M&E manual should come out of those discussions and exchanges. Everyone should acknowledge that this process is progressive and that the program M&E manual may be revised during the course of the program.
- Training sessions, discussions, and exchange workshops will be needed for M&E officers so that most problems are solved in a participatory way. Training needs may include sessions on the theory of change, the logical framework approach, data collection methods, data-processing methods,

bridge and specific software, data and results analysis, main M&E system feeding processes, M&E reporting, and the validation of M&E reports.

Conclusions

This chapter addresses an issue that many projects using a programmatic approach have experienced—namely, how to measure an entire program's achievement toward its strategic objective by using the data and information available from program projects. The USAID stocktaking exercise indicates that developing one-on-one M&E systems without at least minimal dialogue will never succeed. Exchanges have come up with a better way to solve the problem that includes building a program logical framework, building a main program M&E system to which projects' satellite M&E systems will be linked, and training M&E officers to manage and make the whole system work and achieve its goal.

It would probably be better to externalize the main M&E system management to get a better grasp of its entirety in terms of results and impacts. Doing so would solve the consolidation problem and help USAID get a better overview of what everyone is doing in a more coordinated way.

More methodological questions will have to be solved regarding results-based M&E, program outcomes, and impacts, which need to answer the "how" and "when" questions. Making all implementing partners own an M&E culture and engage in practices that are compatible with USAID's programmatic needs and requirements is important but will require that concessions be made.

Bibliography

Chelimsky, E. 1985. "Old Patterns and New Directions in Program Evaluation." In *Program Evaluation: Patterns and Directions*, ed. E. Chelimsky, 1–35. Washington, DC: American Society for Public Administration.

Donaldson, S. 2007. *Program Theory-Driven Evaluation Science: Strategies and Application*. London: Routledge Publishers.

Fitzpatrick, J. L., J. R. Sanders, and B. R. Worthen. 2003. *Program Evaluation: Alternative Approaches and Practical Guidelines*, 3rd ed. Boston: Allyn & Bacon.

Martens, D. 2008. *Transformative Research and Evaluation*. New York: Guilford Press.

Rist, R. C., and L. G. Morra Imas. 2009. *The Road to Results: Designing and Conducting Effective Development Evaluations*. Washington, DC: World Bank, Independent Evaluation Group.

Segsworth, R. V. 1990. "Policy and Program Evaluation in the Government of Canada." In *Program Evaluation and the Management of Government: Patterns and Prospects across Eight Nations*, ed. R. C. Rist, 21–36. Piscataway, NJ: Transaction Publishers.

Smith, N. L., and P. R. Brandon 2008. *Fundamental Issues in Evaluation*. New York: Guilford Press.

CHAPTER 9

Recognizing "Helping" as an Evaluation Capacity Development Strategy

Stephen Porter

The theory of "helping," as conceptualized by Edgar Schein (2009), provides a valuable guide to applying evaluation capacity development work. This chapter argues that when helping is applied, the results of evaluation capacity development are improved. This argument is based on reflections on implementing a community-based project monitoring system.

It is useful to think of the potential of helping in terms of the theater. Putting on a show requires a range of skills from the playwright, director, actors, and audience. In evaluation capacity development, all of these roles

---

The author is particularly grateful to (in alphabetical order) Addis Berhanu, Melusi Ndhlalambi, Phathisiwe Ngwenya, Ravi Ram, Patricia Rogers, and Rita Sonko for their comments on earlier drafts of this chapter, as well as to all of the field staff of AMREF who helped implement the monitoring system, especially Ntombi Mabindisa, Itumeleng Masia, Lovemore Mhuriyengwe, Juju Mlungwana, and Nonhlanhla Mthimkhulu. Thanks also go to all of the contributors to this book for their comments during the expert meeting at IDEA International

need to be played by those leading the change—the helpers. The theory of helping guides the roles of an evaluator: theory applier and model developer are equivalent to playwright and director; advocate and listener are equivalent to actors and the audience.

The beauty of Schein's theory is that it is practical. He states that the essence of relationships can be found in two components: economics and theater. These two components form the basis of a theory of helping. When enacted, the theory of helping guides evaluation capacity development to recognize and react to the relationships being built. For example, evaluators can have 10 evaluation texts on their desks. In implementing program evaluation systems, evaluation professionals may be able to use 15 percent of them. Given the law of diminishing returns, if there is a process to help project staff implement 20–30 percent of selected evaluation theory, larger returns would result from evaluation through improved implementation and use. Schein's theory of helping is one part of an effort to increase the volume of evaluation theory that can be put into practice.

The case to which helping is applied is that of the African and Medical Research Foundation's (AMREF) Bana Barona/Abantwana Bethu project, funded by the U.S. Agency for International Development/U.S. President's Emergency Plan for AIDS Relief (USAID/PEPFAR). Working in two districts in South Africa (Umkhanyakude in KwaZulu-Natal and Sekhukhune in Limpopo), the project aims to ensure that empowered children realize their rights, community-based partners operate effective childcare systems, and local municipalities implement national child policy. Both of these districts are "presidential nodes"—areas of extreme poverty in which indicators such as child and maternal mortality are worse than the national averages. In 2007, the monitoring system of the project was recognized to be in crisis. Eight months later the system was recognized as reporting reliable data. Explaining how this happened using helping as an analytical framework is the main subject of this chapter.

The chapter is structured as follows. The first section defines key terms. The second section describes helping and relates it to other areas of evaluation practice. The third section analyzes key points in the development of the monitoring systems over an 18-month period, using helping as a

---

in Quebec, especially Bali Andriantseheno and Mohammad Jaljouli for their insights. Finally, thanks to all staff from the community organizations, who are too numerous to mention, and the coordinators and data capturers who have stuck with the project and made monitoring happen: Zinhle Gumede, Sbongile Khumalo, Sibongile Mahalngu, Sello Makofane, Tacha Malaza, Joyce Mdluli, Sifiso Mfekayi, Dudu Mhlanga, Jabu Mlambo, Sindi Mthethwa, Zanele Mthombeni, Thembelihle Qwabe, and Phumzile Vilakazi.

reference point. The last section provides some concluding remarks and identifies areas for future work.

Definitions

In this chapter, evaluation is seen as "a key analytical process in all disciplined and practical endeavors" (Scriven 1991, 1). This means that evaluation is applicable to a range of activities from products to programs to personnel and beyond. Scriven (1991, 1) defines evaluation as a "process of determining the merit, worth and value of things." The definition of the Organisation for Economic Co-operation and Development (OECD) for good program evaluation (box 9.1), in alignment with Patton (2008), essentially asks "What? So what? Now what?" The question of "now what?" adds an extra dimension of utilization beyond Scriven's definition. Within this chapter, the OECD definition of evaluation is used because of this extra component. Monitoring is seen as a subset of evaluation. It is a different form of evaluation from, for example, impact evaluation. It helps answer different questions about a program.

A definition of helping, described in the next section, is "a basic relationship that moves things forward" (Schein 2009, ix). This definition covers a wide array of help, which can be placed on a continuum from formal to informal (Schein 2009). Informal help covers giving directions and behaving appropriately toward others (using good manners). Semiformal help involves payment and less personal involvement for some kind of service (purchasing a piece of equipment or providing assistance in using software). Formal help involves formal agreements and the provision of professional expertise (employing a lawyer, doctor, or consultant). In this

---

Box 9.1 The OECD Definition of Evaluation

According to the OECD, "an evaluation is an assessment, as systematic and objective as possible, of an ongoing or completed project, program, or policy; its design; implementation; and results. The aim is to determine the relevance and fulfillment of objectives, developmental efficiency, effectiveness, impact, and sustainability. An evaluation should provide information that is credible and useful, enabling the incorporation of lessons learned into the decision-making process of both recipients and donors."

Source: OECD 1991, 5.

chapter, the main types of help analyzed are semi-informal and formal help, where different roles and forms of inquiry become more pertinent than in informal help.

The Components of Helping

For Schein (2009, 29), the essence of relationships is contained in economics and theater. The "implication for would-be helpers is to become conscious of social economics and the social theater that we all live in, to think clearly about the helper role… and to assess what sort of currency and what kinds of values must be managed to make the relationship fair and equitable." This brief quotation sums up the links between helping and evaluation capacity development. The two components are interactive—the economic exchange is defined by the theatrical roles various players take on. For good evaluation capacity development, the helper needs to know what the demand is for evaluation, what values are to be measured, and how the relationships in the evaluation are to be managed.

In this section, the interaction of economics and theater are expanded upon and related to evaluation practice. The core principles of helping are summarized in box 9.2.

An alternative to helping is understanding the task only in terms of outputs. In practice, sometimes there is pressure to get things done. Success in developing evaluation capacity, for example, may be measured in the number of workshop participants or the budget spent. As Wiesner points out

---

Box 9.2   The Core Principles of Helping

Principle 1. Effective help occurs when both giver and receiver are ready.

Principle 2. Effective help occurs when the helping relationship is perceived to be equitable.

Principle 3. Effective help occurs when the helper is in the proper helping role.

Principle 4. Everything you say or do is an intervention that determines the future of the relationship.

Principle 5. Effective helping starts with pure inquiry.

Principle 6. It is the client who owns the problem.

Principle 7. You never have all the answers.

Source: Schein 2009.

in chapter 2, the effectiveness of evaluation is defined by how the demand is structured for improved results and performance. When short-term goals are the driving force, the direction is inappropriate and rewards are perverse; independent, credible, and useful evaluation capacity cannot be developed. Training and other short-term interventions are valid when the right conditions are established; when they are the sole measures of success, the process can become distorted. One way to establish the right conditions is to work through the social economics and theater involved in defining an intervention (Schein 2009).

The basis of exchange is interactions between people. When economic systems are built on trust and a sense that the exchanges are fair and equitable, confidence and efficiency within a system are supported (Mertens 2009). This basis of exchange can be seen as demand and supply; each side needs the other. The same is true with evaluation capacity development. On the demand side, a decision has been made that evaluation capacity needs to be developed and help has been sought. On the supply side are people who claim to be able to help strengthen evaluation capacity. To some extent, a social process underlies this exchange in which intangibles exist between the supply and demand. Appreciation of the intangibles in a relationship sometimes entails slowing down and seeking understanding rather than pushing to get things done. Schein (2009) recognizes that there is a power imbalance in the relationship between helper and helped that can intrinsically affect the success of an intervention and the changes (outcomes) that can be realized.[1]

Schein (2009) outlines 11 possible pitfalls in establishing a helping relationship, 5 for the client and 6 for the helper. These pitfalls result from genuine anxieties, inequalities, and ambiguities arising in exchange. For example, there can be resentment and defensiveness on the part of those being helped. These attitudes may be expressed as the withdrawal of some participants from a workshop at the last minute. The people supplying evaluation capacities (henceforth called *helpers*) are one up on those demanding it. They are the experts, upon whom, to some extent, the client is dependent. In this formal role of experts, helpers can dispense their wisdom prematurely (Schein 2009). They can uncover too much, shaming current efforts. A better approach is to be an appraiser, treating the program and the staff with respect in a process of dialogue. Schein (2009) moves beyond merely describing the social economics by defining and providing guidance on how to move between different helping roles to work as an appraiser rather than a bully.

Schein (2009, 48) points out that "at the beginning of any helping situation the appropriate roles and the rules of equity are inherently ambiguous . . . both the helper and the client have to develop an identity and choose a part to play." For undertaking evaluation capacity development, it is helpful to think of four roles. Schein (2009) delineates three helping roles: expert, doctor, and process consultant. The liberty is taken here to expand this to four roles to more closely match evaluation capacity development work by breaking out the role of process consultant into audience and actor. The four roles are as follows:

- Playwright: the expert evaluator producing conceptual frames and documents
- Director: the person who moves people through an evaluation system and deploys the tools of evaluation
- Actor: the person playing the evaluation role with the client, working through and demonstrating how things work in practice
- Audience: People watching others conduct the evaluation, giving appropriate praise through cheers and applause.

The helper plays all four of these roles, sometimes in the same day. Acting out tasks with the client leads to reflection; being the playwright means updating the documents. The helper can then return to the audience and watch others play out tasks, then become the director and try out new props and routines. The helper does not take on the problem but facilitates change. The client owns the problem.

It is in the selection of roles that the success of evaluation capacity development is defined. If the client is misread, the work of the helper will be misdirected. Supply will not meet demand. To help reduce the likelihood of miscommunication, Schein (2009, 66) defines *humble inquiry* as "the key to building and maintaining the helping relationship"; approaching evaluation capacity development using humble inquiry equips the helper to enter dynamic situations in "a supportive, ego enhancing way." Schein recommends starting out in a process consultant role as the most effective way to establish fairness and help uncover the real demand for help. In the above schema, this is equivalent to starting off as the audience before moving to humbly working through the current system with the client to create a climate for deeper understanding and trust in which both parties reveal more of themselves (Schein 2009).

Schein augments these roles by defining four forms of inquiry (table 9.1). It is this detail on roles and forms of inquiry that separates Schein from a number of other authors in development and evaluation work. Many authors indicate that having an interactive relationship is a good thing, but they leave it to the practitioner to muddle through how to do so.[2]

Table 9.1 Schein's Four Forms of Inquiry

Type of inquiry	Purpose	Roles	Sample questions
Pure	Build confidence and status of the client. Develop context to reveal anxiety, feelings, and information. Diagnose issues and plan for action.	Audience and actor. Evaluator watches issues play out and at times performs tasks with client (for example, checking data entry together for errors). This passive but attentive role should be balanced by "constructive opportunism," in which significant elements are revealed that enable another form of inquiry.	Tell me more.... When did this last happen? Can you give me some examples?
Diagnostic	Influence client's mental processes by focusing on issues other than the ones the client chose to report, in terms of feelings and reactions, causes and motives, actions taken or completed, and systemic questions.	Audience and actor. Evaluator watches issues play out and at times questions the work of the client (for example, asking why certain data errors keep occurring). This is a passive role, but the evaluator starts to be a more influential actor with the client.	How did you feel about that? (Feeling and reaction) Why do you think you are having this problem? (Cause and motive) What have you tried to do so far? (Action taken) How will your colleagues react? (Systemic question)
Confrontational	Articulate analysis by making suggestions and offering options.	Director and playwright. Actors are directed to take new positions. The playwright may write up and work on new processes.	Did that make you angry? Could you do the following?
Process oriented	Focus on interactions between client and helper to make client conscious of the helper's influence. This can be combined with the other forms of inquiry.	Director. Works through issues with actors, enabling examination of the relationship between the client and the helper.	Are we getting anywhere? Are my questions helping you?

Source: Author.

Recognizing the importance of social economics and theater in these four forms of inquiry provides an accessible and usable approach to developing relations for evaluation capacity development. Helping encompasses developing horizontal relationship between the helper and the helped rather than vertical teacher and student relations. It requires being aware of the small things that take place in the relationship between consultant and client. It guides moments when the helper senses that those being helped recoil because they are close to a change. Helping occurs when helpers become learners, recognizing the limits of their knowledge in a given context. Helping is about being humble about the limits of formal education. It is certainly not micromanagement, as there is give and take in working toward a shared direction. Sharing a journey is a central notion in helping, with a particular emphasis on the challenge of monitoring changes in someone's behavior within a change process.

Helping is largely about utilizing knowledge of social economics and theater in establishing human relationships to incrementally learn together by focusing on the interpersonal responses. Social economics are the expectations on either side of the exchange; theater mediates how the exchange happens. In working from this perspective, helping resonates with other writings on evaluation and development. In chapter 2, Wiesner highlights the importance of the demand for improved results. Boyle and Lemaire (1999) emphasize the importance of the location and structure of evaluation demand and supply. Toulemonde (1999) outlines a framework for thinking about the interaction between demand and supply for evaluation, mixed in with a little theater in describing the use of carrots, sticks, and sermons. Patton's (2008) description of situational responsiveness for evaluation is in many ways a description of how best to match the demand for evaluation while playing different roles. To enable this, Patton takes on the role of the active-reactive-interactive-adaptive evaluator. Chambers (2007) seeks to locate evaluative demand through participatory processes, employing theater through various participatory rural appraisal techniques.

In summary, helping is similar to and compatible with a large variety of research and evaluation practice in the way it describes developing relationships for change. Schein's theory of helping, though not as detailed as the work of Kusek and Rist (2004), Fetterman and Wandersman (2005), Gustavsen (2006), Senge and Scharmer (2006), or Mertens (2009), presents an accessible and usable set of procedures that can be applied to guide practice. The applicability of helping is its major advantage and the reason why it is applied as a prism through which to view the following case study.

Applying Helping to Understand an Evaluation of the Bana Barona/Abantwana Bethu Project

This section examines the experience of developing monitoring capacity in eight grassroots organizations in South Africa. Within a period of eight months, the system moved from being in crisis to being recognized by the donor (USAID/PEPFAR) as in good practice.

Often for things to change and for people to seek help, a crisis is required. This section analyses the implementation of the monitoring system using helping as a prism through which to view how progress was made. It suggests that when helping processes are followed, relationships are built, technical evaluation tools are easier to embed in project design, and results improve. This reflection is based on the experience of the author, who was the monitoring and evaluation (M&E) officer responsible for designing and implementing the system, and reflections from staff, partners, and consultants.

Phase 1: Pure Inquiry and Initial Attempts at Change

The project monitoring system was not started from scratch. Technically, the system was of a reasonable standard. A detailed M&E plan was in place, data-collection forms were being filled in, and a project database had been designed. Despite this, the project had no good idea of what its reach was, where key bottlenecks lay, or how well the project was being implemented. The project had just been reviewed, and data quality was found to be substandard. The system was suffering from a lack of regular help, given that no M&E officer had been in place for six months. The tools that had been developed were not embedded and were not evolving.

Guided by the project staff, the M&E officer tried to get an overview of the system across all sites, through site visits to community partners, review of documents, and interactions with the grant managers of this project, Pact. The outcome of this pure inquiry was the development of some supportive tools and the holding of a training workshop on these tools.

In terms of applying the theory of helping, three points stand out for this phase. First, the initiation of helping followed a process of pure inquiry, with the roles of audience and actor being assumed. From watching how the forms were processed, it was found that the manual counting of service delivery forms, the main method for ascertaining outreach, was a bottleneck. Manual counting was complicated by the need to differentiate between different levels of servicing (a child receiving three or more services was counted differently from a child receiving fewer than three) and different categories of services within a population of about 5,000 children. Doing this meant creating complicated tally charts and lists between which children moved as months progressed. Watching this process, asking questions, and meeting with Pact clarified the demand for evaluation, which came principally from the implementing agency, AMREF, but also from the community organizations, which wanted to reduce the manual counting effort and report their work accurately. AMREF's demand for evaluation stemmed from the need to get a better overview of the project and to report with confidence. This initial period, during which pure inquiry was undertaken, served as a solid foundation for moving forward. Relationships started to be built, system blockages understood, demand for evaluation located, and questions developed.

Second, technical evaluation skills helped frame the capacity development response. The evaluator rapidly moved between the roles of playwright, audience, and actor. In addition to listening, there was also a need to go back to the office to try to make sense of what had been heard. Two tools were valuable in this regard: the Barefoot Collective's (2009) way of thinking about organizational development and the development of a detailed data flow (figure 9.1) based on written and technical support from Pact (McCoy and others 2008).

Third, recognizing the broad phase of organizational development helped tailor the helping assumptions on which the systems development was based. The community organizations being partnered with are in a pioneering phase of organizational development. This phase is characterized by flexibility of approach, very few policies or procedures, a great deal of experimentation, and little planning (Barefoot Collective 2009). Given this new monitoring, processes can be introduced through consultation with a small group of people who work closely with the bottlenecks and are clear on why they demand change. This approach can be contrasted with a more rational type of organization, which is defined by clear leadership, professionalism, plans, policy, and systems (figure 9.2).[3] Within this type of organization, change can be more difficult, because negotiation is with higher-level personnel who "own" the system and may not be directly exposed to the bottlenecks and the demand for change (Barefoot Collective 2009). This knowledge helped direct the first conversations with the organizations and define who needed to buy into the system.

The data-flow process mapped the actions and paper flow that takes place from the identification of a child through the analysis and reporting of the entire project. Mapping the flow of data enabled a single language to be spoken about the bottlenecks in the process. From this mapping, a number of issues could be raised, in more diagnostic-style inquiry, within the project.

The use of these tools demonstrates that technical tools from practical evaluation texts need to underscore the helping process. Initial conversations and the building of relationships will not develop into useful evaluation capacity if, at some stage, the team does not take on the role of playwright.

Figure 9.1 Project Data Flow for AMREF Project

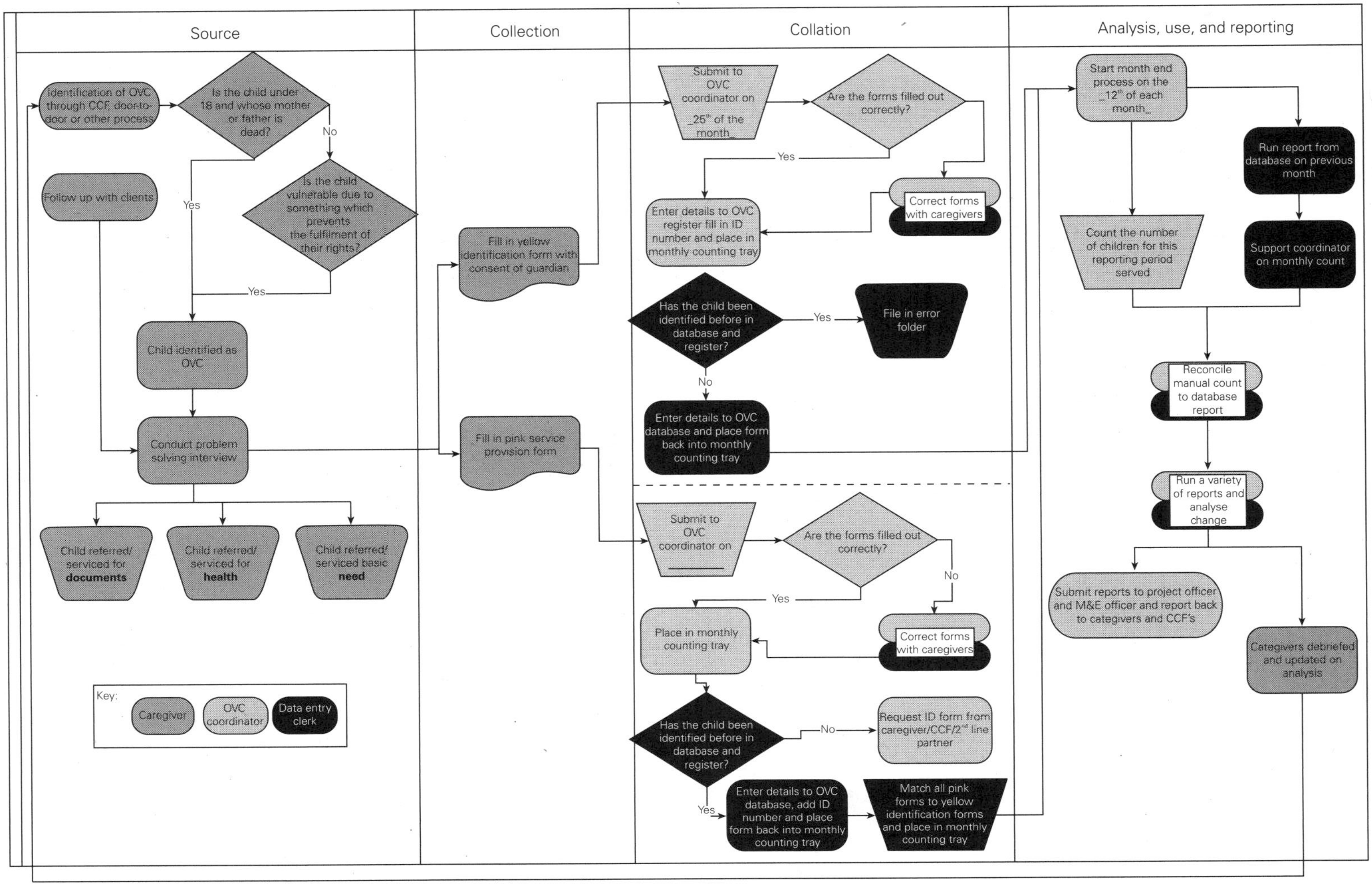

Source: AMREF 2008.

Figure 9.2 The Barefoot Collective's Phases of Organizational Development

Source: Barefoot Collective 2009.

What is necessary is not to be dominated by this form of approach but rather to use it once the process of pure inquiry has been undertaken in association with diagnostic inquiry.

Leading from these two processes—pure inquiry and initial redesign—a workshop was organized to discuss the analysis and support the implementation of the redesigned elements of the system. The workshop covered some basic definitions of M&E and worked through some of the new tools, such as the project data flow. The outcomes of the workshop were mixed. The data flow was taken up as a shared language of the monitoring system. The new manual counting procedures did not work, however. Looking back, it may have been a little early to move from a pure to a more directive, even confrontational, form of inquiry in relation to the counting procedures. The bottleneck was identified, but the context in which it operated was not fully understood. The problem came to light six weeks later, when the next phase of reporting was due and uncertainty over the numbers being reported remained.

In summary, evaluation capacity development workshops need to be tailored to meet issues in context. Doing so requires that the issues first be understood through pure inquiry and then translated into technical evaluation tools.

Phase II: Success after Learning from Others

In the second phase of developing the monitoring system, there was a marked shift in emphasis. More on-site support was provided in which issues were worked through with individuals and organizations. Inspiring this shift of approach was learning from the implementation of a computer database for tracking and monitoring, the Soweto Care System, which was being rolled out across AMREF's community partners at roughly the same time as the manual counting was being completed.[4] The database was a substantial improvement over the previous one. It is a well-designed, off-the-shelf system that reduces the work needed for manual counting and includes easy-to-use backup procedures, allowing the quality of the data to be assessed centrally. As feedback from the field stated, "the database is . . . crucial to us, to know how many children we're servicing at our finger tips. . . . the Soweto Care System was a lifesaver for us, because time was saved from manual counts."

It was not the tool itself but the way the system was rolled out that was all important for the development of evaluation capacity. The implementation of this database followed helping practice. Based on their experience from some 50 organizations, the consultants identified demand as the most important factor for successfully implementing the database. Demand for good data had already been established within AMREF and community partners. During the initial identification of issues in the existing monitoring system, the pure inquiry uncovered some issues regarding the previous database. A diagnostic inquiry process was then undertaken to develop a new database system that addressed these issues. This process culminated in program staff working jointly through the key fields of the Soweto Care System, which was then rolled out. In short, a number of the tools that can be associated with helping were used in the preliminary phases of implementing the system. Following the design workshop, the consultants moved to training at the site level. Training involved data capturers and at least one other member of staff. The consultants took on a director's role, directing others to do the acting, never "touching the keyboard" themselves.

Ongoing support was given by AMREF staff to embed the Soweto Care System and to implement other processes within the data-flow process (see figure 9.1). Managing the implementation of the system using the data flow took about 70 percent of the M&E officer's time for four months, with 50 percent spent on site. The on-site support process used the full range of inquiries described in table 9.1. Looking back at the work done on site, the diagnostic form was used about 50 percent of the time, pure inquiry was used about 30 percent of the time, and confrontational and process-oriented inquiry each took about 10 percent of the time. This support focused on spotting issues in data quality, advising on approaches to remedy issues with data collection, identifying gaps in filing, and verifying issues with the database. Some of the interactions in this process are shown in table 9.2. The confrontational and process inquiry approaches are valuable when used sparingly.

Evaluation capacity development is a change process, which, as Machiavelli pointed out in *The Prince*, can be difficult, doubtful, and dangerous. This means that at times there will be resistance to new behaviors. Sometimes an extra push is required to get through difficult issues. The process of evaluation capacity development in the Bana Barona/Abantwana Bethu project did not follow the helping methodology exactly. Mistakes were made and apologies proffered. At some times, helpers were viewed with joy; at others, they were viewed with suspicion and even anger. Given these reactions, helping can be emotionally draining.

At the operational level, seven of the eight community organizations that AMREF works with were generally committed to the process at any one time. The uncommitted organization changed: when one organization's commitment started to wane, extra effort was put in.

Table 9.2   Examples of On-Site Support Linked to Helping Roles and Inquiry

Interaction	Example	Type of inquiry	Role
Problem solving together	Working through a reconciliation of a database report to the forms. This was an incremental process that helped both parties understand issues in data entry.	Pure and diagnostic	Audience and actor
Laughing about issues	Developing personal relationships with the data capturers based on trust; seeing the humorous side of mistakes (for example, not taking double entries in the database too seriously)	Pure and diagnostic	Audience and actor
Taking issues raised about the database seriously	Recording issues identified by data capturers and escalating them to developers	Diagnostic	Director
Creating some competition between data capturers	Talking about how many entries different data capturers had achieved and using that metric as a yardstick to push people when commitment waned	Confrontational	Director
Pushing through on issues when resistance was met on challenges the community organization's staff could resolve	Repeating exercises of analysis in areas that were difficult, such as data analysis	Confrontational and process oriented	Director

Source: Author.

Help was given mainly to community partner organizations rather than AMREF internal staff. For AMREF staff, this was an unacceptable gap in their own capacity development. The demand for improved monitoring was immediate, as monitoring data had become a critical project issue. Attention was therefore focused at the source of data, the community. As a result, AMREF staff were not helped as extensively during this period.

The initial focus on the community had two unintended longer-term effects. First, information use is still patchy. Some organizations use it solely for reporting, whereas others are starting preliminary analysis of care worker caseloads. Second, because the help was focused at the operational level, the managers of community organizations became less involved. Had local staff been more fully involved, it is possible that they could have better supported information use while getting more buy-in from managers. A theory of helping needs to be applied at different levels of the organizations involved, even when they are at the pioneering phase. Different levels of demand for evaluation have to be taken into account. This speaks to the issues that Heider raises in chapter 5 with respect to establishing an enabling environment for evaluation.

Outweighing these issues are the outcomes. First, the quality audit revealed an immediate improvement in the data. Such an audit is an important process in judging the quality of the monitoring system for USAID/PEPFAR. Data quality is measured in the areas of validity, reliability, integrity, precision, timeliness, and completeness. At the head office level, precision rose from 23 percent to 100 percent, and reliability rose from 79 percent to more than 96 percent; at the community level, validity rose from 79 percent to 92 percent, and precision rose from 59 percent to 87 percent. In the short term, these improvements satisfied the demand for evaluation at the AMREF level. The evaluation team was able to enter into detailed discussions with partners about the way the project operates, how their staff work, and how the management support decisions—all based on up-to-date, reliable evidence.

Second, through the analysis of information, the project team refined its ideas, leading to a new results framework and innovative new projects. The emphasis is now on the importance of the coordination of care by different role players. The monitoring system aided the development of this focus area. Monitoring the project allowed the evaluators to analyze where referrals were breaking down between the community and the health system. In response, community-friendly tools were developed that are being used to support the coordination of care. One such tool is a poster, which was constructed through a process of pure and diagnostic inquiry as monitoring data became available. The poster shows services available within a South

African municipality. This poster is used in a number of ways. For example, care workers use it to discuss with children and guardians the kinds of rights they have. The poster relates to a referral list and could be used in conjunction with a list of telephone numbers of health service providers in local area.

In responding to the monitoring data, mobile technology is being explored for the purposes of developing community health information systems. Through better understanding of the challenges care workers face in working with health services, mobile technology has been developed to help smooth communication and information exchange. The partnerships developed over 12 months reached the stage at which mobile technology is now being piloted.[5]

This technology includes an area-based directory (a toll-free number that provides a directory of area-based service); a health announcements system, which provides SMS airtime to care workers to ask questions and interact with clinics and other service providers, such as schools; and a service rating system, in which clients text a number to rate their satisfaction with a service such as a clinic or police station. These changes demonstrate that although the helping roles of director, actor, and audience require intense communications, the playwright function of those developing evaluation capacity cannot be forgotten. Quiet periods are required to integrate technical evaluation theory into practice to move systems forward.

Coming out of the data analysis processes was recognition of the need to further support changes in quality at the source of information. Service providers are likely to have left formal education early. This means that training processes, forms, and data-collection methods need to be tailored to work with their knowledge base. A training process for implementing service protocols was implemented that drew on the lessons of the past; it was grounded in a solid diagnostic process, mentoring, follow-up, and the involvement of AMREF staff. Interestingly, the training for care workers integrated some of the main tenets of helping. Open-ended questioning and relationship-building techniques were integrated into the training. AMREF staff, care workers, and coordinators report that the training process changed the way they operate with clients, reinforcing the value of recognizing helping as an evaluation capacity development strategy.

This analysis shows that where helping was used, albeit unconsciously, successes in evaluation capacity development occurred. A number of other interventions, such as peer and external support to data capturers and coordinators, were undertaken during this phase to support the development of evaluation capacity. Because of space constraints, it is not possible to describe them here. However, where they were most successful, roles and inquiry were undertaken in the mode suggested by Schein (2009).

Phase III: Ongoing Work

Following from these successes, a third phase is now in process. It can be seen as ongoing development, where the realities of staff turnover and changing context become relevant. Working through a process of developing evaluation capacity does not have an obvious ending point. Systems are in flux, with mixed results. Perhaps the best that can be hoped for is the self-reorganization and regeneration of monitoring systems to higher and lower levels of functioning.

Country-level systems are now being implemented using results-based management (Kusek and Rist 2004) as a guiding frame. Although this is an organization-wide process, demand also comes from within the projects, which want to more systematically collate and analyze their experiences. Within this process, helping can assist with smoothing the recognized implementation and management issues related to results-based management systems (Perrin 1998; Kusek and Rist 2004). Helping is of use because it is specific about the roles that need to be played. For example, the role of actor and audience can be undertaken in the development of outcomes and indicators. Meanwhile, the director can reinforce the demand for the evaluation capacity. The playwright can work behind the scenes, translating the steps within a monitoring plan and framework.

This new phase also needs to be cognizant of some of the limitations of the helping approach, which requires ample resources (people, finances, and time). In addition to the full-time M&E officer, there was the Pact M&E adviser, the AMREF corporate M&E leader, and external advice from RMIT University in Melbourne. About $70,000 (3.6 percent of the budget) was expended over 12 of the 18 months. This money supported one full-time salary for eight months, data capturers, traditional workshops, additional expertise, the rollout of the Soweto Care System, and travel to the site for mentoring. Helping also takes a large amount of time in the field—potentially 40–60 percent, depending on the level of intensity. Given these resource requirements, there is a need to learn from the previous phases and be efficient in implementation.

New challenges exist in using helping in the ongoing development of monitoring systems. Relationships need to be defined, new staff oriented, and resources used effectively and efficiently. In this ongoing work, the roles of audience, actor, director, and playwright will still need to be performed by those developing evaluation capacity. This process will be more conscious of the theory of helping.

Conclusion

Using helping supported the integration of technical evaluation approaches to capacity development work through improved personal relationships. As the outcomes suggest, when the importance of social economics and social theater roles are recognized, even unconsciously, energy is released and new pathways for change opened.

Schein's (2009) theory of helping is useful in developing evaluation capacity. Helping does not replace other strategies and technical approaches; it complements them by assisting them in becoming operational in a given context.

Schein goes beyond other theorists in the accessible way in which he describes how to go about developing evaluation capacity. Schein is accessible to the organizational practitioner. He provides guidance on where to be opportunistic, charismatic, and systematic in a way that can complement other approaches.[6]

Useful work could be undertaken to further evaluate helping. Results for evaluation capacity development can be judged against the standards contained in three OECD evaluation principles: independence, credibility, and utility of evaluations (OECD 1991; see chapter 5 of this book). Using these principles to judge the effectiveness of helping could help go beyond this introductory case study by using a standard evaluative frame for capacity development strategies. In the longer term, doing so will help develop fuller knowledge about the strengths and limits of this approach and others.

One year after the end of the period of intense support, the monitoring system continues to be embedded and is to some extent self-regulating. Many of the gains were retained during a period of program staff changes, although progress was hampered. The robustness of the system and the use of helping are related. This connection will continue to be used in the ongoing development of monitoring systems within AMREF.

Notes

1. The recognition of imbalances in power resembles arguments in Akerlof (1970), where, because of differences in information, incentives exist to supply a lower standard of good. Although this issue is not explored in this chapter, it is an area that requires further exploration.

2. Mertens (2009) is less detailed in her guidance. Bawden (2006) is more academic, describing the "epistemic transformation" of the evaluator.
3. Two additional phases are described in Barefoot Collective (2009): the integrated and associative. These two are not described here, because they are not directly relevant to the case.
4. The database was developed by a volunteer placed with a community organization by Volunteer Services Overseas (VSO) in partnership with VX Company in the Netherlands as part of a corporate social responsibility initiative.
5. Two main partners are involved in the mobile technology project, Cell Life, based in Cape Town, and HIV911, based in Durban.
6. See chapter 5 of this book, on ordered chaos.

Bibliography

Akerlof, G. A. 1970. "The Market for 'Lemons': Quality Uncertainty and the Market Mechanism." *Quarterly Journal of Economics* 84 (3): 488–500.

AMREF (African Medical and Research Foundation). 2008. *How We Care: The Monitoring and Evaluation Plan September 2008–September 2010*. Nairobi: AMREF.

Barefoot Collective. 2009. *The Barefoot Guide to Working with Organisations and Social Change*. Cape Town: Barefoot Collective.

Bawden, R. 2007. "A Systemic Evaluation of an Agricultural Development: A Focus on the Worldview Challenge." In *Systems Concepts in Evaluation: An Expert Anthology*, ed. B. Williams and I. Iman, 35–46. Point Reyes, CA: Edge Press.

Boyle, R., and D. Lemaire, eds. 1999. *Building Effective Evaluation Capacity: Lessons from Practice*. Piscataway, NJ: Transaction Publishers.

Boyle, R., D. Lemaire, and R. C. Rist. 1999. "Introduction: Building Evaluation Capacity." In *Building Effective Evaluation Capacity: Lessons from Practice*, ed. R. Boyle and D. Lemaire, 1–19. Piscataway, NJ: Transaction Publishers.

Chambers, R. 2007. "Poverty Research: Methodologies, Mindsets and Multidimensionality." Working Paper 293, Institute of Development Studies, Brighton, United Kingdom.

Fetterman, D. M., and A. Wandersman. 2005. *Empowerment Evaluation Principles in Practice*. New York: Guilford Press.

Gustavsen, B. 2006. "Theory and Practice: The Mediating Discourse." In *Handbook of Action Research: Concise Paperback Edition*, ed. P. Reason and H. Bradbury, 17–26. Thousand Oaks, CA: Sage.

Kusek, J. Z., and R. C. Rist. 2004. *Ten Steps to a Results-Based Monitoring and Evaluation System: A Handbook for Development Practitioners*. Washington, DC: World Bank.

McCoy, L., N. Njeri, E. E. Krumpe, and R. Sonko. 2008. *Building Monitoring, Evaluation and Reporting Systems for HIV/AIDS Programs*. Washington, DC: Pact.

Mertens, D. M. 2009. *Transformative Research and Evaluation*. New York: Guilford Press, OECD/DAC.

OECD/DAC (Organisation for Economic Co-operation and Development/Development Assistance Committee). 1991. "DAC Principles for Evaluation of Development Assistance." Paris.

Patton, M. Q. 2008. *Utilization-Focused Evaluation*. Thousand Oaks, CA: Sage.

Perrin, B. 1998. "Effective Use and Misuse of Performance Measurement." *American Journal of Evaluation* 19 (3): 367–79.

Schein, E. H. 2009. *Helping: How to Offer, Give, and Receive Help*. San Francisco: Berrett-Koehler.

Scriven, M. 1991. *Evaluation Thesaurus*. Thousand Oaks, CA: Sage.

Senge, M., and C. O. Scharmer. 2006. "Community Action Research: Learning as a Community of Practitioners, Consultants and Researchers." In *Handbook of Action Research: Concise Paperback Edition*, ed. P. Reason and H. Bradbury, 195–206. Thousand Oaks, CA: Sage.

Toulemonde, J. 1999. "Incentives, Constraints and Culture-Building as Instruments for the Development of Evaluation Demand." In *Building Effective Evaluation Capacity*, ed. R. Boyle and D. Lemaire, 153–75. New Brunswick, NJ: Transaction Publishers.

CHAPTER 10

Building Capacities for Results-Based National M&E Systems

Gilles Clotteau, Marie-Helene Boily, Sana Darboe, and Frederic Martin

Monitoring and evaluation (M&E) is one of the five pillars of results-based management (RBM) in the public sector in developing countries, an approach also known as managing for development results (MfDR). The 2005 Paris Declaration on Aid Effectiveness highlighted the importance of improving the M&E of development interventions (High Level Forum 2005). The 2008 Accra Agenda for Action reinforced the commitment of developing countries and donors to demonstrate results through increased accountability and transparency toward the public (Third High Level Forum 2008). Developing countries committed themselves to improve the "quality of policy design, implementation and assessment by improving information systems." Developing countries and donors agreed to develop cost-effective results management instruments to assess the impact of development policies and adjust them as necessary. The MfDR team put

---

The authors thank their colleagues Juan Abreu and Sylvain Lariviere for their suggestions and comments on a draft of this chapter.

together a capacity scan toolkit to help assess progress in national MfDR capacity, including capacity in M&E (OECD/DAC 2009). Evaluation capacity building (ECB) has thus become a priority on the development agenda. In a context of limited public resources, particularly since the 2008/09 financial crisis, the importance of improving national capacities in M&E with approaches that are appropriate, economic, and sustainable cannot be overemphasized.

Two basic considerations are key. First, M&E covers a variety of subareas,[1] as indicated in figure 10.1 (there is no unique way in the literature of defining these subareas). Monitoring informs regularly on progress made in policy, program, and project implementation toward targets and provides information necessary to adjust those targets if necessary. It covers financial and physical implementation as well as outcome and impact indicators, without establishing linkages with the rest of the public value chain.

Evaluation is "the systematic and objective assessment of an ongoing or completed project, program, or policy and of its design, implementation, and results to determine the relevance and fulfillment of objectives,

Figure 10.1 Areas of Monitoring and Evaluation and Their Relationship with the Public Value Chain

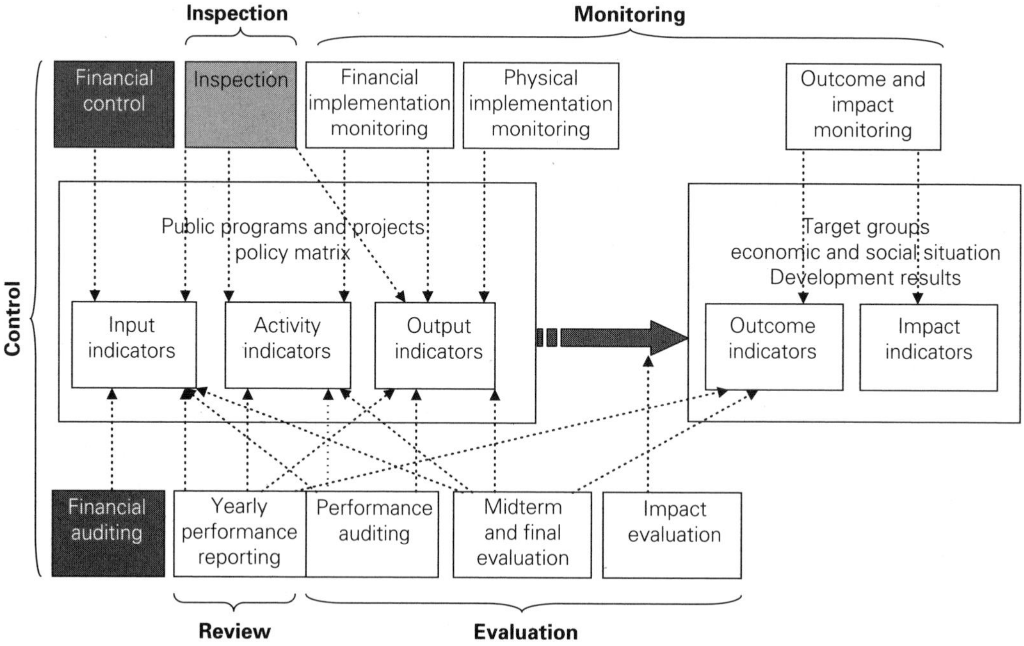

Source: Authors.

development efficiency, effectiveness, impact, and sustainability" (OECD/DAC, 21). It covers classical program and project evaluation, including baseline, midterm, and final evaluation, as well as impact evaluation.

Review through annual performance reports is more and more considered an intermediate area between monitoring and evaluation. Control usually has a financial focus, including financial control and financial audits. Inspection focuses on the completion of standards and rules related to processes and product quality.

Second, ECB is much wider than training. It involves strengthening or building M&E systems, especially country-based systems, so that M&E is regularly conducted and used by countries and organizations themselves (OED 2004).

Various ECB initiatives have been implemented, as components of development projects, through specialized institutions (such as the World Bank Institute [WBI] or the International Development Evaluation Association [IDEAS]) and through specific programs (such as the International Program for Development Evaluation Training [IPDET] or Paris 21). Unfortunately, few ECB initiatives have been subjected to thorough evaluation. The few significant evaluations made—such as the self-evaluation of Evaluation Capacity Development conducted in 2004 by the World Bank's Operations Evaluation Department (OED) (World Bank 2004) and the evaluation of the World Bank's project-based and WBI training conducted in 2007 by the World Bank Independent Evaluation Group (World Bank 2007)—have seriously questioned the effectiveness and impact of ECB initiatives, especially those based exclusively on training.

This chapter draws on the experience of a number of experts from the IDEAS network in supporting developing countries' institutions, programs, and projects in the implementation of RBM in Africa, Asia, and Latin America.[2] The first section outlines major challenges in ECB. The second section draws lessons learned and identifies some best practices in M&E capacity building along with recommendations for more effective and sustainable ECB.

Challenges in ECB

The field experience in a number of countries where IDEAS experts worked is consistent with the results of the few ECB evaluation studies conducted, i.e., mitigated results of capacity-building initiatives, especially through training-only solutions. The human, technical, and financial resource constraints for M&E vary across countries. Unfortunately, M&E

is not yet perceived systematically as a priority in terms of budget allocation. In many countries, M&E units are recent and only partially staffed or staffed with young professionals who may possess the technical know-how but do not necessarily have the experience and political clout to be listened to by technical departments and cabinets.

The lack of properly trained human resources in national institutions (in both number and capacity) not only directly affects their capacity to monitor and evaluate policies, strategies, and programs; it also increases the chances of poor decision making and misallocation of resources when letting nonexperts determine the kind of M&E system, training, and technical assistance needed by national institutions. In addition, this shortage of qualified manpower can reduce opportunities for the transfer of know-how: a reduced staff can make it difficult for staff to get involved in the actual design and implementation of the M&E system and lead to a lack of interest or fear of additional workload. Most of the time, this situation will result in the solution being almost entirely developed by external consultants, limiting ownership—and therefore the sustainability—of the M&E system.

M&E units, along with many public service units, face a major issue of staff turnover. This unfortunate situation comes from a number of factors, including political changes resulting in frequent staff rotation and reassignment; weak financial incentives for civil servants; insufficient integrity and professionalism in hiring and evaluation, which discourages real professionals from remaining in this institutional environment; and the brain drain by international organizations and donor agencies. The end result is the destabilization of already weak institutions and the tendency to come back to square one with the renewal of M&E unit staff.

In fragile states, the situation is complicated by donors who develop project implementation units (PIUs) outside the public sector. These institutional arrangements may help deliver results in the short run and help control financial leakage, but they prevent the development of sustainable national delivery mechanisms and M&E capacity within ministries. In such a donor-driven context, central access to information and coordination of M&E processes by the sector ministries and the ministry of planning become major challenges.

The design of ECB may be faulty. In some cases, M&E was not part of program or project design but was added on later, creating gaps, such as the lack of a systematic baseline at the start of the program or project. Insufficient attention may have been paid to the organizational context and institutional constraints, leading to unrealistic and overambitious objectives. Kusek and Rist (2004) rightly insist that the starting point for the design and implementation of a results-based M&E system should be a readiness assessment, including the validation of the commitment of the organization's leaders to the RBM approach.

In many cases, capacity-building strategies and plans, including a diagnosis of the situation and a needs assessment, were not developed as a component of the M&E system implementation. The result is little knowledge of potential weaknesses and areas of improvement in M&E capacity and an inadequate design of capacity-building activities, which often look like a long list of uncoordinated short-term capacity-building activities.

The selection process of participants to training can also be a problem. In some cases, participants do not have to make much effort to mobilize funds for their participation and are chosen based on their personal relationships with high-level officials rather than the organization's needs; the specific mandate the participant has to fulfill (for example, at strategic level or at operational level); and the person's skills. Such a person may be more interested by institutional tourism than training contents.

Capacity-building activities through training programs tend to have a short-term perspective (one to four weeks at most), with very limited follow-up to ensure the application of new knowledge and techniques in participants' day-to-day work. In many cases, participants come back enthusiastic about what they learned during the training but do not know how to apply their newly acquired knowledge once in the workplace. Without proper follow-up, adequate incentives, and resources for implementation of learning, the daily grind and old habits quickly win over the desire for change, and the temporary capacity gains vanish over time.

Unfortunately, even when capacity-building plans are developed, they are often not the result of a thorough needs analysis and do not factor in the institutional environment (human and material resources) in which the plan will be implemented. In the case of capacity building through the implementation of results-based M&E systems, it is critical to put the institutional environment at the center of the process if a sustainable M&E system is to be implemented.

There is often a limited supply of good in-country training. In many countries, the availability of institutions or experts with adequate training capacity coupled with regional or international experience is insufficient to enable relevant and practical transfer of know-how to participants. National and regional experts may not have sufficient analytical and technical evaluation skills or may not be familiar with lessons learned and best practices from other parts of the world; they may also lack pedagogical skills. International experts brought in from the outside usually have the technical know-how, but they may lack sufficient understanding of institutional and cultural realities to propose appropriate and realistic solutions. Both types of experts may be hampered by a narrow disciplinary approach rather than the approach taken by multidisciplinary teams. The lack of field experience also translates into limited relevance of training material and high training costs for governments with limited resources.

The situation is often particularly difficult in non-Anglophone countries. Non-English speaking professionals enjoy very limited access to good M&E training and information sources, because most resources are available only in English. This problem affects Latin America and particularly Francophone Africa.

Little knowledge of the institutional environment and the inability to identify champions in the organization can also lead to resistance to change, out of fear of the unknown. For instance, in the process of implementing results-based M&E systems, resistance can reflect fear of traditional evaluation schemes, in which "results" were used to blame rather than as a feedback mechanism to enhance performance.

Finally, training results are rarely monitored and evaluated. In a results-based perspective, capacity-building plans should include an M&E component to monitor and evaluate not only outputs (number of trainees, number of trainings) but also outcomes (that is, did training change the behavior and performance at the individual and institutional levels). This is seldom done. It is easier and less time-consuming to report on outputs and direct outcome indicators, such as the level of satisfaction of the participants at the end of the training, than to measure actual outcomes and impacts.

Lessons Learned and Best Practices

The ECB strategies seek to realize four basic objectives:

- Increase the relevance of M&E for policy makers to stimulate their demand for M&E products.
- Improve the quantity and quality of the supply of M&E products.
- Ensure the cost-effectiveness of M&E products.
- Promote the sustainability of M&E systems and institutional arrangements.

The strategies presented below should be considered as complementary building blocks.

Integrating ECB into an M&E System

Training in M&E should not be conducted for the sake of training but rather considered as a catalyst for the implementation of a results-based M&E

system. Anchoring ECB in the actual implementation and improvement of a results-based M&E system helps maintain a sense of the ultimate purpose of ECB—namely, contributing to better public policies and programs. Making progress in the implementation of the results-based M&E system provides an opportunity for learning by doing, thereby reinforcing and building capacities within an organization.

The process of designing and implementing an M&E system should be progressive, as different components are implemented gradually. There is no ready-made, off-the-shelf solution; the approach must be adapted to needs and the existing M&E systems. However, a roadmap is provided by the now standard reference in the field, *Ten Steps to a Results-Based Monitoring and Evaluation System* (Kusek and Rist 2004) (figure 10.2). Tailor-made to the institutional and political context, the needs assessment, the existing M&E system, and available resources, this roadmap has been used in several mandates conducted by IDEA Institute experts and has been proven to provide a relevant and effective framework for ECB.

A good illustration is the design and implementation of a results-based monitoring system at Mexico's Ministry of Social Affairs of Mexico (SEDESOL). Best practices from this experience included the following:

- Active involvement of the organization's personnel in the implementation of the M&E system to reinforce the know-how within the organization and ensure the system's sustainability. Staff involved in the process of implementing the system served as a pool of resources for other programs within the ministry as well as for the development of the

Figure 10.2 Ten Steps to Designing, Building, and Sustaining a Results-Based M&E System

1. Conducting a readiness assessment
2. Agreeing on outcomes to monitor and evaluate
3. Selecting key indicators to monitor outcomes
4. Baseline data on indicators—where are we today?
5. Planning for improvement—selecting results targets
6. Monitoring for results
7. The role of evaluations
8. Reporting findings
9. Using findings
10. Sustaining the M&E system within the organization

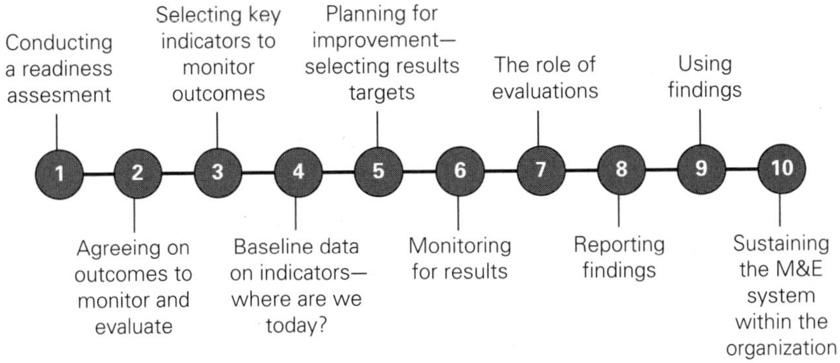

Source: Kusek and Rist 2004.

nationwide M&E system being designed and implemented by the Ministry of Public Service (SFP) with the support of the National Council for the Evaluation of Social Development Policy (CONEVAL) and the Ministry of Finance (SHCP).
- Involvement of all stakeholders at all stages of the process of designing and implementing the M&E system to guarantee their support and ensure the success of the project, resulting in greater sustainability.
- Design and implementation of an M&E system through a pilot in 4 of 27 programs to learn from the experience, while building the organization's capacities for expanding the system, resulting in a reduced reliance on external resources later on.
- An ECB approach based on RBM principles, including a needs assessment, the formulation of M&E capacity-building strategies, the design and implementation of M&E capacity-building action plans, and the M&E of the implementation of capacity-building strategies, action plans, and training effectiveness.

Lessons learned include the following:

- It is important to understand the needs of all stakeholders in terms of data, information systems, reports, and so forth. Often clients themselves do not know exactly what their specific needs are. Either they consider information as a free good and have infinite needs or they have a narrow perspective based on their short-term needs linked to their role in the organization, with little concern for end results. It is the consultant's responsibility to help clients identify their specific needs and suggest, if necessary, different options as a starting point.
- Getting a good grasp of the existing M&E system can be challenging, especially in middle-income countries, where ministries have developed a variety of M&E mechanisms and information systems that are scattered in various parts of the organization, often with little coordination, harmonization, or even information dissemination. For example, the diagnostic made at SEDESOL in 2004 identified 33 information systems in the organization.
- The diagnostic should try to evaluate M&E capacity within the organization and build a training plan as a central component of M&E system implementation to ensure the involvement of personnel throughout the process and to maximize the number of "champions" while limiting the number of potential "opponents."
- Program personnel involved in the design and implementation of the M&E system can sometimes see the new system as a source of additional responsibilities and work, which can cause some frustrations or lack of

interest. Therefore, incentives should be planned to guarantee full participation of stakeholders and personnel throughout the process.
- Enhancing capacity in M&E requires looking at capacity in the other pillars of RBM.[3] Problems encountered at the M&E level often result from faulty design and implementation in other RBM pillars. The SEDESOL program logical frameworks had to be revised for logic; the choice of performance indicators meeting the CREAM+ criteria (clear, relevant, economic, adequate, monitorable; + indicates that the criteria include an added value); and the choice of targets meeting the SMART (specific, measurable, achievable, relevant, timebound) criteria. In many countries, M&E is not considered seriously by many stakeholders until results bear consequences on future budget allocations, which implies linking the M&E process with the budget preparation process.
- M&E goes far beyond technical skills. To act as change agents, M&E officers must have leadership and communication skills to help convince their colleagues in technical departments as well as the ministry cabinet of their self-interest in implementing RBM and push for further reform implementation.

Based on this and other experiences, a checklist of key factors to consider in the design and implementation of results-based M&E system has been developed (table 10.1).

Clearly Identifying the Desired ECB Results

The expected results from ECB should be clearly identified and consensus built among stakeholders. The standard analytical tool is the result chain presented in figure 10.3. Performance indicators need to go beyond outputs to cover outcomes and, whenever measurable, impacts. What matters in the end is that M&E reports and control panels be accessible to decision makers at the strategic (cabinet) level and the operational (program and project) level and that they be used for policy making, program management, and the determination of future budget allocations.

Decision makers are often confused about results. In Senegal, there was much talk about results. Training workshops helped clarify what results really meant at various levels. For example, the director of primary and secondary education realized that classrooms built and teachers trained were outputs of construction projects and teacher training but inputs for his more strategic level. He also had to be concerned with graduation, dropout, and repetition rates; output indicators; and the success of students at the next

Table 10.1 Checklist of Questions to Consider in Designing and Implementing a Results-Based M&E System

Phase	Key questions
Diagnostic—readiness assessment	1. Has the assessment been conducted? Does it need to be updated? If so, does the update follow step 1 of the 10-step methodology? Was the assessment participatory? Internally, did it involve a strategic level and an operational level, technical departments along with the M&E unit, and a regional as well as a central level? Externally, did it include other ministries (especially planning, economy and finance, public service); parliament; civil society; international organizations; and major donors? 2. Have all actors involved in M&E in the organization and other relevant public organizations been identified and their activities and results characterized? 3. Have all major M&E tools and information systems used for M&E by the organization and other relevant public organizations been identified and characterized? 4. If not, what kind of training is needed to conduct a participatory readiness assessment based on the organization's internal resource skills?
Design of the M&E system	1. To what extent can the existing system be capitalized on to design a results-based M&E system? 2. If the system has been designed, does it follow steps 2–7 of the 10-step methodology? 3. To what extent has the design of the M&E system been participatory? 4. Have the major users of the M&E system been clearly identified and their demands in terms of M&E results narrowed down? 5. To what extent will the proposed M&E system respond over time to the needs of the target groups? 6. To what extent are the components of the proposed M&E system coordinated technically and institutionally? 7. To what extent can the proposed M&E system be handled with existing human resources? Have the training and technical assistance needs for M&E implementation been assessed? 8. Are there minimum workable institutional set-ups and incentives for the proposed M&E system to be sustainable? 9. What are the financial requirements of the proposed M&E system over the next three to five years, and can those resources be secured? 10. If the system has not yet been designed, what kind of training and technical assistance is needed to design the system in a participatory way based on the organization's internal resources?
Implementation of the M&E system	1. Is there a clear work plan or at least a roadmap for M&E implementation? 2. If a results-based M&E system is being implemented, at what stage is the institution in the process? 3. Does the system follow steps 8–10 of the 10-step methodology?

continued next page

Table 10.1 *continued*

Phase	Key questions
	4. To what extent is the implementation of the M&E system participatory?
	5. To what extent does the M&E system respond to the needs of the target groups?
	6. To what extent are the components of the M&E system coordinated technically and institutionally?
	7. To what extent can the M&E system be implemented with existing human resources and current training and technical assistance provided?
	8. Is the institutional set-up functional? Are incentives reasonable?
	9. Is the M&E system properly financed?
	10. If the system has not yet been implemented, what kind of training and technical assistance are needed to implement it in a participatory way based on the organization's internal resources?

Source: Authors.

Figure 10.3 ECB Public Value Chain

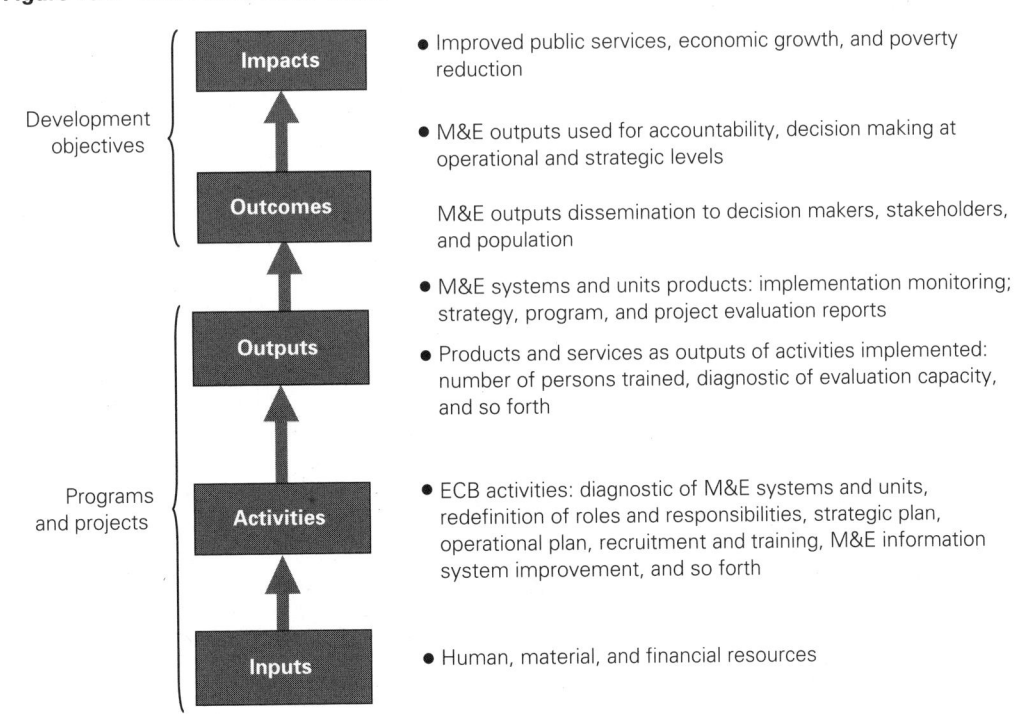

Development objectives:
- Impacts — Improved public services, economic growth, and poverty reduction
- Outcomes — M&E outputs used for accountability, decision making at operational and strategic levels; M&E outputs dissemination to decision makers, stakeholders, and population

Programs and projects:
- Outputs — M&E systems and units products: implementation monitoring; strategy, program, and project evaluation reports; Products and services as outputs of activities implemented: number of persons trained, diagnostic of evaluation capacity, and so forth
- Activities — ECB activities: diagnostic of M&E systems and units, redefinition of roles and responsibilities, strategic plan, operational plan, recruitment and training, M&E information system improvement, and so forth
- Inputs — Human, material, and financial resources

Source: Adapted from OECD 2004.

Building Capacities for Results-Based National M&E Systems

education level, placement rates, and the development of self-employment for graduates.

Key results should also be accessible to other stakeholders for accountability. In Senegal, a wealth of M&E data was available, but there was little coordination or validation by the Direction of Statistics and much frustration on the part of civil servants and civil society with the limited access to results and reports. A new National Agency for Statistics and Demography was established with greater autonomy and power, along with a national Web-based statistical information system.

Using the results chain as an analytical framework helps identify four levels of training evaluation with corresponding means of verification (table 10.2).

Key Factors for Effective Training

Training is an important component of an ECB strategy. As the World Bank (2007, 35) notes:

> One of the strongest determinants of training success is the organizational context in which training is done. For training to be successful, participants must have the resources and incentives to implement acquired skills and knowledge. Where these resources and incentives are not in place prior to training, training must be accompanied by properly sequenced interventions in order to address organizational and institutional constraints.

Experience shows that demand-driven capacity-building activities are usually more sustainable and effective than activities that are not driven by demand. They tend to respond to more specific felt needs, and participants in such training activities tend to be more motivated to learn and then apply what they learn. A demand-driven approach implies designing the training program on the basis of the needs identified in a participatory

Table 10.2 Levels of Training Evaluation

Level	Measure	Means of verification
1	Participant satisfaction	End-of-course participant questionnaires
2	Learning outputs	Posttests, sometimes compared with pretests
3	Performance change outcomes	Observation, interviews, and surveys of participants, colleagues, and supervisors
4	Organizational impact and results	Comparisons with baseline organizational performance measures, surveys, and interviews with key informants

Source: World Bank 2007.

way during the diagnostic and readiness assessment. Figure 10.4 suggests a structured approach for measuring the performance gap and assessing training needs that has been successfully used by the IDEA Institute.

A structured approach also requires carefully selecting participants for each kind of training activity. An ECB plan should consider various

Figure 10.4 A Structured Approach to Assessing Training Needs

Phase 1: Performance gap measurement

- Organization objectives → Desired performance (targets)
- Environment → Current performance (baseline)
- Gaps

Possible causes: Insufficient
- Motivation
- Expectations known and understood
- Management support
- Staff support
- Information, tools, resources available
- Feedback given
- **Competencies**

Possible solutions:
- Increased incentives
- Better documentation
- Staff coaching
- Standard operating procedures revision
- Resource allocation
- Work conditions
- **Training**

Is training part of the solution? — No → Propose other solutions; Yes ↓

Phase 2: Training needs assessment

- Desired competencies by target group, category, and level (targets)
- Current competencies by target group, category, and level (baseline)
- Gaps → Training needs by target group and competencies → Training objectives → Training design

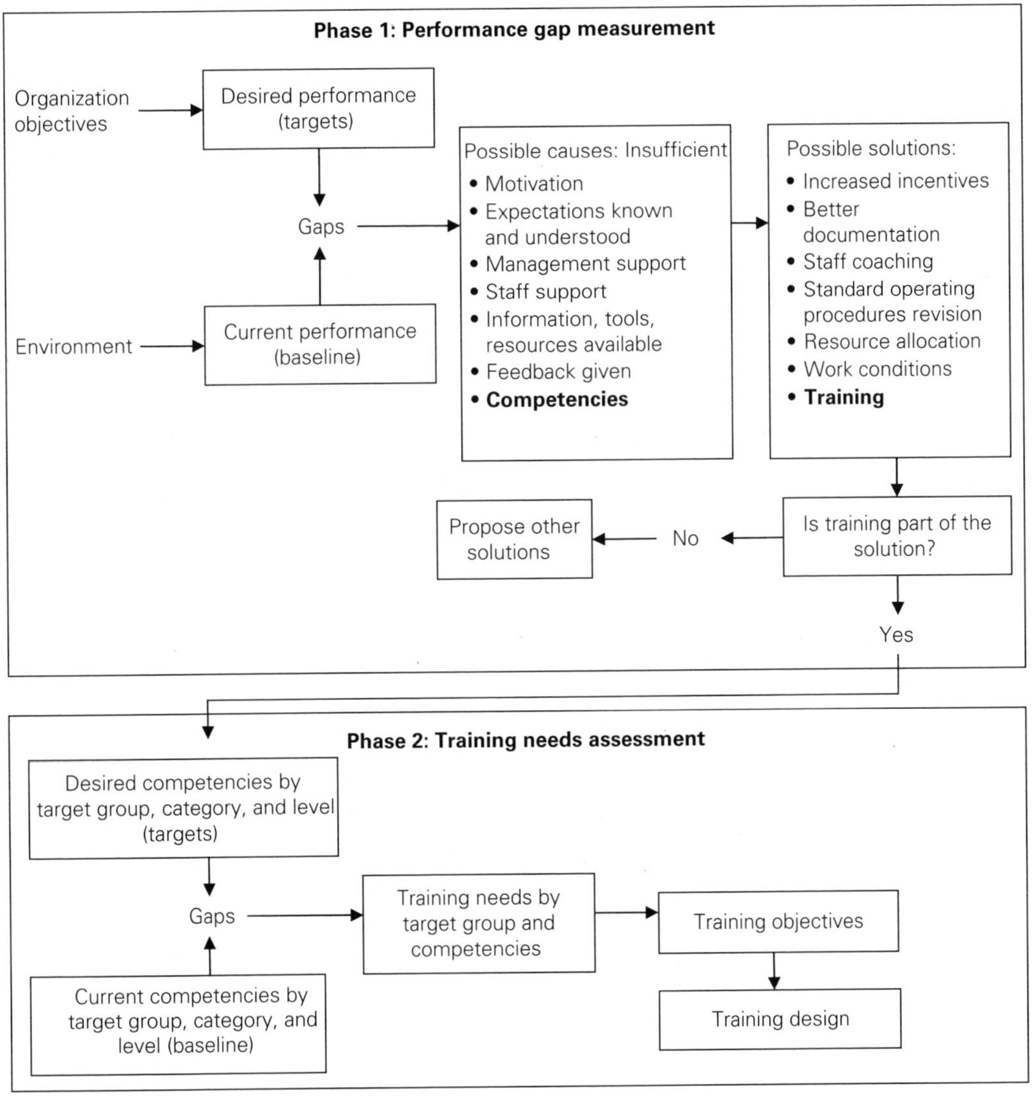

Source: Adapted from Bureau 2000.

kinds of training activities that fit with various categories of participants, objectives, and constraints. Strategic-level participants want to focus on the big picture and have little time. M&E professionals want to understand concepts and master the tools and techniques. The IDEA Institute has helped organize high-level sensitization and discussion seminars of one to two days with small numbers of cabinet members, members of parliament, and donor heads of cooperative organizations. For professionals who want official recognition of their skills through a North American university diploma and have more time and the required financial resources, it offers, with the Université Laval, a master's certificate in RMB, including a certificate in M&E. To facilitate access, this course is offered in various locations (Dakar for francophone Africa, Dar es Salaam for anglophone Africa and Asia, and Panama for Latin America and the Caribbean) in English, French, and Spanish. For professionals who have limited time and money, the institute offers tailor-made technical workshops in its regional centers or in-country on specific M&E topics based on demand. Most workshop participants secure their own funding. Demand is growing, suggesting that a market-driven approach can work.

Training a critical mass of civil servants in M&E offers a number of advantages for a government. It helps deal with staff turnover and attrition to maintain a minimum ECB in M&E units. It creates a common approach among participants who share the same vision, language, and tools and can better communicate among themselves within a community of practices. In several countries, the government asked each ministry to put aside a budget line on capacity building in RBM (specifically M&E) and send their executives to the same training to create this critical mass, thereby creating momentum for moving ahead with RBM-related reforms.

One key factor for effective training is to select a pedagogical strategy that is adapted to the context, the participants, and the intended objectives. The experience of the IDEA Institute is that participants appreciate the use of a variety of pedagogical methods, including a minimum of lectures and a maximum of participatory methods. Training in M&E requires trainers skilled in M&E with both field work experience and pedagogical skills. The IDEA Institute, in association with Université Laval, uses an approach in which a set of competencies is identified for each training target group along with current and desired level of mastery for each competency. A training plan is then designed to establish the linkages between the various training modules and their contribution to competency enhancement.

Executive training requires moving away from theory and concentrating on hands-on training. This does not mean that training becomes a collection of anecdotes: mastering the 10 steps and learning how to use evaluation tools is a must for relevance and credibility. Practical training means

- using many examples
- presenting and discussing success stories through debates with experienced professionals in working group sessions
- helping trainees develop their own M&E systems and tools during training
- taking trainees on study tours (for example, a delegation from Vietnam came to Canada to learn more about municipal performance measurement; a delegation from Benin went to Panama to learn more about M&E of large projects).

Complementary training strategies include participating in a community of practices and international association meetings, such as the IDEAS global conference.

The choice of trainers is another key factor for effective training. All training processes are based on the capacity of the trainer to motivate trainees to open their minds to new concepts, tools, and approaches. Doing so requires a high level of education, a broad range of experience in a variety of institutional and cultural contexts, pedagogical skills, and human skills to handle high-level participants from a variety of backgrounds. Academics tend to focus on advanced technical subtleties of interest to them and their peers that are far too advanced to be relevant for most M&E professionals working in developing countries. Long-term consultants and practitioners tend to talk about their own valuable experiences but may be outdated on methodologies and information technology. Civil servants and national and regional consultants may have trouble distancing themselves from the specificities of the environment and the tools they know, are not necessarily experts in a variety of modern M&E tools and approaches, and may lack the pedagogical skills required of professional trainers. A solution is often to use a team of complementary trainers and make sure that they work together, so that the training is not a piecemeal collection of individual contributions.

One key challenge for the M&E community is how to increase accessibility to quality training in M&E. IPDET trains about 275 participants a year in Canada. This Cadillac of training is doing an outstanding job of training top-notch M&E professionals who will act as champions of change in their organizations upon their return. However, most M&E officers cannot go to IPDET in Canada. One way of bringing training to them is to replicate IPDET. Mini–IPDET courses are offered in various countries in English by IPDET cofounders Rist and Morra Imas (for example, SHIPDET in Shangai and CzechDET in Prague).

Another solution is to build a training program around a "training of trainers" formula. The IDEA Institute recently used such a formula in the Democratic Republic of Congo. For the first phase of two weeks, IDEA experts trained 50 participants. The best were selected for a second phase of training of trainers, deepening their understanding and developing their pedagogical skills. The newly trained trainers gave the training, with technical backup and advice from the IDEA experts. The end result was that, in six weeks, 100 participants and 5 trainers were trained.

A third solution is to develop partnerships with regional and national training institutions to create executive training professional programs leading to certifications. The IDEA Institute has developed a partnership on procurement systems with the Ecole Nationale des Régies Financières (ENAREF), a school based in Ouagadougou, in Burkina Faso, with a mandate to train public finance officers for all eight member countries of the Union Economique et Monétaire Ouest Africain (UEMOA), as well as a partnership on project management with the Tanzania Public Service College in Dar es Salaam, Tanzania.

Another factor for effective training is the follow-up to training. In the IDEA experience, the most effective and sustainable strategy is to design and implement an ECB project over the medium run (two to three years), in which the institute accompanies a national team with a combination of training, technical assistance, and support to data quality and information systems. Activities are organized according to a flexible roadmap that includes the production of intermediate outputs required from the national team, such as progress on policy matrix targets to prepare for World Bank biannual review missions, evaluations of national development plans and Poverty Reduction Strategy Papers, major program impact evaluation studies, yearly performance reviews in line with budget preparation, and Medium-Term Expenditure Framework updating processes. Usually, the program starts with training, then provides technical support missions, then provides on-the-job training. Based on its experiences, IDEA has created a checklist of quality criteria for effective training (table 10.3).

Training is an important component of ECB, but ECB involves an array of other mechanisms as well. These include improving M&E information systems and knowledge management and conducting sensitization and policy dialogue forums.

Table 10.3 **Checklist of Criteria for Effective Training**

Issue	Quality criteria
Training needs assessment and training design	1. Has a training needs assessment been conducted? 2. Has the training design been based on the needs assessment? 3. Has the training design clearly identified target groups, training objectives, and expected results in terms of progress on specific competencies? 4. Are the training targets SMART (specific, measurable, achievable, relevant, timebound)?
Participant selection	1. Have selection criteria been established? 2. Are they professional? 3. Are they consistent with the training objectives? 4. Have participants been selected according to the selection criteria? 5. Have they been involved in securing funding for the training?
Selection of trainers	1. Do the trainers possess the required educational background? 2. Do they possess the required field experience in a variety of institutional and cultural contexts? 3. Do they possess the pedagogical skills for the training?
Pedagogical strategy	1. Has a pedagogical strategy been clearly outlined? 2. If so, does it use a competency-based approach? 3. Does it combine a variety of training methods? 4. Does it emphasize practical applications and active participation by participants? 5. Is it adapted to the target group's interests, skills, and time constraints?
Evaluation and follow-up	1. Is progress made by trainees assessed during or at the end of the training? How is it assessed? 2. What levels of evaluation are being conducted (see table 10.2)? 3. Is the training part of a more comprehensive ECB project? 4. What kind of follow-up is given to the training? When? For how long? 5. Can some participants act as trainers in the future? Does the training include explicit training of trainers activities?

Source: Authors.

Improving M&E Information Systems and Knowledge Management

Information systems can be a very good entry point for ECB. They focus on data collection, data processing and analysis, data quality, and information dissemination and use—all elements with major implications for a comprehensive evaluation and its credibility. Beyond these obvious elements, implementation of a results-based M&E information system can facilitate progress on several key elements of a results-based M&E system.

Figure 10.5 presents a best practice nine-step methodology to implement a results-based M&E information system based on various IDEA Institute experiences. This methodology fits well with the 10-step methodology.

A second best practice is a series of new applications being developed, such as control panels. The IDEA Institute has developed control panels at the sector level (for Mexico's Ministry of Social Affairs, for example) and at the program level (for Panama's National Land Registration Program, for example). It has also developed an attractive information solution, called e@satisfaction, which offers a cost-effective way to measure, process, and analyze data on quality in service delivery on an ongoing basis and feed it back to decision makers rapidly over the Web in a user-friendly way that helps them better pilot programs and projects.

A third best practice is the establishment of knowledge management and learning units in many organizations. Many national and international organizations have realized that many of their experiences, lessons learned, and best practices were not shared among the members of the same organization and were lost when those members left the organization. These units can play a key role in keeping and expanding an institutional memory by collecting information on M&E, documenting it with meta-data, storing it

Figure 10.5 Nine Steps to the Implementation of a Results-Based M&E Information System

1. Readiness assessment and diagnosis of existing M&E system
2. Review of existing program and project logframes and their articulation
3. Evaluation of the demand and information needs
4. Data quality assessment
5. Design and implementation of the data collection and data entry component
6. Design and implementation of the database component
7. Design and implementation of the analysis component (BI tools)
8. Preparation of user and operation manuals and training
9. Finalization of pilot experience and expansion plan

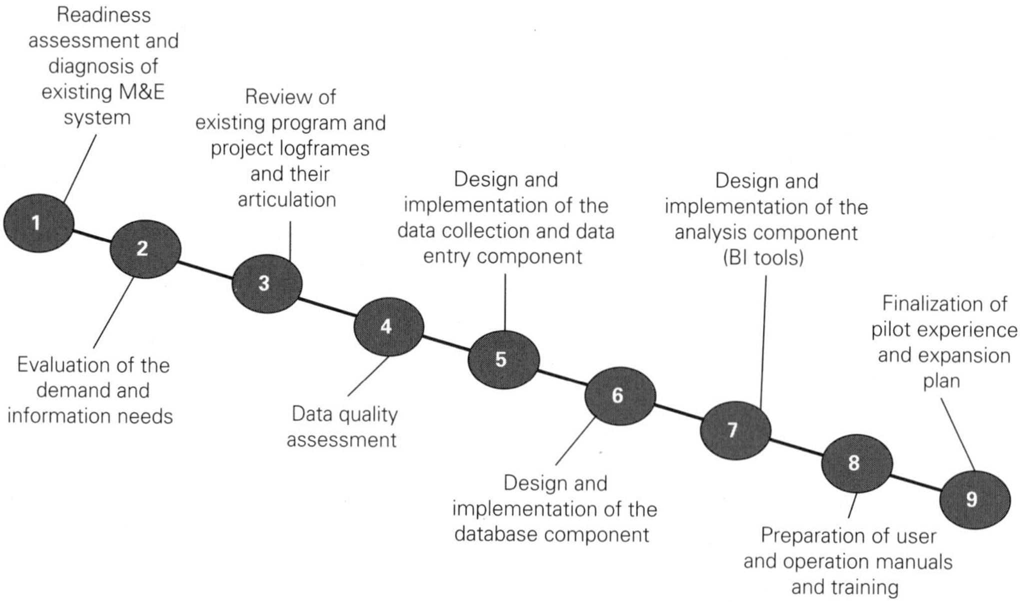

Source: Adapted from Kusek and Rist (2004).

securely and safely, and providing selective access to authorized users. Such units can also facilitate the sharing of experiences from internal and external experts, participate in impact evaluation studies of major programs to learn from failures as well as successes, help orient future policies and programs, and train the organization staff on M&E methods and results. In their new mandate, these units can take advantage of progress in information technology (the Electronic Documentation Management Systems [EDMS]). The IDEA Institute has helped implement such systems in various institutions to maintain huge volumes of administrative and technical documentation with user-friendly retrieval.

Lessons learned from a variety of experiences of the IDEA Institute in many countries include the following:

- In many large public bureaucracies, information is scattered, making it difficult to know where the information lies, who has it, and what it can be used for. It is important to try to identify all information sources, whether they be sophisticated information systems, Excel datasheets, or handwritten reports. This information can be gathered through interviews. It can also emerge as the M&E system design and implementation process progresses.
- In addition to finding where the information is, it is important to understand how this information was gathered or calculated. It is critical to make sure that the information that will be incorporated into the system is of good quality and that its integrity will be ensured. Without this step, an organization could end up with a wealth of useless or inaccurate information. The data quality assessments sponsored by the Millenium Challenge Account being conducted in a number of countries are a welcome initiative. Efforts to revitalize and upgrade national statistical systems under the Paris 21 initiative also add value.
- The results-based M&E information system should be designed by computer specialists under the supervision of M&E experts. The M&E experts should listen to the computer specialists. However, the M&E specialists should keep the focus on the objective, which is a functioning, robust, cost-effective system that delivers on a regular basis the information required by decision makers. Leaving the design to the computer specialists can yield nonoperational costly white elephants and database cemeteries. It is useless to have a complex information system using the latest technology if it is not used in day-to-day program activities and, ultimately, decision making. Computerizing a bad information system only means faster GIGO (garbage in, garbage out). It is better to start small and progressively upgrade and improve the M&E information system.

Improving M&E Information Systems and Knowledge Management

The IDEA Institute has been associated with the establishment, participation, and reinforcement of various kinds of experience-sharing platforms and mechanisms that contribute to ECB. At the country level, there is increased use of joint progress reviews between governments and donors, sector thematic groups, and forums to foster a common vision and strategy (SWAP, or sector-wide approach). In Vietnam, the joint progress review mechanism set up to discuss Program 135, a major poverty reduction program, improved the policy dialogue between the government and development partners and led to a more effective and efficient program. In Cambodia, the Poverty Forum proposed by the IDEA Institute helped share scattered information on poverty and foster a policy dialogue between public institutions and a vibrant nongovernmental organization community. Advocacy initiatives such as short seminars or cabinet retreats can help develop buy-in at a high level and create momentum for results-based M&E under national leadership. The existence of a unit within the public sector dedicated to the promotion, training, and supply of evaluation expertise can facilitate the dissemination of a culture and good practices of evaluation, as it did in the Center of Excellence in Evaluation of the Treasury Board in Canada and CONEVAL in Mexico. Organizing high-level conferences at the national or regional level, involving a combination of ministers, cabinet members, and high-level technical staff and advisers, allows participants to compare national experiences, conduct some benchmarking, and help move toward a common understanding and strategy. Various communities of practices on M&E at the national, regional, and international levels have sprung up, with varying degrees of success and sustainability. If well managed, these communities can facilitate, in a cost-effective way, the sharing of lessons learned and best practices.

Professional evaluation associations also have a significant role to play in ECB. IDEAS, the only international association in development evaluation, has a unique niche and contribution to make in sharing knowledge across regions.

Building Sustainable M&E Units

Training, information system improvements, sensitization, policy dialogue forums, and professional associations are all a means to an end: the creation of sustainable M&E units.[4] To improve the performance and sustainability of the M&E unit, the IDEA Institute has tapped into management approaches that have improved institutional performance and results. These approaches include those of the Baldrige National Quality Program (NIST 2009); Qualimètre (Mouvement Québécois de la Qualité 2009), its Quebec equivalent; and the balanced scorecard approach initially developed for the private sector and then adapted to the public sector (Kaplan 1999).

Figure 10.6 presents the Baldrige criteria for Performance Excellence Framework. Figure 10.7 presents the main concepts underlined in this approach as applied to a public organization such as an M&E unit. The framework's focus on the mission and the target groups of the M&E unit, and its balanced consideration of human resources, financial resources, and the processes of this unit and their linkages, have proven useful in developing the institutional sustainability of the M&E unit.

In fragile states, an important consideration for institutional sustainability is whether the M&E unit should be within or outside the public sector. Setting the unit within a ministry may not be functional if incentives and morale are low. Setting up M&E units within external project implementation units could undermine national sustainable institutions by attracting the few competent human resources available in the public sector by higher pay and better working conditions. An approach used by the IDEA Institute in Cambodia was to help support a Poverty Monitoring Technical Unit at the Ministry of Planning, made up of about 20 young national professionals, each acting as a focal point with a sector ministry. This arrangement proved

Figure 10.6 Baldrige Criteria for Performance Excellence Framework

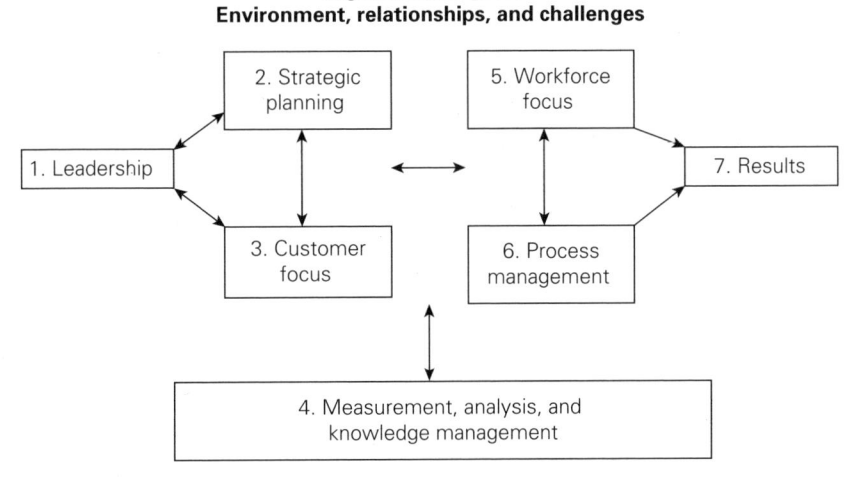

**Organizational profile:
Environment, relationships, and challenges**

- 1. Leadership
- 2. Strategic planning
- 3. Customer focus
- 4. Measurement, analysis, and knowledge management
- 5. Workforce focus
- 6. Process management
- 7. Results

Source: Baldrige National Quality Program 2009.

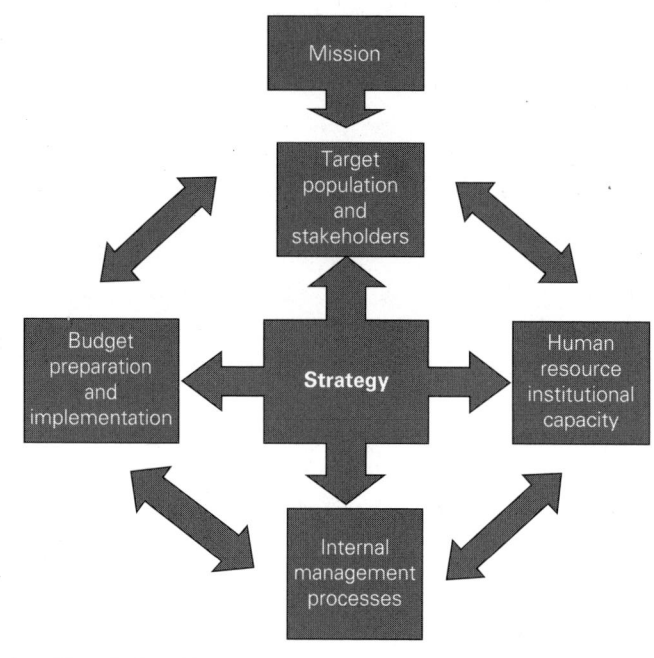

Figure 10.7 Key Components of the Balanced Scorecard Approach

Source: Adapted from Kaplan 2009.

a reasonable compromise between the need to produce short-term M&E products and the desire to boost capacity.

External Evaluation and Accountability

Apart from the central role of M&E units within line ministries, the institutional setup should include other institutions as well as private sector and civil society organizations. In addition to organizations for ex ante and ex post internal control, there is a need for a public body for external control with judiciary independence, the legal power to obtain information, and the human and financial resources to perform good work. The experience of various industrial countries, such as Canada, has demonstrated the significant contribution of an institution such as the office of the auditor general, to the effectiveness and efficiency of public spending.

Beyond a strong audit organization, the culture of results develops itself on the demand as well as the supply side with the implementation of an RBM system in the public sector with performance contracts, public accountability for results by each actor, the dissemination of information on results to the population by communication media and the actors of social society, the follow-up given by the judiciary whenever necessary, the development of an evaluation capacity by the private sector and universities, and so forth. The demand for accountability for public money from the private sector and civil society and the demonstration of public value created go hand in hand with the improvement in the quantity and quality of accountability.

In a mature M&E system, the limits of the two main pillars, internal monitoring for program management and external evaluation for accountability, evolve. As the culture of results pervades public institutions, internal evaluation develops as a self-improvement tool to develop an information-rich learning organization. In addition to traditional baselines, midterm, and final evaluation reports on physical and financial implementation, there is growing development and use of other tools, such as results monitoring, control panels, early warning systems, annual performance reports, performance audits, and combined qualitative and quantitative evaluations (Q^2 approach). The framework to progressively include all these components, modules, and tools is the national M&E system that is built as a result of an articulated midterm M&E plan.

Conclusion

Experience based on lessons learned and best practices shows that significant progress is possible using a variety of ECB mechanisms in a complementary way. More decentralized, effective, and diverse training is a must. Investment in complementary technical assistance; support to information systems; and sensitization, policy discussion, and professional exchange platforms as part of an overall ECB strategy and roadmap defined at the national, sector, and local level can help make an M&E system effective and sustainable and help professionalize the evaluator's job. Continuous improvement needs to be perceived as a key element in the global reform of the public sector toward managing for development results. It requires strong leadership and an increased commitment to a culture of results by governments and development partners.

Notes

1. There is no unique way of defining these subareas in the literature.
2. IDEA is a private institute recognized by the Canadian federal government. For more information, see http://www.idea-international.org.

3. IDB/PRODEV considers the following five pillars for RBM/MfDR: strategic planning, budgeting for results, public finance management, program and project management, and M&E (Garcia Lopez 2008). OECD/DAC follows the following five pillars of MfDR: leadership, evaluation and monitoring, accountability and partnerships, planning and budgeting, and statistics (MfDR 2009).
4. *Unit* is used here in a generic sense and can encompass a variety of institutional setups depending on the country and the organization.

Bibliography

Baldrige National Quality Program. 2009. *2009–2010 Education Criteria for Performance Excellence*. Gaithersburg, MD: National Institute of Standards and Technology.

Bureau, S. 2000. "Analyse des besoins de formation." Développement International Desjardins, Quebec.

Garcia Lopez, R. 2008. "La gestión para resultados y el presupuesto para resultados en América Latina y el Caribe." Paper presented at the International Conference on Budgeting for Results, Mexico City, June 8–9.

High Level Forum. 2005. *Paris Declaration on Aid Effectiveness*. Paris: Organisation for Economic Co-operation and Development/Development Assistance Committee.

Kaplan, R. 1999. "The Balanced Scorecard for Public-Sector Organizations." *Harvard Business Review*, Article Reprint B9911C.

Kusek, J. Z., and R. C. Rist. 2004. *Ten Steps to Results-Based Monitoring and Evaluation Systems: A Handbook for Development Practitioners*. Washington, DC: World Bank.

Mouvement Québécois de la Qualité. 2009. *Le Qualimètre*. http://www.qualite.qc.ca/uploads/files/intro.pdf.

NIST (National Institute of Standards and Technology). 2009. "Baldrige Performance Excellence Program." http://www.quality.nist.gov/.

OECD/DAC (Organisation for Economic Co-operation and Development/Development Assistance Committee). 2009. "Managing for Development Results Capacity Scan: MfDR Capacity Scan." http://www.mfdr.org/Cap-scan/.

OECD/DAC. 2009. Glossary of Key Terms in Evaluation and Results-Based Management. Development Assistance Committee, OECD/DAC, Paris.

OED (Operations Evaluation Department). 2004. "Evaluation Capacity Development: OED Self-Evaluation." OED, World Bank, Washington, DC.

Third High Level Forum on Aid Effectiveness. 2008. "Accra Agenda for Action." Organisation for Economic Co-operation and Development/Development Assistance Committee, Accra, Ghana.

World Bank. 2004. "Evaluation Capacity Development: OED Self-Evaluation." Operations Evaluation Department, Washington, DC.

———. 2007. *Using Training to Build Capacity for Development: An Evaluation of the World Bank's Project-Based and WBI Training*. Washington, DC: World Bank, Independent Evaluation Group.

CHAPTER 11

Where Is Development Evaluation Going?

Robert Picciotto

The Global Assembly held in Johannesburg in March 2009 spawned the articles in this volume. The assembly marked the eighth anniversary of the International Development Evaluation Association (IDEAS). It provided an opportunity to look back at the road traveled by the development community since the launch of the association in Beijing in 2001, an event that, as director general of evaluation at the World Bank, I was privileged to cochair with Khalid Malik, then head of the evaluation function at the United Nations Development Programme.

IDEAS has come a long way since 2002. The Global Assembly offered IDEAS members a forum for exchanging views about the future of development evaluation.

This chapter is based on the keynote speech I was honored to deliver on this topic. Its aim is twofold: to go back to first principles regarding what it means to be a development evaluator and to provoke debate about the evaluation policy implications of recent development trends.

The Origins of IDEAS

Before looking ahead, evaluators are prone to look back. This is why I start by recollecting the circumstances at the creation of IDEAS. The idea of IDEAS germinated at the turn of the 21st century, when a wave of hope and renewal was boosting the development enterprise. A historic watershed was reached in New York at the 2000 Millennium Summit, when 147 monarchs, presidents, and prime ministers committed their nations to the creation of a new development order in which poor countries would assume the responsibility of tackling absolute poverty and rich countries would accept the obligation of helping them do so.

A year and a half later (and six months after the attacks on the World Trade Center), the United Nations Financing for Development Conference at Monterrey (Mexico) focused on the means to achieve these goals. It was agreed that rich countries would provide more and better aid, expanded resources for debt reduction, and greater access to markets, while poor countries would design and implement poverty reduction strategies and reform their governance.

These reciprocal obligations received the unanimous endorsement of all UN members. The shared objectives included measurably reducing poverty, malnutrition, illiteracy, disease, gender discrimination, and environmental stress by 2015. By the time IDEAS was launched, in Beijing in September 2002, the Millennium Development Goals (MDGs) had been unveiled and the notion of managing for results consecrated as an integral part of the new development consensus.

Not coincidentally, these solemn undertakings coincided with an increase in aid flows—for the first time in a decade. Presaging the historic Monterrey Consensus, the London Declaration that crafted the charter of IDEAS had highlighted results management, transparency, good governance, and accountability as the ultimate aims of development evaluation. In pursuit of these goals, capacity building for improved assessments of the outcomes, impacts, and value for money of development interventions was visualized as the core mandate of the new association.

What Is IDEAS About?

Eight years on, the same principles still prevail, and IDEAS is a vibrant reality. In the face of the extraordinary challenges faced by its members—whether they hail from the South, the North, the East, or the West—the Global Assembly demonstrated a shared determination to live up to the mandate of the association. Therefore, it was entirely fitting for the Assembly to revisit the issues of knowledge creation, knowledge transmission, and knowledge synthesis that have animated IDEAS since its establishment.

But what, as evaluators, do we mean by knowledge? In defining what we need to know, we deliberately cross disciplinary boundaries. We do so because our discipline is autonomous; provides analytical tools for all other disciplines; and uses their methods and concepts to assess the merit, worth, and value of public policies, programs, and projects. We reject the notion that there is a gold standard in evaluation methodology, as nowhere more than in development is triangulation of evaluation approaches so critical.

What ties us together is critical thinking. We practice the Socratic approach. We ask and debate policy questions first and gather data, information, and evidence only when relevant questions have been identified. Next we interpret our findings with rigor and fairness and draw inferences about the design and implementation of future policies, programs, and projects with empathy and care.

As evaluators, we are not after any knowledge. Our quest is for useful, instrumental knowledge. We look for propositions that help make things happen. Toward that end, we use methods that allow us to verify outputs, measure outcomes, and assess impacts. This is akin to the scientific method of observation, hypothesis, prediction, and experimentation. But unlike our scientific colleagues, we do not subscribe to the notion of value-free knowledge. Indeed, our work is guided by overarching values that transcend reason and embrace universal ethical norms.

Thus, making ethical assumptions explicit is critical to the integrity of evaluation processes. Development evaluators give privileged attention to what will make a society work for the benefit of the many rather than the few. We celebrate the rights of different societies to adopt distinctive definitions of the common good as a basis for collective action. We believe that principled deliberation, participation, and involvement of stakeholders make our work legitimate. Development evaluation is thus, by its very nature, democratic evaluation. This implies transparency, as development fails if citizens do not have access to the truth. It implies that development evaluators must speak truth to power—calling it like it is without fear or favor despite the perennial threats to independence, whether they be overt and brutal or subtle and exercised through constraints on funding, staffing, programming, data, or peer-group pressure and social isolation. Truth should be secured through rigorous rules of evidence. Evaluation is not advocacy.

Independence is critical to evaluation credibility. As evaluators, we cannot afford to let vested interests influence our agenda, interfere with our investigations, shape our analyses, or suppress our findings. We therefore need to help one another in nurturing and sustaining our independence. Agreed-upon evaluation guidelines, resilient competency standards, and capacity-building actions focused on improved governance and checks and balances are among the professional shields needed to protect ourselves against those who hold power and purse strings and seek to undermine their independence.

With independence comes responsibility. The first imperative of our profession responds to the Hippocratic Oath—first, do no harm. Hence, evaluators cannot be spared from informed and principled criticism. Poor-quality or biased evaluations can be very costly and disruptive. The credibility of the evaluation profession rests on ensuring adequate professional competencies and complying with explicit quality standards in the evaluation process. Evaluators should practice what they preach: detachment, objectivity, and restraint are critical characteristics that evaluators should display to evince public trust in evaluation.

A New Context for Evaluation

Good evaluation practice is not only about process, it is also about context. Our analytical findings are always subject to reinterpretation as new information emerges and the operating environment evolves. Just as scientific models change over time, so do the interpretations offered by evaluation. Because the consequences of human actions depend on the characteristics of the enabling environment, the tools to make informed decisions must reflect the realities of the day.

When the Global Assembly took place, the development context had changed radically since 2002. Business as usual was no longer appropriate for evaluation in the zones of turmoil and transition where the bulk of the world's poor live. When IDEAS was created, the global economy was growing; by the time the Global Assembly took place, the global economy was in an unprecedented state of turmoil. A systemic financial crisis was sweeping the world, coming on the heels of a fuel and food crisis that had ravaged the most vulnerable societies of the planet. The waves generated by the financial crisis that started in New York and London wreaked havoc with the fiscal balances of developing economies, whose foreign exchange positions appeared precarious. For example, the African Development Bank estimated that the current account of African countries would shift from a surplus of 3.8 percent of gross domestic product (GDP) in 2007 to a deficit of 6.0 percent in 2009, as growth estimates were slashed from 6.7 percent to 3.3 percent a year.

Unlike the situation faced in previous crises, during which appropriate remedies could be administered at the national level, it seemed as if only global action would be able to arrest the downturn, because the tentacles of the dysfunctional global international banking and trading system where the crisis originated reach all corners of the world. To be sure, given the global recession, food prices had declined from their 2008 peak, but they were still 20 percent higher than in 2006. By now, as a result of massive injection of public funds, the downturn has been stalled, but uncertainties about the strength and resilience of the recovery still loom and hunger and malnutrition still stalk food-importing countries.

Thus, the promise embedded in the first MDG—according to which the proportion of people going to bed hungry would be cut by half by 2015—will not be met. Even before the recent upheavals in the food market, about 850 million people went to bed hungry every night and severe food scarcity was affecting 33 developing countries. Unlike in previous crises, the economic adjustment problem is now centered in the North rather than the South, and no international institution is mandated to impose discipline on the culprit countries.

The crisis did not induce a fundamental reform of the international financial system. Trillions of dollars have been spent on economic stimulus programs and bank rescues, but the meager flows allocated to aid are widely perceived to be at risk. This is scandalous considering that the South will not be sheltered from the effects of the intense and prolonged economic decline that has its source in the richest and most powerful countries in the world.

Aid flows were already trending down from their 2006 peak when the crisis hit. They amounted to only 0.45 percent of the gross national incomes (GNIs) of rich countries rather than the longstanding 0.7 percent commitment endorsed by the United Nations General Assembly in 1970. Nor are these flows likely to resume their post-Monterrey upswing, given the enormous fiscal burdens of the domestic rescue packages assembled by Organisation for Economic Co-operation and Development (OECD) countries, the large military outlays associated with rising global insecurities, and the centripetal forces of economic nationalism. In fact, the Overseas Development Institute has estimated a drop in aid of about $20 billion compared to commitments.

Private financial flows to emerging economies have been volatile. While now recovering, they fell from U.S.$891 billion in 2008 to U.S.$568 billion in 2009. Spreads on these countries' sovereign bonds are growing. Workers' remittances are also down. Export volumes are dropping, and growth projections are being slashed. Millions of jobs are being lost, and poverty is deepening, with the extreme poor hit the hardest. In February 2009, the World Bank estimated that 53 million more people could be trapped in poverty as global economic growth slows and that 200,000–400,000 more infants could die each year between 2009 and 2015.

A New Spirit among Evaluators

Given this situation, I was not surprised about the palpable sense of urgency that permeated the Global Assembly. But I detected no sign that anyone present had given up on development. I sensed a mood of confidence and determination at all the sessions I attended. The sober but positive mood of this event stood in sharp contrast to that found in other evaluation conferences, dominated by the dismal dogmas of randomization fundamentalists and the defeatist pronouncements of professional aid pessimists.

Indeed, the rich variety of intellectual offerings on display exemplified analytical awareness, critical consciousness, and a shared intellectual conviction that evaluation matters more than ever to poverty reduction. Realism about what development practitioners are up against was everywhere on display. Refreshingly, there was broad-based recognition that the constraints our profession faces—weak institutional foundations, volatile funding, widespread misunderstanding of what evaluation entails—will not vanish overnight.

If the economic crisis raised fundamental questions about development, IDEAS was in familiar territory; as evaluators, its members are used to provocative questions and do not shy away from tough diagnostics. They are hardwired to combine assurance with curiosity, idealism with skepticism, and intellectual engagement with scientific detachment. They know that answers only lead to further questions. They also know that unless they are ready to acknowledge the obstacles associated with the policies and practices that shape the evaluation profession, they will not be part of the solution and will not discover or embrace the possibilities that remain open in a world in crisis.

It was in this spirit that I speculated about the future of development in the first decade of the new millennium. Poised halfway to the finishing line of the MDG race, the development community was faced by grim news. The very heart of the mighty economic engine of the interconnected global economy had been damaged, and the effects of the unfolding crisis were spreading to the periphery.

New Global Insecurities

What can we learn from the recent financial debacle? First, the economic doctrines that we took for granted and the traditional modes of development thinking that we had gotten used to need reconsideration. We will have to forsake the certainties associated with mainstream development economics and acknowledge the new realities of risk and uncertainty, which are systemic and deeply embedded in the integrated global system. They have led to a proliferation of problems without passports.

Indeed, the financial meltdown is only one manifestation of the gap between an increasingly interconnected world and the ramshackle state-centered global governance machinery that was designed for simpler and happier times. Beyond the current financial travails, climate change constitutes an ever-more threatening obstacle to development. It highlights the lack of sustainability of the fossil fuel–based production and consumption patterns that have characterized the development enterprise from its origins.

The fact that human development is inducing temperature rises unknown in human history is not in dispute. There is growing evidence that the ecosystem is under threat given the complex feedback loops associated with the warming and drying of wetlands, the thawing of permafrost regions, and the unabated destruction of rain forests. We are witnessing the rapid destruction of tropical forests, the extinction of land-based species, threats to biodiversity hotspots, the acidification of oceans, and similar problems.

Human security is also threatened by natural disasters, twice as many of which were recorded in the 1990s as in the 1970s. The poorest countries have been the most vulnerable. Evaluations carried out by humanitarian and development agencies have confirmed that disaster preparedness remains a neglected feature of development strategies.

Development practices have been insensitive to conflict, even though since the end of World War II, violent intrastate conflicts have continually erupted—all of them in poor countries. The consequences for development are dramatic. Each war costs $64 billion on average, and most wars take place in poor countries (Collier n.d.). According to the United Nations High Commissioner for Refugees' *Global Trends Report* (UNHCR 2009), the number of people forcibly uprooted by conflict and persecution stood at 42 million, including 16 million refugees and asylum seekers and 26 million internally displaced people within their own countries.

All of these insecurities are concentrated within fragile states, which are home to a third of the absolute poor. Although they desperately need aid to achieve peace and prosperity, these states are being shunned by a development industry intent on avoiding instead of managing risk. Sadly, evaluators may have been part of the problem rather than the solution, as they have promoted development effectiveness concepts that induce risk aversion, do not balance risks and rewards, and, in particular, fail to take account of the enormous benefits of aid targeted to vulnerable countries.

The downside risks of poorly designed economic growth strategies have been amplified by systemic failures in the professions that border evaluation—auditing and research—and their failure to adopt rigorous evaluation methods. For example, the current financial crisis can be traced to inept evaluations of mortgage loan applications and faulty risk valuations of exotic financial instruments. The recent food crisis was exacerbated by the misguided promotion of biofuel production (facilitated by faulty environmental assessments) and intensified by wrong-headed application of the precautionary principle that has retarded the advent of new crop varieties adapted to arid climates.

New Priorities for Development Evaluation

What are the implications for the policy directions of development evaluation? To deal with financial crises, global warming, and other borderless problems that are destroying the prospects for global poverty reduction, evaluation should provide the evidence required for sensible decision making.

In the area of global finance, the lessons of experience should be brought to bear. In the area of climate change, evaluation should help decision makers design mitigation plans and agree on the levels at which emissions should be stabilized; the time period over which stabilization should be achieved; the energy generation options that should be employed; and, through more precise measures of local impacts, the adaptation programs and projects that should be funded.

It would appear that development evaluation has been asymmetrical. It has devoted disproportionate attention to assessing the performance of one side of the global partnership—poor countries. The MDGs demand more of developing countries than they do of developed countries. Most of the indicators (35 out of 48) embedded in the MDGs point south. Vast resources have been mobilized to monitor progress in developing country policies and programs. No similar effort has been put in place to monitor the improvement of policies adopted by rich countries.

New Objects of Evaluation

Currently, the privileged units of account of development evaluation are individual projects and country programs. Evaluations of the global policies and collaborative initiatives that shape the international response to global crises will need increasing attention. Program evaluation theory is well adapted to the assessment of global collaborative programs. Meta-evaluation methods combined with theory-based evaluation techniques are realistic; participatory evaluations are instruments of choice for evaluating such programs.

Arguably, development evaluators focus a disproportionate share of their time and resources on aid operations, as most of the current capacity for development evaluation is lodged in aid agencies. Looking ahead, it would be appropriate to allocate more resources to assessments of all of the transmission belts of globalization (finance, migration, trade, and so forth), as a wide range of policies matter to climate change and other global development challenges.

Part of the development evaluation gap could be filled by systematic assessments of the whole of government policies on a horizontal basis. As the sustainability imperative involves changed behaviors by the private sector, evaluation will need to focus on the social and environmental impact of regulatory regimes and standards. In other words, the move of development evaluation to a higher plane already underway should be accelerated.

New Metrics for Evaluation

The logic of internalizing the externalities implicit in climate change mitigation strategies also argues for the adoption of "triple bottom line" or "green" national accounts, which take account of resource depletion alongside income impacts for various groups and regions. A change in emphasis will also be needed, as the development evaluation ideas with the most traction today (results-based management, experimental methods, and so forth) do not emphasize the distinctive accountabilities of partners in shaping global development outcomes.

Although globalization has generated complex, long-term, and persistent impacts characterized by pervasive risks and uncertainties, the dominant conceptions of development effectiveness today tend to assume linear relationships between means and goals. Yet risk management theory is well equipped to rank threats, whether they originate from global warming, conflict, infectious diseases, natural disasters, and other threats to human welfare.

Cost-benefit analyses combined with probability theory should be deployed to evaluate alternative responses to identified threats. Under certain conditions, game theory and systems analysis could test the resilience of chosen responses. Institutional economics could be put to work to resolve collective action dilemmas and design incentives for cooperation.

The concept of a project as a bundle of contracts offers scope for addressing more explicitly issues of risk assessment and risk sharing. Fiduciary considerations that were once dominant when projects were the main aid instrument will be coming back to center stage, but they will have to be incorporated into the evaluation method instead of treated as add-ons. This approach would be consistent with the concept of development as the expansion of freedom and at the same time would bring to bear the "theory of real options." Legal considerations regulating conflicts of interest could become part of the analysis, just as in project finance. In this context (just as in cost-benefit analysis and evaluation dependent on experimental designs), risks and rewards would imply the identification of a plausible counterfactual, and the value of resource allocations would be based on their opportunity costs (the benefits derived from their alternative uses).

New Institutional Arrangements

Methodological rigor will not be sufficient to ensure the credibility of evaluations. The design of evaluation governance to guarantee independence, objectivity, and value added is of critical importance, because verifiable truth can be ascertained only through iterative processes that recognize the limits of rationality and contestability processes that take on the power of vested interests.

Citizens often misjudge risks or fall prey to risk panics. Professional evaluation should encourage sober reflection and inform public debate. In general, policy priorities are legitimate only if they are set following principled deliberations and safeguarded by checks and balances. At the national level, the debate should involve citizens, their representatives, and the independent judiciary. At the international level, new networks connecting government, the private sector, and voluntary agencies should lend legitimacy and credibility to policy solutions.

Putting Developing Countries in the Driver's Seat

Credible global policy evaluation will imply more efforts to involve developing countries in the process. A major commitment to evaluation capacity development from donors is imperative. Evaluation funding and governance arrangements will have to allocate substantive control of a major segment of the global policy evaluation agenda to developing country governments, organizations, and citizens. Just as development projects and programs executed by poor countries have benefited over the years from evaluations by donor organizations controlled by rich countries, it would make sense for rich country policies that affect poor countries to benefit from evaluations carried out by evaluation organizations controlled by poor countries.

Conclusion

To help find collective solutions to global policy dilemmas, development evaluation should adapt its strategies, instruments, and emphases to new priorities. Development today has less to do with charity than with human security. Tough governance issues, social problems, and economic policy dysfunctions lie at the source of the new threats the world is grappling with.

Throwing the light of reason and bringing the weight of evidence to bear on the management of security and development risks constitutes the new agenda for development evaluation. Bringing this agenda to life is not a job for just anyone. It requires rigor, independence of mind, and courage. These qualities are amply evident in the chapters in this book.

Bibliography

Collier, Paul. n.d. http://users.ox.ac.uk/~econpco/research/conflict.htm.
UNHCR (United Nations High Commissioner for Refugees). 2009. *Global Trends Report*. Geneva: United Nations High Commissioner for Refugees.
World Bank. 2009. "Financial Crisis Could Trap 53 Million More People in Poverty." http://web.worldbank.org/WBSITE/EXTERNAL/NEWS/0,,contentMDK:22068931~pagePK:64257043~piPK:437376~theSitePK:4607,00.html.

CHAPTER 12

Old Challenges and New Frontiers

Elizabeth J. McAllister

The purpose of this overview of the chapters in this volume is to draw out useful ideas for further exploration, support the emphasis on results-based strategy, and discuss two interrelated issues that emerge from the chapters. The first is the interface between the evaluation function and organizational leadership in setting a results strategy. The second is the limitation of results approaches as implemented by the international development community.

This volume brings together the experience and expertise of evaluators from developing countries, international development institutions, a bilateral donor project, and consulting firms. The contributors reaffirm lessons of evaluation practice and public sector reform through managing for development results (MfDR). With a focus on evaluation capacity building (ECB), a number of contributors provide detailed and practical guidance in the form of new conceptual frameworks, models, and checklists. They explore new ideas and disciplines that, in combination with evaluation methodology, can help reinforce a performance culture in public institutions and leverage public sector reforms.

Defining ECB

In its narrowest sense, ECB refers to building the skills and ability (human capital) of evaluators around using systematic research methods to evaluate the performance of projects, programs, country development strategies, and global programs. The international development evaluation community also uses the term in the wider sense of strengthening governance, organizational culture, and administrative support required for a robust evaluation function. The contributors discuss ECB interventions needed to address broad institutional issues at the sector, country, and global levels. Some (particularly Wiesner in chapter 2 and Dimitrov in chapter 3) argue that a modern evaluation function must be mandated to diagnose—and be capable of diagnosing—national and international institutions, through the lens of modern management theory and institutional economics and through advances in the study of political economy.

The chapters chosen for this publication cover a broad spectrum. At the project level, Porter (chapter 9) explores the ECB process with eight grassroots organizations aimed at improving the welfare of rural children in South Africa. He draws from Shein's "helping" concept, a management text inspired by psychology, to reflect on the importance of process and purposeful interpersonal interactions. Porter applies Shein's approach to his experience in helping project staff improve their monitoring techniques.

In chapter 7, Agrawal and Rao examine their experience in the Indian government overseeing major project evaluations. They explore the barriers of organizational culture and mandates of government departments, including their own, that prevent managers from using evaluation to its full potential. In their examination of factors influencing the use of project evaluation, Agrawal and Rao raise an important point about the demand side of evaluation that links to the issue of the enabling environment. Although not a major line of exploration, it is worth capturing here.

As many consultants attest, a good evaluation is a product of excellence in evaluation and of sponsoring agents who have the capacity to write concise terms of reference and stick to them, protect the integrity of the evaluation, and understand how to communicate findings and work with evaluators to craft recommendations that lead to significant action. Capacity-building exercises, then, need to address both sides of the evaluation contract.

In chapter 5, Heider draws on recent research in institutional capacity building to make the case that ECB must embrace the broader institutional environment. She points to the importance of the drive from within the organization (often referred to as a *performance-based culture*); details the attributes of an enabling environment and the institutional arrangements necessary for an effective evaluation function; and outlines practical steps on how to build a high-performance environment that is useful for leaders in government and multilateral institutions.

Training and education remain central to successful ECB. In chapter 10, Clotteau, Boily, Darboe, and Martin stress "the importance of a pedagogical strategy adopted to the context, the participants, and the intended objectives," and provide detailed guidance on how to build successful training programs. They cover the broad range of issues involved in building evaluation capacity, from constraints imposed by the authorizing environment to avoiding the inefficiency of training "development tourists."

Their chapter highlights the importance of both information management and information technology (IT). As organizations downsized the filing room to take advantage of the personal computer, filing systems often became personalized and fragmented. This fractioning of information put organizations at risk of losing valuable knowledge and of duplicating work and data banks. As a result of individualized filing systems, audit and evaluation trails have been compromised.

In performance management (also called *results management*), computerized systems are extremely helpful but are too often seen as the solution rather than the means to a solution. As the authors point out, there are many expensive white elephant systems. Moving too quickly to the IT design stage for results monitoring can lock organizations into expensive systems too quickly and lead to staff frustration and resentment over having to "feed the beast" with data they know will not be used except to track reporting compliance. In turn, managers are often deluged with detailed operational performance data that overwhelm their absorptive capacity without supporting managerial and analytical work. Too often, organizations use the existence of results frameworks in project data systems to assure themselves and others that they are results based—even though the data may be unusable in any serious effort to improve performance at the project level or to support strategic conversations among program management teams at the program or country level.

New Areas for Exploration

A number of areas for further study also become apparent. Taken together, chapters 9 and 10 lead us to consider the psychology of learning and reaffirm the importance of organizational development as underlying concepts for capacity-building curricula, programs, and related interventions.

Two other disciplines have been introduced that are worthy of exploration. One is the use of political economy analysis to understand why some institutions actually fulfill their mandates to serve the public interest while others do so only nominally (see chapter 2). The other is systems theory, as introduced by Heider in her adaptation of emerging approaches to capacity development that are based on systems theory.

Political Economy

Wiesner builds from a recent evaluation of macroeconomic performance in several Latin American countries and draws from institutional economics and the principles of incentive and information theory. He finds that the effectiveness of evaluation is largely a function of the degree to which it is driven by demand for improved results and that this demand is, in turn, a function of accountability and its attendant incentives. He looks to the underlying determinants of political demand to enhance macroeconomic performance, suggesting a move away from evaluation of compliance with "stylized" institutional characteristics. Wiesner concludes that "higher-order" principles of incentive and information theory and recent research in political economy of development are as important to the project, program, and country level as they are to macroeconomic institutions.

Wiesner's inclusion of political economy follows its relatively recent acceptance in official development discourse. Its explicit use in development planning and management was long regarded as too political and as a threat to the neutrality of multilaterals. Yet, as Wiesner suggests, its use is central to understanding the dynamics that create the incentives for appropriate enabling environments for good governance and thus for effective development programming.

Mapping political, social, and economic actors and factors is extremely important to larger-scale evaluations. Not understanding the motivation and power of special interest groups can blind the analysis to institutional rigidities and externalities that raise ethical and conflict-of-interest issues. At the center of development impact analysis is the examination of policy and program impact on the poor. The evaluator's analysis of potential and actual adverse or uneven impacts on different social and economic groups can open a discussion of trade-offs that may have been blocked by special interest groups early in program design and throughout implementation. In the development context, the evaluation community should give voice to the voiceless and should bring the undiscussable into the public forum. Advances in political economy analysis can also serve to depoliticize debate through the use of convincing evidence rather than rhetoric. Speaking truth to power creates discomfort that needs to be handled adroitly even when the independence of the evaluation function is guaranteed. Understanding the interests of different stakeholder power groups can serve the evaluator in crafting recommendations that lead to mutual gain or at least to a more sustainable resolution of contentious issues.

Systems Theory and Complex Adaptive Systems

Wiesner defines institutions as sets of formal and informal rules that shape behavior. He reminds us that the role of institutions and the incentives they contain are believed to be the main determinants of long-term country prosperity. Institutional economics has underscored the importance of incentives, history, politics, and beliefs as determinants in institutional resilience. Taking informal influences into consideration adds considerably to the complexity of evaluation.

Heider's approach to ECB points to the importance of informal and exogenous influences. Building the capacity of the individual evaluator is necessary but not sufficient. To ensure the independence, credibility, and utility of the evaluation function, Heider addresses the importance of ECB in addressing the wider enabling environment, which is determined by a culture of learning and accountability; the institutional framework; and the evaluator's professional development and comportment. The implication is that a wider scope for ECB that includes informal and political systems increases the complexity and importance of the ECB process. Heider notes the inadequacy of blueprints in such complex interventions. She calls for new approaches based on "ordered chaos" (combining high degrees of flexibility with systematic approaches) to allow for planned as well as incremental and emergent approaches.

Both Wiesner and Heider find themselves in conceptual territory claimed by proponents of systems theory and complex adaptive systems thinking. A recent study for the European Center for Development Policy Management (Land, Hauck, and Baser 2009) suggests that donor interventions for capacity building would be improved and donors would better understand what worked and why if they thought of organizations and systems as "human or social systems that evolve organically in unpredictable ways in response to a wide range of stimuli and through multiple interactions." They contrast this way of thinking to the more conventional development paradigm, which is based on detailed, linear design, the charting of cause-and-effect relationships, and planned change.

The implications of the systems approach in Heider's ECB model are significant. She has helpfully charted when more traditional linear approaches would be appropriate and when a fuller systems approach would be more useful. If adopted by the ECB community, the systems approach should also influence concepts of accountability and evaluation methodology. For example, from a systems perspective, in complex development situations it would be unfair to hold staff accountable for their predictions at the beginning of an intervention. Instead, staff should be held accountable for, and have the political authority for, adapting budgets, activities, and even outputs to new situations and influences to attain the expected outcomes. Organizational leadership and the authorizing environment would have to reframe accountability to embrace adaptive management and be more risk tolerant to encourage resilience and innovation.

If good design is based on iteration and accommodation for unplanned processes, monitoring systems need to allow for the adjustment of plans as well as for exploration of the political economy context and for testing different approaches. Evaluation would not test performance against a plan and indicators at entry. Instead, it would focus on how well teams worked with beneficiaries and across teams using constant and deliberate approaches to self-learning. Accountability would be determined by measures of resilience and adaptability, allowing flexibility on how results are achieved but being firm on holding teams responsible for demonstrating the desired, measureable change (improvement in the quality of life, reduction in the number of highway fatalities, increase in productivity) at the outcome level.

Chapters 2, 5, 9, and 10, among others, suggest that the evaluation profession is drawing from a wider range of different disciplines to improve the analytics of traditional social science research. Further exploration of these disciplines could yield significant gains in ECB processes and in the utility of evaluations. Because not every evaluator can master all disciplines, it is often necessary to select and manage multidisciplinary teams. In the current context, characterized by relentless change and the convergence of economic, social, cultural, and environmental systems, the way in which institutions and public officials are measured can have significant effect on their ability to remain relevant while perpetuating the "right" values for public institutions serving the public interest.

Importance of Institutional Results-Based Strategy to Development Outcomes

Several contributors (Andriantseheno, Dimitrov, Jaljouli, and Wijayatilake) point to the importance of high-level strategy and accompanying metrics to unify priorities and align resources from the national, ministry, or regional level to the program and project level to achieve priority objectives. They suggest that there has been a disappointing track record of political and organizational leadership in using results-based strategy development techniques, especially in establishing aligned strategic performance information systems geared to development effectiveness. The contributors provide examples of costly dysfunctions created by a lack of strategy and misplaced ownership of the results agenda

The importance of implementing a unifying strategy is a welcome topic in a collection of articles on ECB. Too often, evaluation methodology tests a specific project or program against its planned objectives, neglecting to take into consideration the higher-order strategy that justifies its existence. Explicit and measurable performance links to the next level must generate incentives and motivation (if not pride) to achieve something bigger—to scale up and replicate lessons learned horizontally across sectors and vertically to spotlight strategy and policy-level systemic changes needed to achieve national or international goals. From an evaluative perspective, the link to higher-order development effectiveness and institutional and partnership strategies must be the ultimate test of the value added of the intervention under examination.

The Cost of the Idiosyncratic Project Approach to Results-Based Monitoring and Evaluation

Andriantseheno (chapter 8) demonstrates the cost of not working within an overarching strategy and its "aligning" metrics. He explores the challenges of taking stock of progress and results across various projects funded by the U.S. Agency for International Development (USAID) for environmental and food security rural development programs in Madagascar. Various implementing partners managed the program for three years. Although from the start there was an effort to develop a strategic and programmatic approach, each project developed its own monitoring and evaluation (M&E) framework. Andriantseheno concludes that "the classical one-on-one program design does not permit the richer consolidation at the higher level for the program itself. When each contractor develops his own M&E in his corner, no one has the possibility to really think about building a consolidated M&E matrix to measure real results and impacts of the program as a whole."

Opportunities were lost. Andriantseheno concludes that shared strategy and metrics would have meant a shared theory of change among management teams, clear expectations and accountabilities throughout the program, better quality control, and a richer and easier consolidation of results and impacts.

Andriantseheno's list of barriers to effective implementation and evaluation are the focus of the Paris Declaration. The program was not harmonized in performance terms with other actors in regional development programs in which the USAID project was active. Coordination even within USAID presented problems.[1]

Agrawal and Rao note the continuing problem of multiple evaluations of the same program: one agency at a time each producing "its own and prescriptions for fixing them," recommendations which are often inconsistent and difficult to reconcile. For the Consultative Group on International Agriculture, the reversal of largely core to largely project funding created another version of the same problem for an international organization. Multiple small projects, each with the same M&E demands as a larger project, created administrative burdens that produced little value. It was not clear that the reports were used by donors for anything more than compliance. Donor-centric financing and reporting displaced the purpose of producing global public goods that donors meant to support (McAllister and others 2008).[2]

At the global, national, and subnational level, multiple idiosyncratic projects disconnected from overarching strategic objectives and metrics disempower leadership. For example, it seems evident from Andriantseheno's chapter that there were no ministry strategic objectives providing the performance magnet for program and project alignment or minister able to demonstrate the consolidated effects of international and domestic investment in regional development. Andriantseheno sets out the necessary elements for effective collaboration in joint evaluation at the program level.

Looking across a sector, in chapter 6, van den Berg notes findings of a meta-evaluation of 400 climate change mitigation and adaptation efforts that evaluations and reports also seemed to be limited in findings and scope, often focusing on a very specific institutional perspective. Many studies have a project basis, with little sense of larger scale programmatic approaches, policy frameworks, or economic, regional and other considerations and drivers of sustainability. The chapters by Andriantseheno, van den Berg, and Agrawal and Rao ask why the development community continues to squander resources and opportunities for more robust monitoring systems linked to higher-order strategy and fails to make better use of joint evaluations for accountability and learning experiences.

The evidence presented in this book and in the External Review of the Consultative Group on International Agricultural Research (CGIAR) system and the World Bank Assistance Strategy-Interim Strategy Note, which lays out the implications to Afghanistan of aid bombardment from 62 donors, many acting with autonomy off budget and off plan, suggests that the Development Assistance Committee (DAC) needs to adjust its evaluation criteria to include synchronization with the country development strategy and its aligned ministry strategies and reinforce efforts to ensure greater policy coherence among donors. The development community needs to build the political will to leave behind the donor-driven, stand-alone project as the modus operandi of development.

Institutional Performance: Developing the Strategy

According to Dimitrov, "Without systemic, if not harmonized, institutional performance evaluations and a commitment to their rigor, impartiality, and follow-up at the highest levels, the use of evaluation work will remain fragmented and underutilized" (chapter 3). He highlights the steps necessary to plan and conduct higher-order institutional performance to enhance an institution's mission orientation and, in his view, motivate collaborative performance improvement. His work is important because too few multilateral institutions are subjected to performance evaluations and current peer review practices pale in comparison with available methodology.

In chapter 4, Jaljouli reports on the initial stages of assisting the Dubai government in developing a holistic city-state strategy. Like Dimitrov and other contributors, he points to the importance of a strategy founded on a high-level, results-based strategic framework with interlinked performance management plans cascading from the highest levels of governance down to the operational level. His goal, like Dimitrov's, is to ensure optimum policy coherence and program coordination to achieve Dubai's three high-level strategic objectives.

In chapter 1, Wijayatilake addresses the importance of a results-based, high-level strategy as the key organizing incentive for the integration of MfDR into the full government-wide institutional planning and management cycle. As the Secretary of the Ministry of Planning Implementation, she encountered obstacles in getting other ministries to develop the necessary ownership of strategies. She is nevertheless optimistic about the three-year experience but has concerns about the full potential of a performance system being realized. Wijayatilake hopes to progress beyond ritualistic reporting, merely because a planning ministry wants it, to creating reports that affect evidence-based decision making.

Strategy and Performance Management Leadership: Whose Job Is It?

The answer to the problem of a ritualistic response to performance measurement systems, noted by Wijayatilake and others, lies partially in Jaljouli's approach. Jaljouli makes the distinction between evaluation practice and strategic management practice, noting that although both rely on the flow of information that enhances the decision-making process, the two concepts differ significantly in terms of ownership and the values driving them.

Jaljouli draws on Kaplan's work on strategic management to argue that the responsibility for developing guiding governance strategy and setting performance frameworks lies squarely with senior leadership and management. He focuses on the importance of their involvement in the process of developing the strategy to create greater ownership and responsibility for achieving the strategic outcomes, suggesting that the resulting sense of ownership among the leadership ensures its role in reinforcing decision making and resource alignment with overall strategic objectives.

The majority of the contributors address institutional-level performance. They are unanimous about the central importance of senior-level leadership in ensuring that evaluation and performance monitoring are taken seriously, not in a routine and perfunctory manner. Building an enabling environment for the use of performance information and evaluation is critical.

The main values that drive strategy management are systematic learning and alignment; all strategy management processes support these two values. The mapping and measuring exercises have to be conducted by a core team representing the organization and approved by the management team. The ownership structure represents the new joint management thinking, taking the organization away from the silo mentality, stressing the fact that the team needs to jointly drive performance, without jeopardizing accountability. In fact, accountability among the management team is even extended to include, in addition to the direct responsibility of functions within each team member's area, the indirect corporate responsibility that each member of the organization's team contributes to. Strategy reviews are well-organized forums in which all performance information against objectives is brought onboard and discussed openly by the owners themselves. Ultimately, through resource alignment processes, performance is reflected in the way people do their day-to-day jobs.

Jaljouli might agree with Dimitrov that institution-wide self-assessment is a good starting point. Wijayatilake would likely agree that an independent evaluation function that addresses institutional performance in a regular and systematic fashion is important as an incentive for the adoption of internal performance management systems and to provide an independent perspective. However, Dimitrov and other contributors who address the importance of overarching strategy and metrics stop short of assigning full stewardship to senior management as the driver behind each phase of the corporate cycle. The chilling effect of having institution-wide performance systems performed by an outsider is not discussed in depth.

Strategy mapping is most useful as a management tool. Jaljouli emphasizes that strategic objectives cannot be achieved as a result of a single functional effort. The management team itself needs to identify the important cross-functional themes that represent value added in all functions of the organization. When the management team does the hard thinking needed to develop the strategy map (called the *strategic results framework* in MfDR), its members establish new accountability structures that ensure appropriate synchronization of the various responsibility centers to achieve common objectives. In doing so, they develop a sense of joint ownership of the strategy.

Evaluators have the measurement skills to develop strategy maps; they cannot induce managers to recognize the benefits of ownership of the process. Too often, organizations give either the evaluation function or external consultants the role of developing strategic objectives and key performance indicators. Therein lies one essential clue about why the ritualistic response to pressure to develop results strategies begets ritualistic reporting.

The Role of the Evaluator and Evaluation in Managing for Development Results

To see why Jaljouli's effort to distinguish management and evaluation practice is important, consider a semantic issue. In its essence, Kaplan's model of strategic management is equivalent to MfDR theory. MfDR in turn stands on the shoulders of the OECD country public sector reforms of the 1980s and 1990s, called *results-based management* (RBM), *performance management and measurement*, and *new public management*. Like its predecessors, MfDR is meant to be what it says it is—management centered in its development (which necessarily requires broad consultation) and citizen centered in its orientation, feedback, and evaluation.

Jaljouli could consider rethinking his use of the term *evaluation practice*. According to the DAC *Glossary of Key Terms in Evaluation and Results-Based Management*, an evaluation is

> the systematic and objective assessment of an on-going or completed project, programme or policy, its design, implementation and results. The aim is

to determine the relevance and fulfillment of objectives, development efficiency, effectiveness, impact and sustainability. An evaluation should provide information that is credible and useful, enabling the incorporation of lessons learned into decision-making process of both recipients and donors.

An evaluation is a study or exercise that can take place before, during, or after a project, program, or development intervention. In 2002, the World Bank, the United Nations Development Programme, and DAC donor members came together to produce the glossary, because there was growing confusion regarding the social research practice of evaluation and public sector reform based on RBM practice. Much of the confusion was based on the terminology. It is important, as Jaljouli suggests, that a distinction be drawn between who owns evaluation and who owns MfDR or strategic management practice. *Evaluation* should refer to episodic reviews conducted by management as part of an effort to verify that it is producing the best mix of outputs to achieve desired results or externally by independent evaluation teams for accountability purposes. The term *managing for development results* should be used for real-time poverty reduction strategy results frameworks and their implementation through adaptive monitoring for continuous learning and adaptation.

The two approaches, MfDR and evaluations, are complementary and interdependent. Managers rely on evaluation to test their outcomes using multiple sources of data and to challenge indicators that are used to test progress. Evaluation depends on an open learning culture and the databases used for smart real-time decision making.

In table 4.1, Jaljouli assigns to the evaluation role "developing a theory of change… and the project logical framework," breaching the management boundary he seeks to establish. When the theory of change is not explicit, the quality of the performance measurement frameworks is poor, there is little evidence of deliberate learning in complex situations, and it is difficult for evaluators to evaluate the development program. But is that not a finding?

The interest by evaluators in building better performance management systems is understandable, but it wrongly places accountability onto those who are charged with building the performance information system. For the same reason, evaluators should not develop results frameworks at the project level; doing so is the role of the project management teams responsible for implementation. The evaluator's role is to judge the quality of the results framework—its effectiveness in aligning resources with priorities, tracking progress, and influencing rapid adaptation by program and project managers when progress is not as predicted, slow, or affected by new circumstances.

The practice of using institutional evaluators to build performance systems, some argue, has sidelined evaluators. The opportunity cost of working on building or advising on results-monitoring systems is that there are fewer resources for carrying out good independent evaluation.

In response to Jaljouli's temperate request for a dialogue on the question of evaluation versus management practice, it is arguable that the role of evaluators is to evaluate results-based strategies and results frameworks using the best strategic management analytics. Their role is not to define strategic objectives or build results chains; it is to diagnose what exists. When no strategic framework exists, or the framework is weak, their findings should reflect as much. An evaluator can assist a management or renewal team in understanding what it means to have a strategy and in discerning what lessons have been learned in the process of developing results-based strategies and frameworks. But it is not the role of evaluators, or even of results-based consultants, to define strategic objectives or key indicators. Assuming this role deprives management teams of an essential collective learning experience—that of defining and accepting collective responsibility for institutional-level priorities.

A good illustration of how the evaluator and management can work together is the recent renewal of the CGIAR lead by World Bank Vice President Kathy Sierra, who chaired the CGIAR, and the simultaneous work by the Independent Panel for the Review of the CGIAR System, which I chaired. The review panel pointed to the need for a results-based strategy and suggested methods for its development. The CGIAR renewal exercise included a wide range of executives in the system, scientists, multilateral organizations, national agricultural research systems, and a range of global and local nongovernmental organizations, all working in multidisciplinary teams to tackle a broad range of strategy, governance, finance, and partnership issues. The exercise developed broadly owned strategic objectives for a new CGIAR. The review panel fed the results of its studies in real time to the renewal exercise, with the provision that with triangulation, its findings could change. The review panel was able to raise previously undiscussable issues and to challenge basic assumptions about how CGIAR operated. The renewal exercise led by Sierra protected the review board's independence and ensured that its voice was always present in the exercise. At no point, however, did the panel suggest what the strategic objectives or indicators should be; it recommended only that concrete objectives and fact-based indicators were necessary and that the existing monitoring system had to be realigned to support a results-based strategy. Leadership of the organizational strategy by the key stakeholders was crucial; the panel's involvement focused on diagnosis, not engagement.

The Interpretation of Results Management by the Development Community

Jaljouli's use of the term *evaluation* as a synonym for MfDR is understandable in the development community, where evaluators have often championed the results approach. And in many cases, management has been quick to hand responsibility for MfDR to staff groups, such as evaluation or quality management departments.

An unfortunate consequence of the confusion between evaluation and management-driven MfDR—as well as the increasing compliance orientation of the donor community—is an overemphasis on reporting on progress toward set indicators at the expense of greater operational learning and flexibility. Results management was meant to give citizens voice by tracking program effects (outcomes) at the citizen level (How was their quality of life improved? Did they use the clinic, and did the treatment make them healthy? Do they trust the financial integrity of the government budget and financial functions?).

For its part, the public sector was meant to be freed of accountability for lockstep compliance with regulations to be more adaptive to specific community needs and rapid changes in the economic and social environment. Management teams were to have the mandate to adjust resource allocation for optimum results and to continuously adapt programs in line with new performance evidence on citizen impact. Indicators were signals that further analysis was required, not an end state. The quid pro quo for greater management or "political" authority was assurance to the authorizing environment, through performance reporting and performance budgeting, that agreed expectations were being met at the lowest cost.

In international development, MfDR has the potential to fulfill the promise of the development partnership while opening it to greater public scrutiny and public understanding of the inevitable tradeoffs. Yet too often, MfDR has served only to burden overworked staff with rigid reporting systems that test their predictive capacity as opposed to their adaptive capacity. Reporting is too often without consequence and disconnected from higher-order objectives (McAllister and others 2008; see also World Bank 2009). Sadly, most reporting focuses on recipient governments rather than on donor behavior or commitments.

The absence of country leadership ownership for development strategies is in some ways understandable. Although ownership progress has been made in some countries, and is supported by Poverty Reduction Strategies and Sectorwide Programs, results systems are too often idiosyncratic to the donor project without informing operational sector strategy performance at the ministry level. This results in a skewed perception that MfDR is largely an accountability or compliance tool for donors. A predictable result is that reports are often crafted to avoid embarrassment rather than to contribute to sector or societal learning. Little attention is paid to the benefits of using results frameworks and reports for real-time communication, motivation, learning, or improvement of cross-project and program performance. Only rarely are performance information systems implemented or used at the management level of the government or the donor to improve everyday decisions or to support policy analysis.

When senior managers focus on and are accountable for institutional outcomes, my experience is that they use their management prerogative, very quickly explore partners at the boundary, and move to a systems approach. Outcomes and impacts can be achieved only in partnership with others. I have observed that, as Jaljouli contends, when organizations are seriously charged to achieve societal outcomes, they are more likely to be open to internal and external partnerships. For example, the New Zealand Road Authority was responsible for providing a good-quality road system. With public sector reform, the government held the authority accountable for reducing road fatalities. The authority had to work seamlessly with police, hospitals, and organizations such as the New Zealand Red Cross (box 12.1.)

Box 12.1   New Zealand Road Authority

In the 1980s, the New Zealand Road Authority, led by Tony Bliss, was contracted to reduce highway deaths. From initially resisting being responsibility for outcomes outside its zone of control, it pioneered a new era of systemwide approaches to managing for results. Progress evolved through these phases:

Phase 1 (1950s and 1960s): Driver interventions: Focus on rules, penalties, education, and training

Phase 2 (1970 and 1980s): Systemic interventions: The "Haddon matrix," focusing on infrastructure, vehicles, and users in precrash, in-crash, and postcrash phases (it is the most commonly-used paradigm in injury prevention).

Phase 4 (late 1990s onward): Long-term elimination of death and long-term injury, systemwide intervention to address human limitation, and shared responsibility for national goals.

The unequivocal long-term goal to eliminate death and serious injury was driven by time-limited outcome and output targets achieved through an exacting strategy for a systemwide, multisectoral intervention based on known safety principles. The result was strengthened, accountable institutional management requiring best practice and continuous innovation across all elements of the road safety management system.

Source: Breene 2008.

Over time, its leaders recognized that outcomes are achieved through partnerships and a whole-system, data-intensive approach to management.

An independent study of the application of a results approach in the international development arena compared with best-practice programs like the New Zealand Road Authority could contribute to reducing the growing frustration with MfDR on the part of people in operations. It could potentially reduce some of the tensions between a systems approach and the more linear interpretation of MfDR that has emerged largely as a legacy of the logic framework analysis thinking that is deeply engrained in the development community's psyche.

Conclusion: Confronting a Political and Leadership Vacuum

Robert Picciotto's opening comments at the conference from which this volume is based emphasize the urgency of improving development effectiveness in a declining global context. He suggests a close examination of the role of evaluation and the evaluator. Taken together, the chapters in this volume push the evaluation community to face old issues and new realities and to explore new fields for research and practice to improve ECB in today's context. In learning about new fields, it is important that the evaluator use new approaches to inform rather than replace management functions.

Many of the vexing issues brought to light in this volume have been around for a very long time. What is to some extent reassuring is that they challenge the development evaluation community to confront a political and leadership vacuum—or at best, resistance—in leading real results-based strategies and programs and using the best methods available for institutional analysis. What is most important about this collection of chapters is that they discuss the obstacles that prevent better performance management and evaluation, including the perspective of developing countries, and open a dialogue for mutual improvement by the donor community and governments.[3]

Notes

1. USAID is not alone in facing internal coordination challenges. The 2008 Independent Review Panel of the Consultative Group for International Agricultural Research (CGIAR) saw that internal coordination within aid agencies presented significant challenges for donor multilateral officers wanting to link the agricultural research they funded through the CGIAR with the agricultural programs

being funded by their country programs. One Centre Director in the CGIAR noted that though he and his colleagues were being admonished to integrate programs with the other 14 agricultural research centers around the world, donors found it hard to get cooperation from colleagues in the same stairwell.
2. The recent reform of the CGIAR has strengthened the mandate of the individual international agricultural research centers by changing the donor-dominated governance structure to include a consortium owned by the centers. The consortium will lead a global strategy development exercise with a view to refocusing the work of scientists and country and civil society partners on three agreed-on strategic objectives, to be achieved through large consolidated programs and a consolidated reporting system for the donor forum.
3. *Synthesis Report of the Evaluation of the Paris Declaration, Phase One* (Wood and others 2008) is a useful companion piece to this volume based on assessments of 8 studies and 11 donor agencies. It addresses progress on implementing the key principles of the Paris Declaration: ownership by countries; alignment with countries' strategies, systems, and procedures; harmonization of donors' actions; managing for results; and mutual accountability. Like the contributors to this book, Wood and others find that some progress has been made on implementing the Paris principles but that country systems, especially the link between national strategies and sector and operation programs and donor coordination, need strengthening. RBM requirements must be made less confusing. High-level political engagement on both sides of the development partnership is critical for achieving aid reforms. Evaluators have a special role to play in bringing evidence to the table to demonstrate how citizens are being served by the global development partnership and what changes are needed to ensure the successful implementation of the Paris Declaration Reforms.

Bibliography

Breene, J. 2008. "Safe System: The New Performance Frontier for Road Safety Management," PowerPoint presentation, Perth, November 6.

Chapman, J. 2002. "System Failure." Demos, London. http://www.demos.co.uk/publications/systemfailure.

Land, T., V. Hauck, and H. Baser. 2009. "Capacity Development: Between Planned Interventions and Emergent Processes." ECDPM Policy Brief 22, European Centre for Development Policy Management, Maastricht, the Netherlands.

McAllister, E., K. Bezanson, G. Chandra, J. Mugabe, and J. Waage. 2008. *Bringing Together the Best of Science and the Best of Development*. Report to the Executive Council of the Consultative Group for International Agricultural Research (CGIAR) by the CGIAR Independent Review Panel. http://www.cgiar.org/externalreview/.

Morra Imas, L. G., and R. C. Rist. 2009. *The Road to Results: Designing and Conducting Effective Development Evaluations*. Washington, DC: World Bank.

Schein, E. H. 2009. *Helping: How to Offer, Give and Receive Help*. San Francisco: Berret-Koehler Publishers.

Wood, B., D. Kabel, F. Sagasti, and N. Muwanga. 2008. *Synthesis Report of the Evaluation of the Implementation of the Paris Declaration: Phase One.* Copenhagen: Ministry of Foreign Affairs of Denmark.

World Bank. 1999. *The Drive to Partnership, Aid Coordination and the World Bank.* Washington, DC: World Bank, Operations Evaluation Department.

——. 2006. *Annual Report in Operations Evaluation.* Washington, DC: World Bank, Independent Evaluation Group.

——. 2007. *Sourcebook for Evaluating Global and Regional Partnerships.* Washington, DC: World Bank.

——. 2009. *Annual Review on Development Effectiveness.* Washington, DC: World Bank.

CHAPTER 13

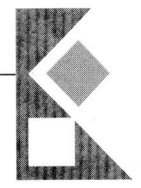

Perspectives on Evaluation Capacity Building

Steffen Bohni Nielsen and Karin Attström

This volume introduces a number of different perspectives on evaluation capacity building (ECB). Some offer analytical and theoretical frameworks; others emphasize the empirical content of efforts to build evaluation capacity. Different perspectives are offered on what constitutes evaluation capacity and ECB.

In the seminal volume on ECB in *New Directions for Evaluation* (Baizerman, Compton, and Stockdill 2002a), the editors note that important lessons can be learned from the field of development aid, where a longer tradition for (evaluation) capacity building has been formed and conceptualized. The contributions in this volume may inform, inspire, or otherwise guide the emerging practice of ECB.

This chapter reflects on the contributors' perspectives on ECB. It does so in three steps:

- surveying the literature on ECB
- mapping the perspectives offered by the contributors in terms of scope, purpose, definitions, and methods

- relating the key findings and recommendations to a common ECB framework.

The Literature on Evaluation Capacity Building

Within the evaluation field, the concepts *evaluation capacity* and *ECB* are relatively new.[1] Although the national strands of evaluation may have lagged the development aid strand, there is now a considerable focus globally on ECB, in both evaluation practice and academia.

Arguably, the themes of the 2001 and 2002 American Evaluation Association (AEA) conferences—Evaluation Capacity Building and Mainstreaming Evaluation—directed a broader and more sustained degree of professional attention to this topic. In 2008, more than half of the AEA's members who responded to a survey reported that they were engaged in ECB efforts (Preskill and Boyle 2008).

As these concepts are being explored, their boundaries are being probed and ambiguities concerning their precise meaning are being revealed (Compton and Baizerman 2007). Indeed, a review of the literature reveals four trends: widespread conceptual pluralism, differing opinions regarding the purpose of ECB, the lack of a comprehensive empirical base for the various models, and a focus on approaches to and methods for tackling capacity building. Less attention is being paid to what capacity building comprises.

Conceptual Pluralism

The term *evaluation capacity* has been applied at the macro (societal) level (Furubo and Sandahl 2002; Mackay 2002); the meso (organizational) level (King and Volkov 2005; Preskill and Boyle 2008); and the micro (individual) level (Taut 2007a). Some scholars and practitioners (Boyle and Lemaire 1999; Milstein and Cotton 2000) focus exclusively on the supply side (developing human capital, tools, and resources). Others (Boyle, Lemaire, and Rist 1999; Mackay 2002; Dabelstein 2003; McDonald, Rogers, and Kefford 2003) emphasize the importance of the demand side (policies, plans, organizational structures, processes, culture).

Purpose of ECB

The aim and purpose of ECB are also issues of contention. One prevalent definition of capacity building is that of Stockdill, Baizerman, and Compton (2002, 8), who define ECB as "a context-dependent, intentional action system of guided processes and practices for bringing about and sustaining a state of affairs in which high-quality program evaluation and its appropriate uses are ordinary and ongoing practices within and/or between one or more organizations/programs/sites." Together with Milstein and Cotton (2000), they emphasize both the ability to carry out and sustain high-quality program evaluation and the ability to use the evaluation appropriately.

Mackay (2002), among others, argues that this view is too narrow, that ECB must have a wider scope and become a cornerstone in ensuring that knowledge from monitoring and evaluation (M&E) is applied as part of sound public governance. This view seems to dominate the development aid perspectives on ECB. Mackay (2002, 83) proposes that ECB should encompass "a broad range of evaluative tools and approaches that include but go beyond program evaluation. The purpose of the (World) Bank's ECB efforts is not to build M&E capacities per se; capacity building is simply one step along a 'results chain.'"

In this sense, Mackay supports a line of argument also proposed by others (de Lancer 2006; Mayne and Rist 2006; Rist 2006; Stame 2006; Nielsen and Ejler 2008) to the effect that the scope of evaluation and evaluation practice should be broadened from consisting merely of studies to becoming streams of evaluative knowledge that are applied in sound public governance. In this view, evaluation should generate more than high-quality program evaluation studies; it should engage in wider practices that produce and apply evaluative knowledge that is integral to the entire policy cycle. Arguably, then, the different conceptions and purposes of evaluation capacity and ECB stem, at least in part, from different understandings of the actual role and purpose of evaluation as a management tool in organizations, as a research tool for understanding interventions in society, and as an accountability tool (Mayne, Divorski, and Lemaire 1999).

Limited Empirical Base

The empirical bases of the models differ. Generally, most contributions on evaluation capacity and ECB are grounded and informed by a qualitative research design driven by one or more case studies. This means that analytical but not statistical generalizability can be inferred from them.

Approaches to and Methods for Tackling Capacity Building

The lion's share of attention has been focused on methods for, and roles in, building evaluation capacity (see, for example, Stockdill, Baizerman, and

Compton 2002; Baizerman, Compton, and Stockdill 2002c; Huffman, Thomas, and Lawrenz 2008). Much less attention has been paid to the nature of evaluation capacity. Naccarella and others (2007, 232) correctly point to the consequences of this focus in noting that "differing definitions of evaluation capacity result in varying conceptualizations of ECB. This is not surprising—if there are different views about what is being built, there will inevitably be different views about how to build it."

Only some contributions can be regarded as systematic attempts to conceptualize evaluation capacity (Preskill and Torres 1999; World Bank 1999; Furubo and Sandahl 2002; Stufflebeam 2002; King and Volkov 2005; Stufflebeam and Wingate 2005; Taut 2007b; Preskill and Boyle 2008; Taylor-Powell and Boyd 2008; Russ-Eft and Preskill 2009). Even among them, differences in scope are marked. Many models focus on evaluation capacity either at the macro (societal) level (World Bank 1999; Furubo and Sandahl 2002); the meso (organizational) level (Stufflebeam 2002; King and Volkov 2005; Preskill and Boyle 2008; Taylor-Powell and Boyd 2008); or the micro (individual) level (Stufflebeam and Wingate 2005; Taut 2007b). In this sense, the theoretical developments have not yet been consolidated around a few predominant theoretical and methodological conceptions of what constitutes evaluation capacity or ECB.

ECB Perspectives Offered by the Contributors

This section maps the perspectives on evaluation capacity and ECB offered in this volume. The contributions differ significantly in scope and content, making a synthesized analysis difficult. This heterogeneity underlines the point that differing conceptualizations dominate the field. The contributions are based on a comparative framework structured around six categories: scope, geographical and institutional coverage, purpose, definition, methods used, and findings (table 13.1).

Purpose

Like the scope of the chapters, differences exist in conceptualizations of evaluation capacity and ECB. Almost all contributions are written in the context of developing countries or emerging economies. It appears that all authors agree that the purpose of ECB efforts is ultimately to achieve better governance; all of the contributors thus offer support to the framework proposed by the Organisation for Economic Co-operation and Development/ Development Assistance Committee (OECD/DAC 2009).

Table 13.1 Main Features of Each Chapter

Author/chapter	Scope	Geographic and institutional coverage	Purpose of ECB	Definition	Methods used	Findings
Agrawal and Rao (chapter 7)	Argues for national-level systematic ECB program to increase evaluation utilization; presents case study on three rounds of evaluation of an employment generation scheme	India, program-level case study	Emphasis on strong supply side when building evaluation capacity	None offered	Emphasizes both demand side and availability of training to strengthen capacity	Centralized, high-powered institution must look at various evaluation studies, ensure proper study of recommendations, and track follow-up action taken on each recommendation.
Andriantseheno (chapter 8)	Identifies factors for internalizing programmatic approach to M&E system	Madagascar, program-level case study	To help build, use, and sustain a program- and project-level M&E system	None offered	Training, technical assistance	To make program- and project-level M&E systems work, considerable ECB investments (training, tools, and approaches) must be made in terms of structures, processes, and human capital.

continued

Table 13.1 *continued*

Author/chapter	Scope	Geographic and institutional coverage	Purpose of ECB	Definition	Methods used	Findings
Clotteau and others (chapter 10)	Outlines major challenges in ECB, identifies lessons learned and best practices in M&E capacity building	General, developing countries	M&E capacity is central in MfDR framework; ECB is necessary to support better governance	ECB involves strengthening or building M&E systems so that M&E is regularly conducted and used by the country/organization itself.	ECB approach based on RBM principles, including more decentralized and diverse training; the use of well-established tools; technical assistance; supporting information systems; and various sensitization, policy discussion, and professional exchange platforms as part of overall ECB strategy and road map	ECB is key element in more global reform of public sector toward managing for development results. Evaluation capacity should be built by targeted, balanced use of variety of methods. It also requires strong leadership and increased commitment by governments and development partners.
Dimitrov (chapter 3)	Reviews evaluation of development organizations and proposes ways to surmount common barriers	Development aid, organizational level	None offered	None offered	None offered	Focus is on key factors that make institutional review difficult. Lessons learned on successfully planning, conducting, and following up evaluations of institutional performance are presented.

Heider (chapter 5)	Suggests ways to make use of good practice in capacity development and applies them to ECB	General	To create better governance, provide input to institutional capacity building in general	None offered, but necessary to address the three levels of capacities	Overview and analysis of good practice from capacity development and ECB interventions and theory; combines and integrates evaluation capacity and capacity development approaches, defining capacities and capabilities needed at each level	Prescribes good practice in capacity development and shows how it may be applicable for ECB. Capacity building must take place at multiple levels, including enabling environment, institutional capacity, and individual capacity.
Jaljouli (chapter 4)	Seeks to open dialogue between M&E practices and strategy management in public and private sectors	Dubai, local government		None offered	None offered	M&E and strategy management can be integrated by creating strategy maps and theories of change and by using evaluation techniques in evaluating strategic themes and high-level outcomes.

continued

Table 13.1 continued

Author/chapter	Scope	Geographic and institutional coverage	Purpose of ECB	Definition	Methods used	Findings
Picciotto (chapter 11)	Discusses challenges facing evaluation of development aid	General development aid	None offered	None offered	None offered	Development evaluation must reconsider its strategies, instruments, and emphases, recognizing that development today has less to do with charity than with human security. Global developments challenge role of evaluation in governance and in relation to other disciplines.
Porter (chapter 9)	Finds that conceptualization of "helping" in personal relationships between helper and helped throughout ECB efforts may improve results	South Africa, eight not-for-profit organizations	To build capacity to manage, use, and sustain M&E system	None offered	Development of horizontal relationship between helper and helped rather than vertical teacher and student relations; different forms of inquiry and dialogue (pure, diagnostic, confrontational, process-oriented); training and technical assistance	Helping supported integration of technical evaluation approaches into ECB work by improving relationships between experts and recipients. Schein's theory of helping should be used as strategy in ECB.

Wiesner (chapter 2)	Relates evaluation of macroeconomic performance in Latin American countries to evaluation capacity	Latin America, macroinstitutional	To increase effectiveness through demand-driven evaluation and ECB	Same as World Bank (Mackay 2002)	Not stated, but implication is that strong demand side with needs for high-quality information will create supply	Effectiveness of evaluation in enhancing results is largely a function of degree to which it is driven by demand for improved results rather than supply side.
Wijayatilake (chapter 1)	Outlines efforts to institutionalize a results-based M&E system in Sri Lanka	Sri Lanka, whole of government	To build capacity to establish, manage, use, and sustain a government-wide M&E system	None offered	Various tools, databases, and incentives to support development and implementation of MfDR	Quality of results frameworks, availability of data, and good reporting are technically important elements. Also important are ownership, leadership, need for integrated processes, and time for implementation to take effect.

Source: Author.

Note: Not all chapters were available at the time this chapter was written.

Definition

Conceptual pluralism, which is widespread in the field, is evidenced in this volume. None of the articles discusses the theoretical basis of evaluation capacity or ECB. There is thus little focus on definitions.[2] ECB efforts to strengthen M&E frameworks to improve governance suggests that the use of evaluative knowledge is key. Heider (chapter 5) argues that capacity must be conceptualized in the context of the larger environment, the institutional framework, and the individual level. These distinctions are similar to the distinctions between the macro, meso, and micro levels discussed in chapter 5. At the same time, Heider's capacity development framework goes much further than the ECB discussion, as it conceptualizes several levels and has a more operational perspective than the more theoretical discussions.

Other authors discuss ECB in the context of a macro (societal) perspective (Agrawal and Rao, Clotteau and others, Picciotto, Wiesner, Wijayatilake). Andriantseheno, Dimitrov, Jaljouli, and Porter conceive of ECB at the meso (organizational) level. None of the authors discusses ECB purely at the micro (individual) level.

The authors hold different views on the relative importance of the demand and supply sides in ECB. Wiesner (chapter 2) places strong emphasis on the demand side, arguing that

> the effectiveness of evaluation in enhancing results is a function of the degree to which it is driven more by the demand for improved results than by supply side considerations and origins... Accountability is the ultimate incentive driving the quality of evaluations and attendant learning... [E]valuation capacity building is a process that requires—and results from—the demand for improved results.

Heider (chapter 5) and Wijayatilake (chapter 1) emphasize the strategies, structures, and processes that drive demand for evaluative knowledge and evaluation capacity. While acknowledging the demand side, Clotteau and others (chapter 10) and Agrawal and Rao (chapter 7) argue that fostering evaluation capacity requires adequate and accessible training and human capital. Andriantseheno (chapter 8) argues that a strong supply side is critical to the internalization and use of evaluative knowledge.

Key Findings in a Common ECB Framework

Notions concerning the purpose, macro/meso/micro level, and demand/supply side all concern the very conceptualization of ECB. The conceptual pluralism becomes increasingly evident when considering evaluation capacity.

Heider's framework for conceptualizing evaluation is based on studies on the levels important for capacity development in general. As she notes in chapter 5, "Capacity development practitioners highlight the importance of working at three levels, which—when applied to the world of evaluation—illustrate the need to institutionalize the evaluation principles with measures that go beyond the individual but span the institutional framework and the enabling environment for evaluation." Combined with the three principles deemed central for evaluation (independence, credibility, and utility), the three constructs create the framework adopted here to reveal the authors' respective emphases when discussing ECB.

Figure 13.1 shows significant variety in the range of issues encompassed in the contributors' discussions of evaluation capacity and ECB. Although this may partially be explained by the different scopes of the chapters, it also pinpoints the conceptual pluralism that dominates the ECB field.

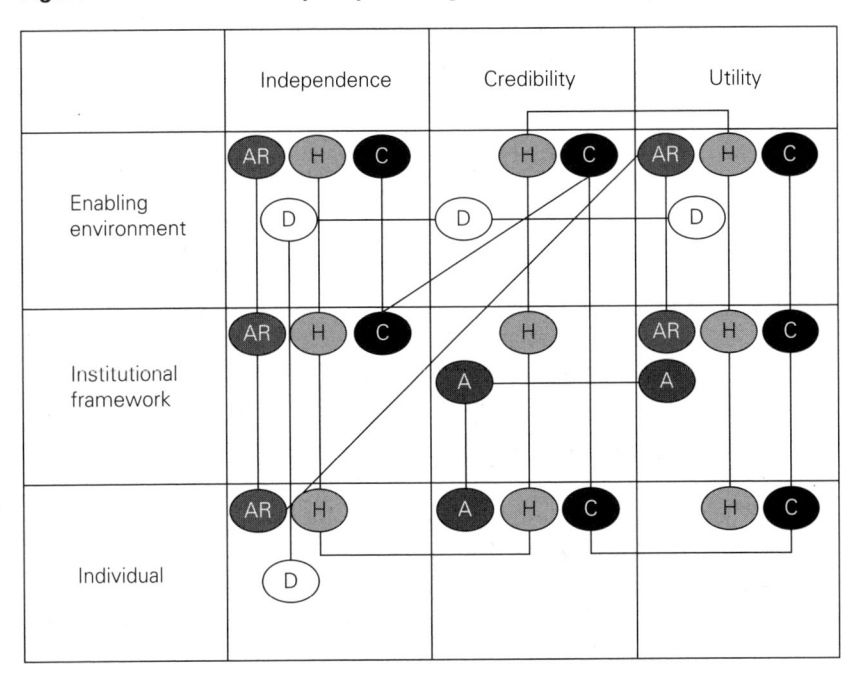

Figure 13.1 Evaluation Capacity Building Issues Covered by the Authors

	Independence	Credibility	Utility
Enabling environment	AR, H, C, D	H, C, D	AR, H, C, D
Institutional framework	AR, H, C	H, A	AR, H, C, A
Individual	AR, H, D	A, H, C	H, C

Source: Author.

Note: A: Andrianteheno; AR: Agrawal and Rao; C: Clotteau and others; D: Dimitrov; H: Heider.

Perspectives on Evaluation Capacity Building

All authors touch on utility issues with regard to ECB efforts, especially with regard to the enabling environment and institutional framework that foster a demand for evaluative knowledge. To varying extents, the authors discuss issues concerning credibility and the enabling environment. In contrast, little attention is given to practices concerning credibility within the institutional framework. Among the three core principles in evaluation, the least attention is devoted to evaluators' independence.

Methods

The conceptualizations of evaluation capacity and ECB differ substantially across chapters. Consequently, the tools prescribed or applied to ECB also differ. Preskill and Boyle (2008) chart a number of learning strategies or methods to build evaluation capacity. The methods proposed by the contributors can be identified using this framework (table 13.2).

Not surprisingly, chapters dealing most comprehensively with ECB (chapter 5, 9, and 10) prescribe a diversity of methods needed to build evaluation capacity, whereas those dealing with ECB either tersely or in a circumscribed manner do not broach the issue of methods or they mention only a few methods. The crucial point is the authors' recognition that several methods and approaches are needed to achieve the ECB objectives. This finding is reflected in recent findings in the ECB literature as well (see Huffman, Thomas, and Lawrenz 2008; Preskill and Boyle 2008).

The Empirical Base

Despite efforts in recent years, the lack of a systematic empirical base for ECB remains a problem (Dabelstein 2003; World Bank 2005). Three chapters in this volume stand out. In chapter 5, Heider draws from extensive reviews of good practice for capacity development and makes the inference that good practices should be applied in the field of ECB. However, she does not provide concrete evidence of the effectiveness of the framework. In chapter 10, the authors base their recommended practices on studies, their consultancy experience, and consultation with collaborators in ECB efforts. The analysis is well constructed but does not appear to be based on a rigorous study supporting the validity of the recommended practices. In chapter 2, Wiesner refers in passing to an evaluation of macroeconomic performance but does not present the actual evidence. The remaining contributions that offer empirical evidence are based on case-based narratives or studies. They thus add to the body of single case studies that dominate the empirically based ECB literature.

Table 13.2 Methods for Evaluation Capacity Building Prescribed or Applied by the Authors

Method	Agrawal and Rao	Andriantseheno	Heider	Wijayatilake	Wiesner	Clotteau, Boily Darboe, and Martin	Jallouli	Picciotto	Porter	Dimitrov
Internship: Participating in a formal program that provides practical evaluation experience for novices	✓ (by implication, through formal education)				n.a.		n.a.	n.a.		n.a.
Written materials: Reading and using documents about evaluation processes and findings			✓	✓	n.a.	✓ (by implication, through formal training)	n.a.	n.a.		n.a.
Technology: Using online resources such as Web sites and e-learning programs to learn from and about evaluation			✓	✓	n.a.	✓ (by implication, using established tools)	n.a.	n.a.		n.a.
Meetings: Allocating time and space to discuss evaluation activities specifically for the purpose of learning from and about evaluation			✓	✓	n.a.		n.a.	n.a.	✓	n.a.
Appreciative inquiry: Using an assets-based, collaborative, narrative approach to learning about evaluation that focuses on strengths within the organization					n.a.		n.a.	n.a.		n.a.
Communities of practice: Sharing evaluation experiences, practices, information, and readings among members with common interests and needs (sometimes called learning circles)			✓	✓	n.a.	✓	n.a.	n.a.		n.a.

continued

Table 13.2 continued

Method	Agrawal and Rao	Andriantseheno	Heider	Wijayatilake	Wiesner	Clotteau, Boily Darboe, and Martin	Jallouli	Picciotto	Porter	Dimitrov
Training: Attending courses, workshops, and seminars on evaluation	✓ (based on formal, university-based education)	✓	✓	✓	n.a.	✓	n.a.	n.a.	✓	n.a.
Involvement in an evaluation process: Participating in the design or implementation of an evaluation			✓	✓	n.a.		n.a.	n.a.	✓	n.a.
Technical assistance: Receiving help from an internal or external evaluator		✓	✓	✓	n.a.	✓	n.a.	n.a.	✓	n.a.
Coaching or mentoring: Building a relationship with an evaluation expert who provides individualized technical and professional support			✓		n.a.		n.a.	n.a.	✓	n.a.

Source: Author.

Note: n.a. = Not applicable

Conclusion

The field of ECB is highly heterogeneous. The chapters in this volume reflect the same trends as revealed in the literature—namely, widespread conceptual pluralism, differing opinions regarding the purpose of ECB, the lack of a comprehensive empirical base for the various models, and a focus on approaches and methods for tackling capacity building. By illustrating these trends, this anthology contributes to the body of knowledge on ECB. It does not offer evidence that supports conclusive conceptualizations or a more unified understanding of ECB.

The chapters in this volume share some important commonalities. ECB must ultimately lead to better governance. The use of evaluative knowledge is critical in capacity-building efforts, which require that multiple methods be deployed.

While acknowledging the evolving nature of evaluation capacity as well as capacity development, the contributors to this volume highlight a few issues for further consideration, gained from practical work in capacity development within evaluation and results-based management. The OECD's *Working towards Good Practice* (OECD/DAC 2006, 13) states that "the enabling environment influences the behavior of organizations and individuals in large part by means of the incentives it creates." Incentives are not only created by rational and conscious processes, they often emerge from invisible mechanisms, such as culture and tradition, which form a part of the norm system of societies as well as organizations. Intrinsically, normative incentive systems, which are not based on accountability, will display resistance to change, given the effect a stronger focus on rational accountability would entail. These mechanisms are a challenge to any capacity development intervention, particularly when the stated objective is ECB and increased accountability.

Another important feature that merits further exploration is the linkage between the demand and supply sides. There is a tendency in the literature, including this volume, to lean toward one side or the other in the approach to ECB. Developing supply-side and technical skills will not create demand by itself, but demand that is not met with high-quality and reliable evaluative knowledge will eventually wither. A concern is the time required to build evaluative systems that provide sufficient information to allow for longitudinal analysis and value added in policy and decision making. A thorough understanding of the interrelation and interaction between the supply and demand sides is thus essential to realize the benefits of ECB.

Notes

1. The comparative analysis must be treated with caution, as the publications and proposed models serve different purposes and conceptualizations (for example, institutionalization or capacity building); are at different stages of finalization; and are based on different methods and empirical evidence.
2. Only Clotteau and others (chapter 10) and Wiesner (chapter 2) define *evaluation*.

Bibliography

Baizerman, M., D. W. Compton, and S. H. Stockdill. 2002a. "Editors' Notes." *New Directions for Evaluation* 93 (Spring): 1–6.

———. 2002b. "New Directions for ECB." *New Directions for Evaluation* 93 (Spring): 109–19.

———. 2002c. "Summary and Analysis of the Case Studies: Themes across the Cases." *New Directions for Evaluation* 93 (Spring): 101–108.

Boyle, R., and D. Lemaire, eds. 1999. *Building Effective Evaluation Capacity: Lessons from Practice.* Piscataway, NJ: Transaction Publishers.

Boyle, R., D. Lemaire, and R. C. Rist. 1999. "Introduction: Building Evaluation Capacity." In *Building Effective Evaluation Capacity: Lessons from Practice*, ed. R. Boyle and D. Lemaire, 1–19. Piscataway, NJ: Transaction Publishers.

Compton, D., and M. Baizerman. 2007. "Defining Evaluation Capacity Building." *American Journal of Evaluation* 28 (1): 118–19.

Dabelstein, N. 2003: "Evaluation Capacity Development: Lessons Learned." *Evaluation* 9 (3): 365–69.

De Lancer, J. 2006. "Performance Measurement: An Effective Tool for Government Accountability? The Debate Goes On." *Evaluation* 12 (2): 219–35.

Furubo, J.-E., and R. Sandahl. 2002: "A Diffusion Perspective on Global Developments in Evaluation." In *International Atlas of Evaluation*, ed. J-E. Furubo, R. C. Rist, and R. Sandahl, 1–23. Piscataway, NJ: Transaction Publishers.

Huffman, D., K. Thomas, and F. Lawrenz. 2008. "A Collaborative Immersion Approach to Evaluation Capacity Building." *American Journal of Evaluation* 29 (3): 358–68.

King, J. A., and B. Volkov. 2005. "A Framework for Building Evaluation Capacity Based on the Experiences of Three Organizations." *CURA Reporter* 35 (3): 10–16.

Mackay, K. 2002. "The World Bank's ECB Experience." *New Directions for Evaluation* 93 (Spring): 81–99.

Mayne, J., S. Divorski, and D. Lemaire. 1999. "Locating Evaluation: Anchoring Evaluation in the Executive or the Legislature, or Both or Elsewhere?" In *Building Evaluation Capacity: Lessons from Practice*, ed. R. Boyle and D. Lemaire, 23–52. Piscataway, NJ: Transaction Publishers.

Mayne, J., and R. Rist. 2006. "Studies Are Not Enough: The Necessary Transformation of Evaluation." *Canadian Journal of Program Evaluation* 21 (3): 93–120.

McDonald, B., P. Rogers, and B. Kefford. 2003. "Teaching People to Fish? Building the Evaluation Capability of Public Sector Organizations." *Evaluation* 9 (1): 9–29.

Milstein, B., and D. Cotton. 2000. *Defining Concepts for the Presidential Strand on Building Evaluation Capacity*. Fairhaven, MA: American Evaluation Association.

Naccarella, L., J. Pirkis, F. Kohn, B. Morley, P. Burgess, and G. Blashki. 2007. "Building Evaluation Capacity: Definitional and Practical Implications from an Australian Case Study." *Evaluation and Program Planning* 30 (3): 231–36.

Nielsen, S. B., and N. Ejler. 2008. "Improving Performance? Exploring the Complementarities between Evaluation and Performance." *Evaluation* 14 (2): 171–92.

Nielsen, S. B., and S. T. Lemire. n.d. "Measuring Evaluation Capacity: Results and Implications of a Danish Study." Ramboll Management, Copenhagen.

OECD/DAC (Organisation for Economic Co-operation and Development/Development Assistance Committee). 2006. *The Challenge of Capacity Development: Working towards Good Practice*. Paris: OECD/DAC. http://www.oecd.org/dataoecd/4/36/36326495.pdf.

———. 2009. "Managing for Development Results Capacity Scan: MfDR Capacity Scan." http://www.mfdr.org/Cap-scan/.

Preskill, H., and S. Boyle. 2008. "A Multidisciplinary Model of Evaluation Capacity Building." *American Journal of Evaluation* 29 (4): 443–59.

Preskill, H., and R. Torres. 1999. *Evaluative Inquiry for Learning in Organizations*. Thousand Oaks, CA: Sage

Rist, R. C. 2006. "The 'E' in Monitoring and Evaluation: Using Evaluative Knowledge to Support a Results-Based Management System." In *From Studies to Streams: Managing Evaluative Systems,* ed. R. C. Rist and N. Stame, 3–22. Piscataway, NJ: Transaction Publishers.

Russ-Eft, D., and H. Preskill. 2009. *Evaluation in Organizations: A Systematic Approach to Enhancing, Learning, Performance, and Change*. New York: Basic Books.

Stame, N. 2006. "Introduction: Streams of Evaluative Knowledge." In *From Studies to Streams: Managing Evaluative Systems*, ed. R. C. Rist and N. Stame, vii–xxi. Piscataway, NJ: Transaction Publishers.

Stockdill, S. H., M. Baizerman, and D. Compton. 2002. "Toward a Definition of Evaluation Capacity Building Process: A Conversation with the Evaluation Capacity Building Literature."*New Directions for Evaluation* 93 (Spring): 7–26.

Stufflebeam, D. 2002. "Institutionalizing Evaluation Checklist." Evaluation Center, Western Michigan University, Kalamazoo. http://www.wmich.edu/evalctr/archive_checklists/institutionalizingeval.pdf.

Stufflebeam, D. L., and L. A. Wingate. 2005. "A Self-Assessment Procedure for Use in Evaluation Training." *American Journal of Evaluation* 26 (4): 544–61.

Taut, S. 2007a. "Defining Evaluation Capacity Building: Utility Considerations." *American Journal of Evaluation* 28 (1): 120.

———. 2007b. "Studying Self-Evaluation Capacity Building in a Large International Development Organization." *American Journal of Evaluation* 28 (1): 45–59.

Taylor-Powell, E., and H. Boyd. 2008. "Evaluation Capacity Building in Complex Organizations." *New Directions for Evaluation* 120 (Winter): 55–69.

World Bank. 1999. "Evaluation Capacity Development: A Diagnostic Guide and Action Framework." ECD Working Paper 6, Operations Evaluation Department, Washington, DC.

———. 2005. "Evaluation Capacity Development: Building Country Capacity for Monitoring and Evaluation in the Public Sector: Selected Lessons of International Experience." ECD Working Paper 13, Operations Evaluation Department, Washington, DC.

CHAPTER 14

Lessons Learned in Capacity Building: Where Do We Go from Here?

Stefan Dahlgren

The chapters reviewed here provide a wide range of examples and lessons learned—implicit and explicit—of capacity building for evaluation. What they have in common is a keen interest in improving capacity and competence in the field. Where they differ is in the level of application, uniqueness or replicability, environment or context, and relation between monitoring and evaluation.

The chapters fall largely into two groups. One group comprises case studies, which provide examples of more or less successful initiatives and of analyses of problems and their remedies. The other group attempts to synthesize, drawing generalized conclusions and lessons learned and identifying trends or prescriptions.

One can read these contributions from different perspectives. Of course, these chapters are not a representative sample of how monitoring and evaluation look at the moment in developing countries, but to make it simple for the time being, let us pretend that they are. For the case studies, we ask questions about representativeness, possibilities to generalize, and so forth. From the syntheses, we want to know the extent to which these generalized views can be applied to specific countries or contexts, how approaches can be better implemented, and whether new aspects of problem analysis are possible.

The chapters can also be grouped by those that take a "Western" or donors' view and those that provide a developing country or recipients' perspective. Most of the cases are written by authors from developing countries, and most of the syntheses are written by Western authors. What is noteworthy is that there are so many interesting cases from which to learn. This was not the case 10 years ago. In contrast, today one does not have to go very far to find real cases from which to learn.

A third sorting principle is to see if a chapter discusses mainly monitoring or evaluation. Almost all of the contributors talk about monitoring or evaluation, but they differ in terms of their emphasis. Not surprisingly, most of the developing country contributions are about monitoring. I do not believe that monitoring somehow must precede evaluation or that monitoring must be performed to conduct an evaluation; evaluations are often conducted without proper monitoring. Monitoring is easier, more straightforward, and more "natural" than evaluation. One will almost automatically want to follow up on what one finds.

The chapters show a change from projects to programs to ongoing, continuous, and "normal" government budget execution and service delivery and perhaps even governance. Running schools and hospitals is a day-to-day activity, not a project or a program, but a normal service government should provide. It needs monitoring as well as evaluation from time to time.

A word of caution is warranted regarding the meaning of concepts and terms. In the development cooperation business, the terms *monitoring* and *evaluation* are normally used in relation to projects and programs—that is, activities that are limited in time with respect to resources allocated and space. Years ago, one "evaluated" the effects and "monitored" implementation progress. However, with the change of perspective from donor to developing country and the increased importance of sector programs and broader poverty reduction measures, the term *monitor* has taken on a slightly different and more general meaning. Evaluators now follow different areas of social development over time and monitor long-term indicators of interventions that are not always funded by donors. Attention is shifting from limited interventions to continuous, routine, public sector operations. Confusion will arise if these meanings are not kept apart.

In the following sections, I highlight some of the interesting features of each chapter and discuss different aspects of what is presented.[1] Arriving at a conclusion is not possible—the selection is too diverse for that—but a few issues that arise are discussed in the last section, including some aspects that seem to be missing.

Working toward Development Results: The Case of Sri Lanka

Dhara Wijayatilake

In chapter 1, Dhara Wijayatilake relates an impressive story about the introduction of a monitoring and evaluation (M&E) system in Sri Lanka that was implemented in 35 ministries during a very short period of time. Despite starting from a very basic level of monitoring only expenditure, the system was made to work. It is particularly interesting to learn about the starting points—what M&E was performed (and not performed) before mid-2007—and the limited resources that were available. The main conclusion—that it is possible to carry out such a scheme without massive financial input—is striking. The most essential resources are a clear vision and strategy, reliable political backup, and sufficient latent competence in the form of a number of well-educated civil servants who could be trained and convinced to redirect their efforts toward this new endeavor. Large financial investments were not necessary, although presumably some manpower had to be redirected for data collection and analysis.

What was created was a comprehensive monitoring system that focused on results. It seems that the crucial element was to change what was monitored from looking at inputs (that is, budget allocations and expenditures) to outputs (that is, the production of services and infrastructure). Doing so is both simple and revolutionary. Like governments everywhere, the government of Sri Lanka has an elaborate accounting system that keeps track of where the money goes. What was needed was a similar system to keep track of what the money buys. Creating such a system may be complicated initially, as new data collection mechanisms have to be established and results are measured in different "currencies" (pupils, patients treated, kilometers of roads built), at least as primary data. A unified "currency" (for example, percentage accomplished against targets or something similar) needs to be created to measure performance. As for financial monitoring, auditing is needed to ensure the quality and reliability of the reporting. And, as Wijayatilake points out, "the most important challenge is not to lose sight of the fact that even this initiative should be results based."

The main lesson from this story is that such an endeavor is possible. A second lesson is that it is essential to assess the situation before the new system is implemented, so that the right preconditions are created and the relevant resources allocated.

Two other interesting lessons are noted in the chapter. The first is to go rather slowly. Two years may be long enough to implement a systemwide approach. There may be a temptation to move more quickly, leaving some people and institutions behind.

The second lesson is to build capacity incrementally rather than begin with a large training program while everything is kept on hold. This lesson is consistent with the notion that change is not that difficult to implement once the idea and the vision are clear.

The chapter probably tells only half the story. One would like to know more about the political environment that enabled capacity to be built. Did some triggering factor make it possible or unavoidable? Was there growing dissatisfaction about government performance that had been simmering for a while and threatened to boil over? Or was there some feature in Sri Lanka's government structure that made this success possible? To judge replicability and sustainability, one would like the answers to such questions.

Chapter 1 is essentially about monitoring. Evaluation—in the sense that fundamental, critical questions are asked by people with little stake in the possible answers—is still needed. To some extent, the media, lawmakers, and academic researchers pose questions. But systematic, fact-based evaluations have a role to play as well.

The Evaluation of Macroeconomic Institutional Arrangements in Latin America

Eduardo Wiesner

In chapter 2, Eduardo Wiesner provides both a case study of evaluation of macroeconomic policy management and a generalized statement on the importance of evaluation being governed by demand. Wiesner wants to convey two messages. The first is that policy evaluation must be demand driven to be effective. The second message is that accountability is the key incentive driving the effectiveness of capacity building. His interest focuses on policy institutions' performance. The case used for illustration compares macroeconomic achievements across Latin American countries.

According to Wiesner, evaluators should not hesitate to attack complicated, macro-political issues, even those that border on research. Reluctance to do so often makes evaluators and their commissioning agencies shy away from greater challenges in evaluation.

Wiesner places great emphasis on accountability. His is the only chapter that discusses accountability at length. Some readers may find his argument that accountability is the ultimate driving force toward quality in evaluation a bit idealistic. Evaluation does require an open attitude and a genuine will to find out how things really work, but only good-quality reports can withstand the scrutiny of stakeholders with different interests and points of view.

The importance put on demand may also seem idealistic, but Wiesner points out that demand may be based on a more or less explicit search for lower transactions costs and thereby have quite a practical motivation. Even so, as Wiesner notes, the self-interest of individuals and groups can hamper efforts to find out about results of a given policy.

Accountability as one of the two main reasons to carry out evaluations (the other is learning) is usually associated with moral obligations to tell stakeholders what is being done with the money. It is also behind Wiesner's argument, but his way of introducing the discussion of transactions costs is interesting.

From Evaluating Projects toward Assessing Institutional Performance

Todor Dimitrov

Measuring institutional performance is not easy; doing so as a self-evaluation can be particularly tricky. In chapter 3, Todor Dimitrov describes how an international development bank measured such performance. He argues that doing so is not only possible, but, all else equal, also preferable to doing so through external consultants.

Dimitrov describes recent changes regarding multilateral development banks and the somewhat surprising lack of performance assessments by these institutions. Only two comprehensive evaluations of UN organizations (the International Fund for Agricultural Development [IFAD] and the Food and Agriculture Organization [FAO]) have been conducted. Donors have assessed the performance of multilateral institutions, mainly UN organizations, with some, such as Canada, Sweden, and the United Kingdom, creating ranking systems. For a few years, the evaluation function at multilateral institutions has been subject to peer reviews by donors based on the belief that the quality of evaluations and their use is strategically important to ensure proper feedback on the international organizations' own activities.

One advantage of carrying out a self-assessment of the kind described in chapter 3 is that ownership stimulates better learning. Another important factor is cost: keeping an evaluation in-house reduces direct costs. Moreover, once the method is established, it is possible to repeat the exercise from time to time with less preparation and cost. A drawback is, of course, that fewer resources will be available for evaluations of the activities the institution is financing.

At first sight, one may ask how an evaluation of a development bank differs from any other organizational review. The first difference is that most organizations use external expertise for such reviews, partly because they normally do not have evaluations departments or similar functions (apart from internal audit departments, which is another matter).

A second difference is that development banks are partly responsible for the results of the projects and programs they finance; conventional banks limit their attention to the financial aspects of a loan (interest, collateral, and repayment). Performance must therefore include what employees do to ensure successful performance of the projects they finance. The typical organization consultant probably does not have sufficient insight into what is needed for judgments regarding development projects. For this reason, self-evaluation may be a reasonable option. As Dimitrov points out, the question is whether the self-evaluation is rigorous, independent, and open enough. Openness is probably the key.

In many ways this self-evaluation is a peer review. Even if colleagues are not evaluators, they are familiar with many of the aspects covered by the study, not least because some of the problems they meet when they work with loans are similar, thus putting them in a position to judge or at least understand the approach and methodology. They will probably also have a sense of the degree of independence of the review, because they know something about the organization's problems, mistakes, and successes and will immediately see if such things are properly handled in the review. Nevertheless, it may be appropriate to formulate and share in advance explicit criteria for the independence of the unit and the self-evaluation itself.

The biggest problem to overcome may be the behavior of top management. If findings are very negative or not implemented, the evaluators may lose credibility. An absolute requirement must be that once the review is launched, it cannot be stopped. The solution is openness.

Whether self-evaluations are appropriate for a particular organization is difficult to say. At certain times in an organization's life, a self-evaluation may be the right thing to do; on other occasions, an external review may be a better or the only viable option.

Evaluation Systems as Strategy Management Tools: Building Dubai's Institutional Learning Capacity

Mohammad A. Jaljouli

By comparing and finding ways to merge planning and follow-up methods from the public sector with strategy management tools from the private sector, Mohammad Jaljouli wants to stimulate evaluation and institutional learning based on experiences from highly business-oriented Dubai. As he points out in chapter 4, both approaches are built on a basic feedback loop (plan → do → check → act), but they differ in certain ways. The main differences are in ownership or the degree of detachment from the feedback; in the degree of emphasis on the feedback process itself; and in the way information influences decisions. Some of these differences stem from how Jaljouli describes conventional monitoring and evaluation and strategy management. The differences may be perceived to exist because the strategy follow-up is essentially a monitoring mechanism, whereas "conventional" follow-up is more of a stand-alone evaluation.

According to Jaljouli, the strategy feedback is organically built into the strategy process during both its creation and its implementation. The people transforming the strategy into concrete work plans and activities are also reporting back on results and involved in acting on those results. In conventional development aid, those processes are separated; consultants often carry out evaluations, which are normally initiated and thus "owned" by the foreign development agencies. The advantages of the strategy management approach are obvious, according to the author, particularly in a fast-growing economy like Dubai.

From this difference follows the strategy management emphasis on the process as a continuous flow of information from the center to the implementation level and back again to be directly acted upon at different levels. In the development cooperation area, there are often two separate tracks, with planning and execution following one track and feedback, particularly proper evaluations, following another. This does not mean that the twain shall never meet; it does mean that deliberate measures need to be taken for them to do so. Because most people find that planning and creation are much more fun than checking what really happens, planning and creation usually get considerably more attention in most organizations than follow-up, particularly as follow-up often causes a change of plans, a cumbersome and boring thing to do for most people.

The issue of ownership is important: the Paris Declaration and Accra Agreement are emphatic that ownership should be transferred to host countries. This is fairly easy when administrative capacity and political will are present, but it has much to do with the source of the money: Dubai generates its own income, whereas most developing countries still depend on external resources, which foreigners are eager to keep track of.

Recent trends in monitoring and evaluation suggest moving from studies to streams, but stand-alone systems are nevertheless still important. I believe that the difference has less to do with different views on follow-up mechanisms and more to do with the shift from projects to the ongoing "production" of public services. Running schools or hospitals year after year are not projects that are limited in time and budget but streams, which, in principle, never stop (certain streams will change course many times). From this it follows naturally that monitoring and continuous feedback, usually linked to budget execution, are the normal form of follow-up. In my view, evaluations have to be precisely such stand-alone undertakings to bring added value; they should be detached and "foreign," in the sense of being able to look at things with fresh eyes.

Jaljouli states that there is a big difference in follow-up mechanisms in conventionally financed activities in most developing countries and the domestically created and financed development plans in Dubai. He does not, however, sufficiently distinguish between monitoring and evaluation when pointing out the advantages of the strategy management approach. Nevertheless, he argues convincingly that learning, one distinguishing mark of evaluations in contrast to monitoring, can be achieved in the strategy management world. One reason for this is probably that Dubai's government system may have more similarities with a large corporate setup than with the political and administrative structure in countries with multiparty systems. This difference presumably makes it possible for Dubai to have a more streamlined decision-making mechanism.

A Conceptual Framework for Developing Evaluation Capacities: Building on Good Practice

Caroline Heider

Caroline Heider's excellent chapter on combining overall quality requirements of an evaluation function with a comprehensive view of capacity building provides a constructive basis for further efforts in the area of developing evaluation in organizations and even at the national level. She uses the three interrelated concepts of independence, credibility, and utility as a normative theory and a starting point, emphasizing that training is only one of several necessary building blocks for an effective evaluation function. The trick is to combine tangible efforts such as formal training, organizational setup, and so forth with less tangible norms and values, without which neither effective learning from nor proper accountability for successes and failures will be possible.

Heider shows that the three concepts are interrelated but need to be defined and applied separately. The purpose of evaluations is, of course, to use them; if evaluations are not credible, stakeholders will not use them. The chain is not a simple one, in which independence creates credibility and so forth. Although independence is a prerequisite for credibility, credibility needs its own set of defining elements.

What makes the three concepts particularly interesting is that there may be tensions among them. The proper application of the three normative principles is a constant balancing act, in which independence may lead to isolation, to the detriment of both credibility and utility, and credibility may suffer if independence is perceived to be lacking.

Many in-house evaluation departments find themselves in exactly this position. Being part of an organization no doubt makes it easier to understand potential problems and time evaluations, and improve the possibilities for communicating findings and recommendations. However, for outsiders, the general public, and sometimes even colleagues, an evaluation that is conducted by the organization is automatically less credible than one executed by an outside party. Many people consider independence an absolute value that should not be compromised; it takes a great deal of work to explain that things are never black or white. Independence concerns not only organizational issues but also the individual evaluator; evaluators who move from the operational parts of an organization to evaluation may create doubts about their integrity. This is ironic, as the credibility of an evaluator who worked in operations should be higher than that of one who did not.

Increasingly in development cooperation agencies—and probably also in national evaluation commissions and the like—evaluations are carried out not by full-time evaluators but by contracted consultants. The organizations' evaluators are instead evaluation managers, who plan and design evaluations, make them happen, and disseminate their results. The in-house evaluation manager works as a kind of interface between potential users and other stakeholders within and outside the organization on the one hand and the consultants who conduct the evaluation on the other. Having the evaluation conducted by people who are outside the institution should improve the credibility of an evaluation (although a popular view is that consultants are dependent on further contracts and thus dare not be too critical).

An essential point in Heider's chapter is that the development of evaluation capacity is not linear; a number of processes take place in parallel. As she notes, "Capacities do not develop following a blueprint." Evaluation requires keen attention and flexibility to simultaneously adopt to circumstances and adhere to established values.

Table 5.1—in which the three principles of independence, credibility, and utility are combined with the three levels of conditions (the enabling environment, the institutional framework, and the individual's competence and capacity)—is very instructive. It indirectly invites the reader to fill in the cells, making it an interactive tool for analysis of needs for developing a successful evaluation function. This tool could be used for training purposes.

Capacity Building: The Indian Experience

Rashmi Agrawal and Banda V L N Rao

Chapter 7, by Rashmi Agrawal and BVLN Rao, discusses the preparation of evaluations in India. The authors identify several actual or potential obstacles, which can be overcome primarily by increasing capacity and competence among evaluators as well as by greater involvement of the government agency that is most connected to the evaluated project or program.

Although evaluation and systematic follow-up has been established in the Indian administration, according to the authors it has never played the role it should in informing decision makers and the general public about results. Instead, it seems to have become a routine and rather mechanical exercise that few people are interested in and even fewer are using to improve performance or question activities.

Uneven quality—caused by a combination of low capacity to undertake methodologically sound and conceptually interesting evaluations—and a lack of interest in reports that are carried out too far away from the agencies concerned may explain the lack of relevance of evaluations. Thus, there is no real demand for evaluations.

To the authors, the obvious ways to remedy the situation are to improve the competence of the evaluators, both individually and institutionally, and to better target potential users, which would stimulate real demand. The solutions are interlinked: greater competence yields better evaluations, which are more useful and used, and greater usage of evaluations creates greater demand, which, in turn, makes evaluators try harder.

There is a third and even more crucial part of the solution: involving users more in the entire process. It is likely that an evaluation that involves users will be based on more realistic and relevant assumptions with better knowledge by evaluators of the intervention logic. Moreover, the evaluation will be received by potential users not as a foreign matter that no one seems to know how to deal with but as something familiar. Users may have been engaged in the formulation of recommendations, making them "owned," more relevant, and probably less threatening. This engagement has to be balanced against the integrity and independence of the evaluators, which should be part of an evaluator's competence. The basic principles are well known and firmly based in evaluation guidelines and rules.

The authors' analysis seems reasonable, but it is also fairly conventional these days, when everyone advocates ownership and involvement. To be really useful and lead to realistic remedies, one has to go into details. The chapter does this to some extent by listing a number of factors that negatively influence the use of evaluations. One such factor, which they consider fundamental, is failure to identify the user in advance. As Weiss (2004) indicates, "If you cannot identify and articulate the primary intended users and uses of the evaluation, you should not conduct the evaluation. Unused evaluation is a waste of precious human and financial resources."

This quotation must be contextualized, as it may be risky to reduce the quality of an evaluation by overemphasizing its instrumental use and simply linking it to immediate actions. Policy-level or thematic evaluations may run less of a risk of falling into the instrumental trap; project-related evaluations may easily do so. When identifying users, one assumes that they will undertake certain actions (this lies in the user definition), which will, in turn, influence the evaluation design. By too narrowly defining users, the evaluator may unintentionally limit its scope.

In contrast to monitoring, evaluations must leave room for reflection. Of the five Development Assistance Committee (DAC) evaluation criteria, relevance is what really makes an evaluation. If evaluators define the user in a limited way, they may never ask if they are examining the right questions. Of course, involving stakeholders means that evaluators identify potential users. The point is to be careful about users; defining them too narrowly may limit the evaluation and its use.

Implicit in this reasoning is the problem of how far the evaluator should go in creating use for ("selling") the product. A good evaluator should have a fair view of where the problems may lie in a program and what issues tend to be avoided when reports are written or plans drawn. A certain amount of advocacy is both prudent and desirable.

The more fundamental the questions asked are, the higher the quality required from the evaluation. This does not necessarily mean harder, numerical data; it does mean clear logic, verifiable facts, and honesty about when and where the weaknesses may be in an evaluation.

Among factors detrimental to evaluations, the authors mention evaluations carried out as a mandatory process, which become routine and mechanical without a clear relation to current problems or successes. Many organizations set rules for when an evaluation must be undertaken (either after a certain amount of time or above a certain level of money). The idea is to guarantee that resources are not spent without control, but such evaluations are about as exciting as annual reviews.

Auditors—evaluators' cousins—establish their work plans from a simple formula: risk and importance. Importance is usually the equivalent of "a lot of money," but an activity with a high level of risk does not need to include a high level of funds. It is the combination of risk and size that determines whether to conduct an audit. Evaluations could be decided upon by using similar principles, but "importance" could have another meaning—namely, implications for the future. Using implications for the future as a criterion could lead to evaluation of even small projects and programs, particularly pilots, because the learning potential is great.

It is easy to accept the chapter's critique of mechanical rather than context- or problem-oriented evaluations. But one could also ask if the problem really lies only with reutilized evaluations. It may be that something is wrong with an administrative and political machinery that is able to make decisions without the input that was once deemed necessary. Apparently, the flow of information runs along other routes and may not consist of verified facts.

Multiple evaluations of programs, which are mentioned in the chapter as a problem, could very well turn out to useful, by creating a more nuanced picture and stimulating reflection. If all of the evaluations are badly done and produce only bland findings and conclusions, they are indeed a waste of resources and can generate only indifference or even aversion to evaluations.

Fault-finding evaluations are indeed the bane of any evaluation activity. Little learning will come out of such an approach, and it may yield no gain from the accountability point of view, as partial successes may be underestimated or underanalysed. Failures are seldom complete failures.

Timing, timeliness, and the dissemination of information are sometimes even more important than good quality. The evaluation is never just the report. Evaluation is a process that begins with the idea of conducting an evaluation; it never really ends, because some evaluations may be used long after the report was published. Charting the whole process in advance and taking precautions at each step in relation to the potential for quality and future use is the key to success with an evaluation.

The Environmental/Rural Development and Food Security Program in Madagascar

Balsama Andriantseheno

The chapter by Bali Andriantseheno describes a new and previously untested method for evaluative data collection and the analysis. People connected to the program, most of them working with implementing partners, were invited to write publishable articles on their experiences from the program and to formulate lessons learned from its implementation and design. The method was labeled a "stocktaking exercise" rather than an evaluation, but to some extent, it was apparently partly used as an evaluation.

The invitation yielded almost 30 articles focusing on national, cross-regional, and regional issues. Articles describing the central level of government discussed policy and strategy analysis. At the regional level and farther from the center, the discussion was mainly on practical implementation issues. These different focuses proved to be a problem, as the assumed complementarities of the articles from different levels did not lead to the broad overview that was expected. Andriantseheno notes that traditional M&E setups in the program did not help, because they were developed separately for different parts of the program and it was not possible to combine the reporting to produce a comprehensive picture and overview of the program.

Despite the disappointment regarding the overall perspective, the exercise was worthwhile, according to the author, because it was very much a participatory approach, it stimulated analysis at all levels, and it created a knowledge base that may lead to other evaluative studies.

This is indeed an interesting method, whose learning potential seems great. In some ways, it resembles focus group interviews, but the element of reflection and analysis by the participants is more emphasized. A problem is to find the right balance between maintaining openness and capturing many aspects on the one hand and retaining enough focus to provide the most relevant and useful information on the other.

As a stocktaking exercise, the article writing only partly fulfilled the objective. The coverage seemed too scattered, and one may assume that the data on which the articles were based varied much in quality.

The author finds the approach useful, particularly in relation to the monitoring that already existed within the program, which apparently differed widely between subprograms and individual projects. However, the chapter's conclusions are more about improvement of more conventional M&E systems. They never really elaborate on how an exercise of this kind can be integrated with more conventional approaches.

Recognizing "Helping" as an Evaluation Capacity Development Strategy

Stephen Porter

Stephen Porter's story about "helping" as a way to build monitoring capacity in a small development project in South Africa challenges established ways of carrying out tasks. The author argues that a true sense of what monitoring entails is not just a technical skill; it is also a way to gain insight into the purpose of an evaluation exercise and the nature of bringing about change.

Helping takes time and resources—in the case of the project in South Africa, 7 percent of a $2 million budget. To be effective, it must comprise a substantial element of person-to-person relationship. Porter argues that the same degree of achievement would never have taken place if the organization had relied on conventional training courses.

The questions the chapter raises are whether it was worth the large investment and whether this model can be replicated and scaled up. Figures are presented about improvements, but perhaps substantial changes could have been accomplished at much lower costs. How much is enough? I come back to that question in the next section.

Building Capacities for Results-Based National M&E Systems

Gilles Clotteau, Marie-Helene Boily, Sana Darboe, and Frederic Martin

The chapter by Clotteau, Boily, Darboe, and Martin is based on experiences from a number of recent efforts in evaluation capacity building (ECB) in several countries. The aim of the chapter seems to be to summarize the accumulated experiences by International Development Evaluation Association (IDEAS) and other practitioners and to provide guidance to people, particularly external consultants and advisers, engaged with ECB. The chapter should be very valuable for developing country officials and politicians involved with these issues.

The great value of the chapter is that it is based on practical experiences in a range of situations. This is particularly important in the light of what the authors say about the absence of evaluations regarding ECB in general.

The chapter refers mainly to evaluation, but the definition of evaluation makes the reader a bit uncertain about how much the authors distinguish between evaluation and monitoring. Included in the list of components of evaluation are audit and annual performance reports, together with "classical" evaluation and "impact" evaluation. The authors seem to be stretching the definition too far, running the risk of not separating the roles of actors when reporting is being done. Of course, a performance audit is often similar to an evaluation, but the term *audit* usually refers to financial procedural issues, where rules, regulations, and laws are the yardstick. Annual reports are normally management products. They seldom highlight problems and shortcomings, focusing instead on achievements, which make such reports less useful as independent assessments of an activity. It is not clear why impact evaluations are separated from "classical" project or program evaluations; the difference is mainly that evaluations that look for impact use a longer perspective than evaluations dealing with outcome.

The authors note that ECB has become a priority on the development agenda and that ECB may be included in international agreements. In practice, it is not even included in most donors' portfolios, let alone being high on the agenda. Compared with the attention given to public financial management and audit, evaluation still ranks low on donors' priority lists, and monitoring is normally supported as part of a program rather than a skill in itself. It is true that some support goes to evaluation training, but contributions so far have been financed out of the evaluation budget rather than from governance support allocations.

It is interesting to compare this chapter with the chapter by Heider, which addresses the same topic. Chapter 10 focuses on training, albeit in a wider perspective, which is well described in a number of diagrams. Chapter 5 is more about how to analyze a situation and create the prerequisites for ECB. Chapter 10 is more prescriptive; chapter 5 suggests a way to conduct an initial analysis (which could very well be a self-analysis). The two chapters are thus complementary.

Where Is Development Evaluation Going?

Robert Picciotto

Robert Picciotto's well-written and well-argued chapter about the future of evaluation generates two main comments. One is that he presents in an excellent way what could be called a spiritual or ideological manifesto for evaluators, pointing out the importance of independence and integrity as well as the concurrent requirement of responsibility. His description of the evaluator as "hardwired to combine assurance with curiosity, idealism with skepticism and intellectual engagement with scientific detachment" is indeed difficult to formulate better; it captures both what drives evaluators and the balancing act that every evaluator has to perform.

The other comment is about Picciotto's second theme, the introduction of a wider context for evaluators. Picciotto may be correct that circumstances do change and that evaluators need to keep in mind certain overarching issues to get the evaluations right. But his message has implications that are not easy to implement. I suppose what he means is that the dimension of relevance must be widened and always linked to certain general conditions, not only to local, national, or regional conditions.

Should it really be the responsibility of evaluators to include climate change and similar issues in their analyses? Such aspects should have been addressed when the objectives of a program were formulated and thus automatically included in the evaluation. One can always argue that any well-designed evaluation task leaves room for the evaluation team to introduce dimensions not explicitly mentioned in the terms of reference.

I am not sure whom Picciotto addresses with his proposal to include a wider perspective. If he is referring to commissioning agencies, his point is well taken. For individual evaluators, it may be more difficult to maintain detachment and not be viewed as an advocate for certain points of view.

Picciotto's chapter is an important contribution to the debate over and development of the evaluation profession and the function of evaluation. It is hoped that this strand of discussion will be maintained in future IDEAS conferences and other evaluation forums.

Discussion

Competence and quality are obvious considerations when building evaluation capacity in a developing country. Other issues also need to be considered.

Almost as important are the political and institutional context, costs, relative importance of learning and accountability, and differences and similarities between monitoring and evaluation.

A political context that is supportive of openness and self-criticism is a prerequisite for a successful large-scale evaluation. When this context is discussed in the chapters, it is done so mainly from a technical or administrative perspective (for example, the need for better capacity to improve quality). Chapter 1 emphasizes the importance of support from the highest political level. I would have liked to know more about the political considerations that made such support possible. Success stories with some kind of political analysis would be welcome in the future.

Another largely absent theme is cost, which is discussed only indirectly in the chapters by Porter and Wijayatilake. There is surprisingly little discussion among evaluators about how much resources should be allocated for follow-up and what gains are possible through proper follow-up and lessons learned. Some organizations allocate a percentage of project costs or prescribe that project and programs above a certain budget level or length of time should be evaluated. Creators of such rules are presumably less motivated by the desire for greater efficiency than by the urge to maintain better control over and reduce the risks associated with very large amounts of money.

One can speculate about what amounts should be the norm. The Swedish Development Cooperation Agency (Sida) spends about SKr 30 million a year on its evaluation department, including salaries for staff and expenditures for evaluation consultants. This is about 0.2 percent of SIDA's total budget of SKr 15 billion. Is this amount reasonable? If this effort in knowledge gathering would yield, say, 1 percent greater efficiency in the development cooperation budget a year, it would be a hugely profitable investment. It would be worth discussing the level of evaluation expenditure and how much should be spent on capacity building in this area.

Evaluation is traditionally motivated by the objectives of increasing accountability and generating learning. Several chapters touch on accountability; learning receives far more attention, possibly because accountability is largely political, whereas learning can be seen as a "safer" and more technical aspect of evaluation.

As noted at the beginning of these comments, all of the authors almost always refer to monitoring and evaluation (M&E). I believe that always linking the two and indiscriminately mentioning them together is a disadvantage for both. With one or two exceptions—notably Heider's chapter—none of the authors discusses differences or connections between monitoring and evaluation except in passing.

Although the distinction between monitoring and evaluation in relation to development programs is not always clear-cut, it is useful to consider the two activities as different forms of follow-up, with partly separate functions and purposes (see Sida). Unfortunately, it is common to lump them together and talk about M&E or M&E systems (implying an elaborate setup with established procedures for handling of data linked to decision making). *System* is such a convenient, vague, and yet correct-sounding term that it is not surprising that it is widely used.

As most people in the evaluation business know, M&E systems, if they exist, are almost invariably about "M" rather than "E." Such systems are far from being systems, in the sense that the monitoring data can easily be fed into evaluations and used to make decisions. Monitoring and evaluation normally require different sets of evidence. One cannot just aggregate monitoring data over a longer period and call a report an evaluation. The concept of M&E systems is therefore doubtful in both theory and in practice.

A World Bank–OED report (Hauge 2003) on ECB in Uganda illustrates the situation. The report points out that although much data collection and reporting (that is, monitoring) is going on, the quality of the data are generally low and analyses are lacking. According to the report, "Within Uganda's public sector, existing M&E systems are generally not geared toward understanding causality and attribution between the stages of development change. The evaluation function is relatively underdeveloped" (Hauge 2003, 169). Although the report was written some years ago, there is reason to believe that this statement is still valid and not limited to one country.

Perhaps a more adequate term would be *institution*, in the sense of the established norms, values, and behavior that constitute the framework and the practical execution of evaluations and of monitoring. *Institution* is admittedly a general and vague term, but it does not imply a machinery with smoothly running, interlocking parts.

Note

1. The contributions of several authors were not available when this chapter was written.

Bibliography

Hauge, Arild. 2003. "The Development of Monitoring and Evaluation Capacities to Improve Government Performance in Uganda." Evaluation Capacity

Development Working Paper 10, World Bank, Operations and Evaluation Department, Washington, DC.

Sida (Swedish International Development Cooperation Agency). *Looking Back, Moving Forward*. Stockholm: Sida.

Weiss, C. 2004. "Identifying the Intended Use(s) of an Evaluation." Evaluation Guideline 6, International Research Center, Ottawa. http://www.idrc.ca/uploads/user=s/11564499841Guideline.pdf.

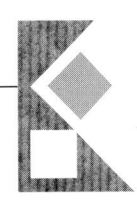

Index

A

Abdelhamid, Doha, 114
accessibility
  definition, 105 *Annex* 5.A
  to quality training in M&E, 185–86
accountability, 259
  definition, 2, 105 *Annex* 5.A
  and enabling environment, 89–90, 107*nn*10–11
  and external evaluations, 192–93
  and institutional framework for evaluation, 90–92, 95*t*5.2
  link to incentives, 24, 30–31, 34, 35*n*3, 36*nn*16–19
  and MfDR, 220–21
  and review of institutional arrangements case study, 246–47
  and strategy management, 66
accounting systems, 246
Accra Agenda for Action, 86, 88
ADAPT, 144
adaptation indicators, 118
adaptive systems, 211–12
AEA. *See* American Evaluation Association (AEA)

AFD. *See* Agence Française de Développement (AFD)
Africa
  Bana Barona/Abantwana Bethu project, 152, 158–68, 169*nn*3–5
  GDP of, 198
African and Medical Research Foundation (AMREE), 152
  See also Bana Barona/Abantwana Bethu project
African Development Bank, 198
Agence Française de Développement (AFD), 113–14
Agency Results Framework (ARF), Sri Lanka, 17–18, 19
Agrawal, Rashmi, 123–39, 208, 214, 252–55
agricultural research centers, 223*n*2
American Evaluation Association (AEA), 226
AMREE. *See* African and Medical Research Foundation (AMREE)
Andriantseheno, Balsama, 141–50, 213, 255–56
ARF. *See* Agency Results Framework (ARF), Sri Lanka

263

ASK. *See* Association for Stimulating Know-How (ASK)
assessments
  of data quality, 189
  and development framework for evaluation capacity, 4–9, 10n2
Association for Stimulating Know-How (ASK), 135
Attström, Karin, 225–42
audits and auditors, 165, 192, 254

B

balanced scorecard approach, 191, 192f10.7
Baldrige National Quality Program, 191
Bana Barona/Abantwana Bethu project, 152, 158–68, 169nn3–5
Barbut, Monique, 116
Barefoot Collective, 160, 162, 169n3
best practices
  and collaboration with IDEAS and other evaluation associations, 120–21
  identification of, 112
  and interactive software of evaluations, 119–20
Bibliotheca Alexandrina, Arab Republic of Egypt, 114, 116
Black Sea Trade and Development Bank, evaluation of, 53–54b3.1
blame game, 68
Boily, Marie-Helene, 1–12, 171–94, 209, 256–57
budgets, results-based, 18–19

C

Cambodia, Poverty Forum, 190, 191–92
Canadian International Development Agency (CIDA), 65
capabilities, for evaluation capacity building, 92–96, 107n13
capacity building, 15–16
  for better utilization of evaluations, 132–34
  case study in India, 134–36
  conclusions concerning utilization of evaluations, 136–37
  and demand-driven process, 30–32, 36nn20–22
  evaluation of, 24
  Sri Lanka, 245–46
  See also evaluation capacity building (ECB)
capacity development, 85–86, 106n1
  from capacities to capabilities, 92–96, 107n13
  and enabling environment, 89–90, 93t5.1, 94, 95t5.2, 100, 107nn10–11
  importance of process, 96–98
  and institutional framework for evaluation, 90–92, 93t5.1, 94, 95t5.2
  overview of concept, 88–89, 106–7nn7–9
  See also evaluation capacity building (ECB)
cascading of strategy management, 63–64, 74–76, 83n2
Center of Excellence in Evaluation of the Treasury Board, Canada, 190
CGIAR. *See* Consultative Group on International Agricultural Research (CGIAR)
change
  drivers of, 64–65, 66
  and evaluation capacity development, 164
  in Latin America, 32
  theory of, 218
child welfare, 152
CIDA. *See* Canadian International Development Agency (CIDA)
clear, relevant, economic, adequate, monitorable (CREAM), 179
climate change, 201, 202, 203, 214
  evaluations of, 115
  international conference on, 114, 116–17, 121n1
  mitigation of, 116–17, 118
Clotteau, Gilles, 171–94, 209, 256–57
collective action, 97
commitment, 97
Common Performance Assessment System (COMPAS), 42, 55n1
communication
  role in IPEs, 51–52
  of strategy management, 63, 80
community organizations, and evaluation capacity building, 160, 164
COMPAS. *See* Common Performance Assessment System (COMPAS)
competence, definition, 105 *Annex* 5.A
computer specialists, 189
conceptual pluralism, 226, 234–35, 239
CONEVAL. *See* National Council for Evaluation of Social Development Policy (CONEVAL)
conflicts, costs of, 201

conflicts of interest, 204
Consultative Group on International Agricultural Research (CGIAR), 55*n*2, 214–15, 219, 222–23*nn*1–2
control panels, 188
corporate social responsibilities, 169*n*4
cost–benefit analyses, 203
costs, 256
    of conflicts, 201
    and ECB, 259
    of IPEs, 50–51, 248
    transaction costs, 24, 31, 35*n*4, 36*n*2
country-level systems, 167
CREAM. *See* clear, relevant, economic, adequate, monitorable (CREAM)
credibility, 251
    definition, 105 *Annex* 5.A
    of evaluations, 86–88, 93*t*5.1, 100–104
    and independence of evaluators, 197–98
custodianship of evaluation process, 68–70

D

DAC. *See* Development Assistance Committee (DAC)
Dahlgren, Stefan, 243–61
DANIDA. *See* Danish International Development Agency (DANIDA)
Danish International Development Agency (DANIDA), 65
Darboe, Sana, 171–94, 209, 256–57
data and databases
    collection of and evaluation results, 129
    control panels, 188
    for DSP, 78, 82–83
    e@satisfaction, 188
    EIS, 18, 21
    and manual counting, 159, 162, 163
    to monitor performance, 19–20
    post-conference surveys, 119
    quality of, 66–67, 189
    and Soweto Care System, 163
    specific to ARFs, 19
    used in AMREE's project, 160–66
DEAC. *See* Development Evaluation Advisory Committee (DEAC)
decision making, 7
    evidence-based, 15
    and politics, 29
    and use of evaluation results, 30
    See also policies
demand-driven evaluations, conclusions concerning, 246–47

demand-driven process, 234
    and capacity building, 30–32, 36*nn*20–22
    conclusions concerning, 34
    and incentives, 24, 29–30, 34, 35*n*3, 36*nn*16–19
    support for evaluations, 33
Democratic Republic of Congo, 186
Department for International Development (DfID), United Kingdom, 114, 115
design mechanisms, 27, 35*n*12, 36*n*18
developing countries, and global policy evaluations, 204–5
development
    and collaboration with IDEAS and other evaluation associations, 120–21
    and evaluation of institutions, 24–26, 35*n*8
    and global insecurities, 201–2
    and inventory of evaluations for conference, 115
    multiple evaluations of development programs, 130–31
    Sri Lanka, 15
    sustainable development, 111–18
development aid, 15–19, 59
    decrease in, 199
    increase in, 196
    integration with strategy management and evaluation processes, 71–73
    See also Dubai Strategic Plan (DSP)
Development Assistance Committee (DAC), 2, 3*f*1, 215, 218, 228, 253
development banks
    assessing performance of, 42–43, 55*n*2
    evaluation of, 53–54*b*3.1
    harmonization of, 45, 55*n*4
    and MfDR, 42
    review of performance assessments, 247–48
Development Evaluation Advisory Committee (DEAC), 127
development evaluations, 111–13, 115
    future of, 258
    institutional mechanisms for in India, 126–27
    new context for, 198–200
    priorities for, 202
development institutions, 41
    closing IPE gaps between reality and intentions, 42–43, 55*n*2
    environment to facilitate evaluations of, 43–45, 55*nn*3–4

development institutions *(continued)*
  scope of evaluations of, 42, 55*n*1
  steps in preparation of IPEs, 45–54
Development of Women and Children in Rural Areas (DWACRA), 136
DfID. *See* Department for International Development (DfID), United Kingdom
diagnostic process for evaluation capacity development, 98
Dimitrov, Todor, 41–57, 208, 215, 216–17, 247–48
disaster preparedness, 201
dissemination of evaluation findings, 131–32
donor–funded programs, 64–65
  and ECB, 257
  Jordan, 64*b*4.1
  See also development aid
Dubai
  conclusions concerning strategy management tools, 249–50
  government structure, 83*n*2
  and institutional learning capacity, 99–100
Dubai Strategic Plan (DSP)
  challenges to, 80–83
  mapping of, 76–78, 79*b*4.2
  measuring of, 78, 82–83
  overview, 73–74
  performance reports and reviews of, 79–80
  system architecture, 74–76, 83*n*2
DWACRA. *See* Development of Women and Children in Rural Areas (DWACRA)

E

e@satisfaction, 188
ECB. *See* evaluation capacity building (ECB)
Ecole Nationale des Régies Financières (ENAREF), 186
economic growth, Latin America, 25–26, 27*f*2.2, 35*n*8
ecosystems, 201
EDMS. *See* Electronic Documentation Management Systems (EDMS)
education, and rules-based management certification, 184
EIS. *See* Evaluation Information System (EIS), Sri Lanka
Electronic Documentation Management Systems (EDMS), 189
electronic project monitoring system (e–PMS), 14–15, 20
electronic repositories for evaluations, 119
enabling environment
  and capacity development, 88, 89–90, 93*t*5.1, 94, 95*t*5.2, 107*n*8, 107*nn*10–11
  reinforcing of, 100
ENAREF. *See* Ecole Nationale des Régies Financières (ENAREF)
English–speaking professionals, 176
Enhanced Productivity Program, Jordan, 64*b*4.1
environmental impact assessments, 113
environmental issues
  collaboration with IDEAS and other evaluation associations, 120–21
  evaluation challenges, 112–13
  international conference for, 113–15
  inventory of evaluations for, 115
  publication of conference papers, 117–18
Environmental/Rural Development and Food Security program, Madagascar, 213
  conclusions concerning, 149
  issues raised during stocktaking exercise, 145
  lessons learned from, 146–47
  overview, 141–43
  recommendations for, 147–49
  review of Andriantseheno's analysis, 255–56
  roles and responsibilities of team for, 144–45
  stocktaking exercise for, 143–44
e–PMS. *See* electronic project monitoring system (e–PMS)
European Center for Development Policy Management, 96, 211
evaluation associations, 106*n*3, 114, 116, 190
  See also International Development Evaluation Association (IDEAS)
evaluation capacity
  on climate change issues, 116–17
  conceptual pluralism of, 226, 234–35, 239
  developing assessment framework for, 4–9, 10*n*2
  issues identified by IPDET, 9
evaluation capacity building (ECB), 1, 85, 151, 172
  approaches to and methods for, 227–28
  and Bana Barona/Abantwana Bethu project, 158–68, 169*nn*3–5
  challenges in, 173–76

and community organizations, 160, 164
conclusions concerning, 34, 222,
    223n3, 239
definition, 208–9, 234, 240n2
demand-driven requirements of, 30–32,
    36nn20–22
design of, 174–75, 177
developing assessment framework for,
    4–9, 10n2
empirical base for, 236
findings in framework for, 234–38
and helping theory, 154–58,
    168–69nn1–2
identification of results of, 179–82
issues to consider in, 258–60
and key factors for training, 182–87
limited empirical base of models of, 227
literature review of, 4, 226–28, 240n1
and M&E systems, 2–3, 4
    improvement of, 187–93, 194n4
    integrating into, 176–79, 194n3
    review of, 256–57
methods for, 236, 237–38t13.2
objectives of strategies for, 176
perspectives of, 228–34, 243–45
purpose of, 226–33
review of Heider's framework
    for, 250–52
review of Porter's analysis of helping
    strategy for, 256
review of Witjayatilake's case study in
    Sri Lanka, 245–46
starting point for, 98–104, 107nn14–15
systems approach to, 211–12
tips for developing institutional
    framework for, 101
Evaluation Cooperation Group, 113
Evaluation Information System (EIS),
    Sri Lanka, 18, 21
Evaluation Network, 113
evaluation professionals, 86, 89–90,
    106nn2–3, 251–52
evaluations, 24–26, 35n8, 202–4, 244
    acceptance of reports, 132
    and accountability link to learning and
        incentives, 30
    and application of helping theory to,
        158–68, 169nn3–5
    from capacities to capabilities
        for, 92–96, 107n13
    collaboration with IDEAS and other
        evaluation associations, 120–21
    and complex adaptive systems, 211–12

conclusions concerning
    in Latin America, 34
    utilization of, 136–37
definition, 3, 105–6 Annex 5.A, 153–54,
    172–73, 217–18, 257
and demand-driven process, 30–32,
    36nn20–22
dissemination of findings, 131–32
electronic repositories for, 119
external evaluations and
    accountability, 192–93
of global policies by developing
    countries, 204–5
heads of evaluation offices, 101–2
identification of practices
    and standards for
    evaluation of sustainable
    development, 111–13
impact of financial crisis on, 32–33
institutional framework for, 90–92,
    93t5.1, 94, 95t5.2
and institutional learning capacity
    measuring of the DSP, 78, 82–83
    overview, 73–74
    performance reports and
        reviews, 79–80
    system architecture, 74–76, 83n2
integration with strategy management
    processes, 71–73
international conference on climate
    change and development, 113–18
link to research, 31, 36n21
multiple evaluations, 130–31
need-based, 128–29
in NGOs, 112
overview of use of, 123–24
PMRY scheme, 134–36
and political economy, 210–11
principles of, 86–88, 93t5.1, 99–103,
    106n2, 107n14, 168
priorities of, 24–26, 35n8
processes of, 70–73
professional evaluation networks, 103–4
and review of capacity building, 242–55
role of in managing development
    results, 217–19
sponsors of, 130
systems theory, 211–12
value of, 15
versus strategy management, 64–71, 83n1
views of, 27
virtual community of practices
    of, 119–20

evaluations *(continued)*
 See also demand-driven process; development evaluations; institutional performance evaluations (IPEs); monitoring and evaluation (M&E); utility of evaluations
evaluators, 244
 associations for, 114
 from capacities to capabilities for evaluation development, 92–96, 107*n*13
 competencies of, 128–30
 and development strategies, 201–2
 in-house, 251–52
 knowledge role for, 197–98
 networks for, 113
 professional evaluation networks, 103–4
 review of in India capacity building case study, 252–55
 roles of, 156–57, 169*n*2, 217–19, 223*n*3
 and system theory, 211–12
 tips for developing skills and knowledge of, 103–4
evidence-based decision making, 15
evidence-based evaluations, 67
exchange, basis of, 155
executive training, 185
external shocks, 34

F

FAO. *See* Food and Agriculture Organization (FAO)
feasibility, asssessment of IPE feasibility, 48–49
feedback, 103
FFEM. *See* Fonds Français pour l'Environment Mondial (FFEM)
financial capital, 6*f*3, 8, 18–19
 See also development aid
financial crisis, 32–33, 34, 198–200, 202
follow-up strategies
 feedback, 103
 of IPEs, 52, 54–55
 and performance reports, 63, 79–80
 in training, 186
Fonds Français pour l'Environment Mondial (FFEM), 113–14
Food and Agriculture Organization (FAO), 55*n*2, 90*b*5.1
food crisis, 199, 202
food security, in Madagascar, 141–50, 213, 255–56

foreign aid
 effectiveness of in Sri Lanka, 15–19
 See also development aid
fundraising, for international conference on environment and development, 114–15

G

game theory, 36*nn*17–18
GDP. *See* gross domestic product (GDP)
GEF. *See* Global Environment Facility (GEF)
GEF Evaluation Office
 conference on environment and sustainable development, 113–18, 121*n*1
 identification of practices and standards for evaluation of sustainable development, 111–13
Global Environment Facility (GEF), 55*n*2, 111–12
globalization, 203
governance, 215, 239
 and enabling environment, 89–90
 and evaluation capacities, 99–100, 107*n*14
 of evaluation process, 68–70
 framework for, 5
 global governance machinery, 201
government, whole of government approach, 13
government structures, 69, 80, 83*n*2
greenhouse gases, 116–17
gross domestic product (GDP), 25, 26*t*2.1, 27*f*2.2
 African countries, 198
 changes in world GDP, 32–33
 Dubai, 73
gross national incomes (GNIs), 199

H

harmonization, of development banks, 45, 55*n*4
Heider, Caroline, 85–110, 208–9, 211–12, 250–52
helping and helping theory
 components of, 154–58, 168–69*nn*1–2
 conclusions concerning, 168
 definitions used, 153–54
 and evaluation capacity building, 151–53
 and evaluation of Bana Barona/ Abantwana Bethu project, 158–68, 169*nn*3–5
 principles of, 154
 review of Porter's analysis of, 256

human capital, 6f3, 7–8, 10n2
human resources, 148
human rights, 116

I

IDEA Institute, 183, 184, 186, 188, 189–91
IDEAS. *See* International Development Evaluation Association (IDEAS)
IDRC. *See* International Development Research Centre (IDRC), Canada
IFAD. *See* International Fund for Agricultural Development (IFAD)
ignorance, veil of, 29, 36n19
Imas, Morra, 186
impartiality, definition, 105 *Annex* 5.A
implementation, of results–based M&E systems, 179, 180–81t10.1, 188f10.5
incentives, 239
  and accountability, 30–31, 34, 36nn16–19
  and demand–driven evaluations, 24, 29–30, 34, 35n3, 36nn16–19
  for performance, 18–19
  to stakeholders, 179
independence, 251
  definition, 105 *Annex* 5.A
  as evaluation principle, 86–88, 93t5.1, 100–103, 106n4
  of evaluators, 89–90, 258
  as key to credibility of evaluations, 197–98
India
  case study in capacity building, 134–36
  conclusions concerning utilization of evaluations in, 136–37
  factors influencing utilization of evaluations, 128–34
  institutional mechanisms for development evaluation in, 126–27
  review of capacity building case study, 242–55
information
  about evaluation process, 103
  critical to evaluations, 24, 35n2
  health information and mobile technology, 166, 169n5
  and macroeconomic reforms, 33
  sources for, 189
information systems, 178, 187–93, 221
information technology (IT), 209
infrastructure, 15–16
initiatives, for strategy management, 62, 66
inquiry, and Bana Barona/Abantwana Bethu project, 159–65, 169n2, 169n3
Institute of Applied Manpower Research, 135
institutional capital, 5–7
institutional development, 88, 107n8
institutional learning, 60, 65–66, 70
  Dubai, 99–100
  challenges of DSP, 80–83
  mapping of DSP, 76–78, 79b4.2
  measuring of DSP, 78, 82–83
  overview, 73–74
  performance reports and strategic reviews, 79–80
  system architecture, 74–76, 83n2
institutional mechanisms
  for development evaluation in India, 126–27
  tips for development of for evaluations, 101
institutional memory, 188–89
institutional performance evaluations (IPEs), 215
  Black Sea Trade and Development Bank, 53–54b3.1
  closing performance gaps in, 42–43, 55n2
  environment to facilitate, 43–45, 55nn3–4
  framework for, 44–45, 49
  of international development institutions, 42, 55n1
  preparation of, 45–54
institutions
  demand-driven approach to arrangement of, 30–32, 36nn20–22
  design mechanisms for, 27, 35n12
  and ECB, 211–12
  environment of, 175–76
  evaluations of, 24–26, 35n8
  implications of financial crisis on, 32–33
  importance of results–based strategy to outcomes, 212–13
  and institutional arrangements, 25, 26–28, 35–36nn10–11
    new institutional arrangements for evaluation, 204
    review of case study, 246–47
  institutional framework for evaluation, 90–92, 93t5.1, 94, 95t5.2, 211–12
  linking performance with institutional characteristics, 28–29
  and manpower trained in evaluation, 174

institutions (continued)
  review of performance
    assessments, 247–48
  role in economic growth, 25, 35n8
  term use, 260
  See also development institutions;
    institutional performance
    evaluations (IPEs)
Integrated Rural Development Program, 136
intentionality, definition, 105 Annex 5.A
interactive software, challenges of, 119–20
International Development Evaluation
    Association (IDEAS), 1, 114–15, 134,
    173, 193n2, 195, 257
  collaboration with, 120–21
  and determination of evaluators, 200–205
  and new context for evaluation, 198–200
  origins of, 196
  review of association principles, 196–97
International Development Research Centre
    (IDRC), Canada, 55n3, 114, 134
International Food Policy Research
    Institute, 125
International Fund for Agricultural
    Development (IFAD), 55n2, 103,
    107n15
International Program Evaluation Network
    (IPEN), 120–21
International Program for Development
    Evaluation Training (IPDET), 9, 134,
    173, 185–86
interpersonal relationships. See
    relationships
IPDET. See International Program for
    Development Evaluation Training
    (IPDET)
IPEN. See International Program
    Evaluation Network (IPEN)
IPEs. See institutional performance
    evaluations (IPEs)
IT. See information technology (IT)
IUCN. See World Conservation Union
    (IUCN)

J

Jaljouli, Mohammad A., 59–84, 215, 216,
    218, 220–21, 249–50
joint progress review mechanisms, 190

K

knowledge
  improvement of management of, 187–93
  role of for evaluators, 197–98

L

Latin America
  economic growth in, 25–26, 27f2.2, 35n8
  impact of financial crisis on, 32–33, 34
  overview of evaluation in, 23–24,
    34nn1–4
  and political demand for change, 32
  review of features of case study,
    246–47
leadership, 97
  link to strategy and performance
    management, 216–17
  organizational, 212, 213
  ownership of, 220–22
  role in IPEs, 51–52
  Sri Lanka
    fostering of, 20–21
    to initiate MfDR in, 15–16, 20
    whole of government approach, 13,
      16–18
  to support M&E, 7
learning
  definition, 105 Annex 5.A
  and enabling environment, 89–90,
    107nn10–11
  institutional, 60, 65–66, 70
  link to accountability and incentives, 30
  units of, 188–89

M

macroeconomic institutional arrangements,
    25, 26–28, 35–36nn10–14
macroeconomic performance, 28–29, 33
Madagascar, Environmental/Rural
    Development and Food Security
    Program, 141–50, 213, 255–56
Malik, Khalid, 195
managing for development results
    (MfDR), 171–72, 215, 217, 220–22
  and development banks, 42
  pillars of, 179, 194n3
  Sri Lanka, 13, 15–19, 21–22
manual counting, 159, 162, 163
mapping of strategy management, 60–62,
    76–78, 79b4.2, 217
Martin, Frederic, 1–12, 171–94, 209, 256–57
McAllister, Elizabeth J., 207–24
MDGs. See Millennium Development
    Goals (MDGs)
M&E. See monitoring and evaluation (M&E)
measurements
  of DSP, 78, 82–83
  of outcomes, 62, 66

Medium-Term Expenditure Framework
 (MTEF), Sri Lanka, 15
Mexico, 177-79
MfDR. *See* managing for development
 results (MfDR)
Millennium Challenge, 143, 188
Millennium Development Goals (MDGs),
 17, 42, 55*n*1, 196, 199, 200, 202
Ministry of Finance (SHCP), Mexico, 178
Ministry of Plan Implementation (MPI),
 Sri Lanka, 14-15
 accomplishments of, 21
 challenges to institutionalization of
  MfDR, 19-21
 future plans of, 21-22
 institutionalizing MfDR in, 15-19
Ministry of Public Service (SFP),
 Mexico, 178
Ministry of Social Affairs (SEDESOL),
 Mexico, 177-79
mobile technology, 166, 169*n*5
monitoring, 244
 AMREE project, 152
 audits used to judge quality of, 165
 definition, 3, 172, 257
 electronic project monitoring
  system, 14-15
 as subset of evaluation, 153
monitoring and evaluation (M&E), 2, 213-14
 building units of, 190, 194*n*4
 challenges for, 185-86
 definition, 2-3
 design and implementation of, 179,
  180-81*t*10.1
 distinction between, 259-60
 and ECB, 2-3, 4
  identification of desired ECB
   results, 179-82
  integrating M&E into, 176-79, 194*n*3
 Environmental/Rural Development and
  Food Security Program in
  Madagascar, 141-50
 external, 192-93
 improvement of information systems and
  knowledge management for, 187-93
 perceptions of, 173-74
 as pillar of RBM, 171-72, 173
 programmatic approach to, 141-50, 214
 requirements for system of, 4-9
 results-based, 213-14,
  222-23*n*1, 256-57
 review of Witjayatilake's case study in
  Sri Lanka, 245-46

 in Sri Lanka, 14-15
 staffing of units of, 174
 subareas of, 172, 195*n*1
 See also evaluations; GEF Evaluation
  Office; monitoring; results-based
  management (RBM)
motivation, 97
MPI. *See* Ministry of Plan Implementation
 (MPI), Sri Lanka
MTEF. *See* Medium-Term Expenditure
 Framework (MTEF), Sri Lanka
Mubarak, Suzanne, 116
multilateral institutions, 42-43, 45, 55*n*4
 assessment of, 247-48
 See also development banks; institutions

N

National Council for Evaluation of Social
 Development Policy (CONEVAL),
 178, 190
natural disasters, 201
need-based evaluations, 128-29
networking, 119
new institutional economics, 25
New Zealand Road Authority, 221-22
NGOs. *See* nongovernmental organizations
 (NGOs)
Nielsen, Steffen Bohni, 225-42
nominal institutional characteristics, vs.
 real characteristics, 28
non-English speaking professionals, 176
nongovernmental organizations
  (NGOs), 41
 evaluators in, 112
 use of IPEs, 43-45
not-for-profit organizations, 69

O

OECD. *See* Organisation for Economic
 Co-operation and Development
 (OECD) countries
on-site support, 162-64
Organisation for Economic Co-operation
 and Development (OECD)
 countries, 119
 definition for evaluation, 153
 domestic rescue packages, 199
 and evaluation principles, 168
 pillars of RBM, 2, 3*f*1
 See also Development Assistance
  Committee (DAC)
organizational development, 160,
 162, 169*n*3

Index

outcomes
  accountability for, 221
  importance of institutional results-based strategy to, 212-13
  measurement of, 62-66
outputs
  focus on, 14, 15
  world output, 32-33
Overseas Development Institute, 199
ownership structures, 62-63, 97, 215, 253
  and drivers of change, 64-65, 66
  Dubai, 81
  and evaluation systems, 249-50
  and leadership for development strategies, 220-22
  of M&E systems, 173
  of process custodianship and governance, 68-70

P

Paris Declaration, 223n3
participatory approach, Madagascar case study, 141-50, 255
partnerships, with training institutions, 186
pedagogical methods, 184, 186
PEO. *See* Program Evaluation Organisation (PEO), India
performance
  Baldrige criteria for, 191
  definition, 2
  of development banks, 42-45, 55n2
  environment to facilitate evaluations of, 43-45, 55nn3-4
  leadership link to, 216-17
  macroeconomic, 28-29
  management of, 71, 217-18
  monitoring of, 19-20
  See also institutional performance evaluations (IPEs)
performance appraisal systems, Sri Lanka, 18-19
performance reports, 19-20, 63, 173, 220
  for DSP, 79-80
  Dubai, 74-76, 82n2
Picciotto, Robert, 116, 117, 121n1, 195-205, 222, 258
PIUs. *See* project implementation units (PIUs)
PMRY. *See* Prime Minister Rojgar Yojana (PMRY) scheme
policies
  developing countries and global policy evaluation, 204-5
  and evaluation principles, 88, 106n5
  global, 202-3
  and political demand for economic stability, 29
  See also decision making
political economy, 210-11
politics, 246
  and decision making, 29
  and demand for macroeconomic stability, 28-29, 31-32
  and ECB, 259
  and evaluation professionals, 89-90
  role in evaluations, 27, 35nn10-11
  Sri Lanka, 15-16, 20
  to support evaluations of institutions and performance, 33
Porter, Stephen, 151-70, 208, 256
practitioners of capacity development, 85, 106n1
Prime Minister Rojgar Yojana (PMRY) scheme, 134-36
private sector, and strategy management, 63-64
profiles of management strategy, 62
Program Evaluation Organisation (PEO), India, 127, 128
programmatic approach to monitoring and evaluation, 141-50, 214
project implementation units (PIUs), 174
public sector, and quality of data, 67
public service, 16
public value, 79b4.2
public value chains, 172f10.1, 179, 181f10.3

R

Rao, Banda V L N, 123-39, 208, 214, 252-55
RBM. *See* results-based management (RBM)
readiness assessments, 175
real per capita growth rate, Latin America, 25
relationships, and helping theory, 152, 154-58, 168-69nn1-2
reports and reporting. *See* performance reports
research, and evaluations, 31, 36n21
results
  evaluation and accountability for, 192-93
  identification of desired ECB results, 179-82
  and results chains, 179, 181f10.3, 182t10.2
  in Sri Lanka case study, 245

results-based management (RBM), 167,
    171–72, 184, 209, 215, 217, 220
  certification in, 184
  challenges in ECB, 173–74
  design and implementation of, 179,
    180–81*t*10.1
  importance of for institutions, 212–13
  and improving M&E information systems
    and knowledge management,
    187–93, 194*n*4
  and integrating ECB into M&E system,
    176–79, 194*n*3
  key concepts of, 2
  pillars of, 179, 194*n*3
  requirements for, 223*n*3
  See also monitoring; strategy
    management
Results Focus, 18, 21
review meetings, 80
risk, 203–4, 254
Rist, Ray C., 1–12, 186
rules
  link to incentives and accountability,
    30–31, 34, 36*nn*16–19
  rules-based management
    certification, 184
rural development, Environmental/Rural
    Development and Food
    Security Program in
    Madagascar, 141–50

S

Sampoorna Grameen Swarozgar Yojana
    (SGSY), India, 136
Schein, Edgar, 151–52
sector management, Dubai, 78
security, and environmental
    evaluations, 116, 117
SEDESOL. *See* Ministry of Social Affairs
    (SEDESOL), Mexico
self-employment, India, 134–36
self-evaluations, 106*n*6, 173, 247, 248
Senegal, and results of evaluation capacity
    building, 179, 182
Serageldin, Ismail, 116
SFP. *See* Ministry of Public Service (SFP),
    Mexico
SGSY. *See* Sampoorna Grameen Swarozgar
    Yojana (SGSY), India
Sida. *See* Swedish International
    Development Cooperation
    Agency (Sida)
Sierra, Kathy, 219

SMART. *See* specific, measurable,
    achievable, relevant, timebound
    (SMART)
social economics and theater, and helping
    theory components, 154–58,
    168–69*nn*1–2
socioeconomics, Sri Lanka, 13–14
Soliman, Salah A., 114
South Africa, review of Porter's helping
    strategy, 256
Soweto Care System, 163–65
specific, measurable, achievable, relevant,
    timebound (SMART), 179
Sri Lanka, 15–22
  M&E as of *2006*, 14–15
  overview, 13–14
  review of Witjayatilake's case study in
    Sri Lanka, 245–46
stakeholders
  from capacities to capabilities for
    evaluations, 94
  and developing evaluators' skills and
    knowledge, 103–4
  and developing institutional framework
    for evaluation, 101
  and evaluation principles, 87–88,
    106*nn*5–6
  to implement MfDR in Sri Lanka,
    16, 18, 22*n*2
  involvement of, 178–79, 253
  and M&E systems, 178–79
  and reinforcing enabling environment
    for evaluation, 100
stocktaking exercise for environmental/
    rural development in Madagascar,
    143–49, 255
strategic planning, and IPEs, 52, 54–55
strategic reviews, 63
strategy management, 59, 213, 215, 218
  challenges to, 80–83
  concept and processes of, 60–64
  link to leadership, 216–27
  mapping of, 60–62, 76–78, 79*b*4.2
  and performance reports and
    reviews, 79–80
  processes of, 70–73
  review of Jaljouli's case study, 249–50
  vs. evaluations, 64–71, 83*n*1
  See also Dubai Strategic Plan (DSP)
supply and demand framework
  for ECB, 4–9, 239
  and helping theory, 155, 156, 158
support teams, Dubai, 81–82

surveys, postconference, 119
Swedish International Development Cooperation Agency (Sida), 65, 259
Synthesis Report of the Evaluation of the Paris Declaration, Phase One, 223n3
systemic frameworks, 67–68, 83n1
systems theory, 211–12

T

Tanzania, 186
technical capital, 6f3, 8
technical evaluation skills, 160
Ten Steps to a Results–Based Monitoring and Evaluation System, 177
Ten-Year Development Framework (TYDF), Sri Lanka, 15, 17
Terms of Reference (ToR), 130, 132
theme management
   Dubai, 76–78
   strategy management themes, 61–62, 63–64
theory–based evaluations, 66
timeliness, definition, 106 Annex 5.A
ToR. *See* Terms of Reference (ToR)
training, 256, 257
   assessing needs for, 183–84
   and capacity development, 88, 106n7
   of care workers, 166
   choice of trainers, 185–86
   as component of M&E, 174
   developing evaluators' skills and knowledge of, 103–4
   executive, 185
   follow–up, 186
   in–country, 175–76
   and integrating ECB into M&E system, 176–79, 194n3
   key factors for, 182–87
   participant selection for, 175
   and results chain, 179, 181f10.3, 182t10.2
Training of Rural Youth for Self-Employment (TRYSEM), India, 136
transaction costs, 24, 31, 35n4, 36n2
Translinks, 144
transparency, definition, 106 Annex 5.A
TRYSEM. *See* Training of Rural Youth for Self-Employment (TRYSEM), India
TYDF. *See* Ten-Year Development Framework (TYDF), Sri Lanka
typology, Dubai, 83n2

U

UEMOA. *See* Union Economique et Monétaire Ouest Africain (UEMOA)
Uganda, 260
UNDP. *See* United Nations Development Programme (UNDP)
UNEP. *See* United Nations Environment Programme (UNEP)
UN Evaluation Group, 113
UNICEF. *See* United Nations Children's Fund (UNICEF)
Union Economique et Monétaire Ouest Africain (UEMOA), 186
United Nations Children's Fund (UNICEF), 124
United Nations Development Programme (UNDP), 90b5.1, 112
United Nations Environment Programme (UNEP), 112
United Nations Financing for Development Conference, Monterrey, 196
United Nations High Commissioner for Refugees, 201
Universalia Management Group, 55n3
U.S. Agency for International Development (USAID), 115, 213, 222–23n1
   Environmental/Rural Development and Food Security Program in Madagascar, 141–50, 213
U.S. Agency for International Development/U.S. President's Emergency Plan for AIDS Relief (USAID/PEPFAR), 152, 165
USAID. *See* U.S. Agency for International Development (USAID)
USAID/PEPFAR. *See* U.S. Agency for International Development/U.S. President's Emergency Plan for AIDS Relief (USAID/PEPFAR)
user–friendly evaluation products, 125–26
users of evaluations, 253
utility of evaluations, 87, 93t5.1, 100–103, 251
   definition, 106 Annex 5.A
   and enabling environment, 90, 107n11
Utilization-Focused Evaluation, 125
utilization of evaluations, 124, 125–26
   capacity building for better utilization of, 132–34
   case study in India, 134–36

conclusions concerning, 136–37
factors influencing in India, 128–34
selective utilization, 131
views of, 124–26

V

values
    to drive evaluations and strategy management, 65–66
    value creation theory, 81
van den Berg, Rob D., 111–21, 214
verticality, 67
Vietnam, 190
virtual communities, 119–20
Volunteer Services Overseas (VSO), 169n4
VX Company, Netherlands, 169n4

W

WBI. *See* World Bank Institute (WBI)
Western Province, Sri Lanka, 14, 22n1
whole of government approach, 13, 15–19
Wiesner, Eduardo, 23–40, 208, 210, 211, 246–47
Wijayatilake, Dhara, 13–22, 215, 216, 245–46
Working towards Good Practice, 239
World Bank, 65, 112, 114
World Bank Institute (WBI), 173
World Conservation Union (IUCN), 113–14
world crisis. *See* financial crisis
World Food Programme, 102–3, 107n14

Y

Yojana, Rojgar, 134–36

ECO-AUDIT
Environmental Benefits Statement

The World Bank is committed to preserving endangered forests and natural resources. The Office of the Publisher has chosen to print *Influencing Change: Building Evaluation Capacity to Strengthen Governance* on recycled paper with 50 percent postconsumer fiber in accordance with the recommended standards for paper usage set by the Green Press Initiative, a nonprofit program supporting publishers in using fiber that is not sourced from endangered forests. For more information, visit www.greenpressinitiative.org.

Saved:
- 17 trees
- 5 million BTUs of total energy
- 1,630 lbs. of net greenhouse gases
- 7,849 gallons of waste water
- 477 lbs. of solid waste

green press INITIATIVE